Contrasting Arguments

This book is part of the Peter Lang Education list.
Every volume is peer reviewed and meets
the highest quality standards for content and production.

PETER LANG
New York • Bern • Berlin
Brussels • Vienna • Oxford • Warsaw

Oscar Pemantle

Contrasting Arguments

The Culture War and the Clash in Education

PETER LANG
New York • Bern • Berlin
Brussels • Vienna • Oxford • Warsaw

Library of Congress Cataloging-in-Publication Data
Names: Pemantle, Oscar, author.
Title: Contrasting arguments: the culture war and the clash in education / Oscar Pemantle.
Description: New York: Peter Lang, 2019.
Includes bibliographical references.
Identifiers: LCCN 2018034361 | ISBN 978-1-4331-5165-1 (hardback: alk. paper)
ISBN 978-1-4331-5166-8 (ebook pdf) | ISBN 978-1-4331-5167-5 (epub)
ISBN 978-1-4331-5168-2 (mobi)
Subjects: LCSH: Education—Philosophy—History. | Culture conflict—History.
Classification: LCC LB14.7.P46 2018 | DDC 370.1—dc23
LC record available at https://lccn.loc.gov/2018034361
DOI 10.3726/b14661

Bibliographic information published by **Die Deutsche Nationalbibliothek**.
Die Deutsche Nationalbibliothek lists this publication in the "Deutsche
Nationalbibliografie"; detailed bibliographic data are available
on the Internet at http://dnb.d-nb.de/.

© 2019 Peter Lang Publishing, Inc., New York
29 Broadway, 18th floor, New York, NY 10006
www.peterlang.com

All rights reserved.
Reprint or reproduction, even partially, in all forms such as microfilm,
xerography, microfiche, microcard, and offset strictly prohibited.

To my mother

TABLE OF CONTENTS

	Introduction	1
Chapter 1:	The Transformation of Antonio Gramsci: A Study in Retrieval	5
Chapter 2:	"The Magic of Marxism": Paulo Freire Pro and Contra	27
Chapter 3:	The Two Codes: Origins and Meaning of the Culture War in Education	43
Chapter 4:	The Traditional Mistake of the Traditional Educator	61
Chapter 5:	How Myths Are Made: The Mythic Power of Marxism	75
Chapter 6:	Truths, Half Truths, and One and a Half Truths: From Diane Ravitch to Sheldon S. Wolin	85
Chapter 7:	Bertrand Russell and the Eureka Syndrome: Kekule's Dream	109
Chapter 8:	Where Ends Collide: The Liberal-Conservative Debate in Philosophy	147
Chapter 9:	The Conservative Critique	161
Chapter 10:	Closing Comments	`183
	Final Remarks	213
	Conclusion: The Argument in Model Form	221

INTRODUCTION

The *Dissoi Logoi* is an ancient Greek document dating back, perhaps, to the seventh century BC. Its author is as unknown as its date of publication. And it is not for its contents, which are understandably primitive, that it invites our attention here. It is for its form which is consistently dialectical from the opening argument to the close of the study. Indeed, it is the first such book in the history of Western man. And not until Plato, some two centuries later, was there another. Its title is happily translated as Contrasting Arguments and sets the theme for the structure of the present work on the historic debate in education and the culture clash which underlies it in the culture wars of the modern world.

So I begin with the controversial teaching of Antonio Gramsci and its received interpretation by the conservative side and the radical reception to which it was a most scholarly response. This critical difference poses a problem and raises the question: Who is right? I bracket the two together, labeling this "the counter position" and question the counter position with a series of contrasting arguments. The counter position envisages the universe of Gramsci on education as a universe of objects. By contrast, I contend that it is a universe of subjects. And that is the argument in a nutshell, once more raising the question: Who is right, the counter position or the critic?

I follow essentially the same procedure in the next chapter on Paulo Freire in "The Magic of Marxism," and so on through the book. *The Pedagogy of the Oppressed* evoked many a strong response, and I consider the most recent as a paradigmatic example. And once again, I bracket the two together to form the counter position and present the contrasting arguments, first that the *Pedagogy* has nothing to do with education, except for the first two pages of the second chapter. And, second, that it is, on the contrary, a book on consciousness-raising among the workers and peasants of Brazil, the oppressed of the title to whom it extends a hand in "the politics of friendship" characteristics of the revolutionary movement in its first and earliest phase. How this transformed itself into an autocracy, a despotism over the people, is a question each reader must answer for him or herself. In general, I follow this form throughout the book. Grasp the form and the rest will follow whether or not you agree with the specific arguments made. The grand alternative posed by the book, the ultimate contrast, is between the form of education here called "Plato" and dominated by the lecture, and the form of education here called "Socrates" which elevates the dialogue, conversation with the student as fellow subject, to the central position in the search for "new truths," new that is to the beginning student in our schools and colleges. This can only be a community decision in forging a way through the culture wars and the most a book writer can do is to point the way.

If the foregoing excursus is correct it casts two features of the debate into bold relief. First, the critic who disregards the esoteric teaching and the elements of which it is composed has simply said "Goodbye text" and left no common universe of discourse between us. This makes the text and with it the politics of friendship incomprehensible to the mind shaped by market morality. A striking example of this incomprehension is provided by the Hearings of the House Committee featuring Whittaker Chambers. How much did Alger Hiss charge him for his two months residence in the Hiss apartment and meals at his house on P Street, etc.? When Chambers explained that it was not a commercial arrangement, Committee members like Nixon and McDowell were uncomprehending.[1] It was a Party relationship and based on fraternity, Chambers later explained (1934). This sense of fraternity is at the heart of the politics of friendship whether it comes from the corporate left or right and is incomprehensible to the center from the Congressmen to the critics.

Second, this incomprehension and the misunderstandings to which it leads point to a deeper problem at the heart of this study. In my first mention of Mario Puzo's novel, *The Godfather,* I was sketching the outlines of a counter argument, a different way of seeing things as Puzo does. I was not advocating a thesis or making an attempt to convince the reader. Here, what I was saying is the counter argument and it is now for you to judge. Where we come to a problem from two radically different horizons, say Plato's and Nietzsche's, purely rational discussion will not resolve the difference. You must choose the horizon, the objective pole, expressive of your vision, your character, and personality as a subject, and only you can make the decision which at the margin is made in fear and trembling. This sets the limit of rational discourse, and this limit provides the rationale for a study made up of contrasting arguments which by their very structure demand a choice by the reader.

So, let me set out the structure of the argument made by the best on the two sides and invite the critic to make his choice. The fact that I am on one side makes no difference. Everyone has to be on one side or the other. But listen to the best and choose your side.

Note

1. Testimony of Alger Hiss and Whittaker Chambers before the House Committee on Un-American Activities, August 25, 1948. https://www.famous-trials.com/algerhiss/653-8-25testimony

· 1 ·

THE TRANSFORMATION OF ANTONIO GRAMSCI

A Study in Retrieval

The Problem

When contemplating Gramsci's views "On Education" an intriguing puzzle confronts the educator. In the literature on the topic Gramsci emerges as the hero with two faces, two heads facing in precisely opposite directions.

The views of Antonio Gramsci on education present a problem to the scholar, the educator, the teacher, and the enlightened citizen concerned about the fate of education as a casualty in the war on culture. His views have been subject to extensive analysis by partisans on both sides for over a generation. They involve writers of prominence, men who would all appear to know what they are talking about. Yet, the essential Gramsci seems to slip through their fingers. To the Left, he emerges as the incarnation of the educator as radical and visionary, while to the Right, he takes shape as the beau ideal of traditional and conservative education. Each case is forcefully argued and, at its best, displays wide familiarity with his writing and the literature surrounding it.

Disputes of this kind are not unknown in political science. In a celebrated article Sir Isaiah Berlin summarizes the centuries-old "question of Machiavelli."[1] And in the introduction to what is the most precise and imaginative translation of the Social Contract Willmore Kendall tells us that the interpretation of Rousseau's masterpiece has, despite "its engaging sentence-by-sentence simplicity," become a tangle of conflicting opinions. But *The Prince* has long signaled its problematic character by the sudden change in the last chapter. And Rousseau's great work is pitched on a hair-raising level of abstraction and complexity. By contrast, Gramsci's essay, his most explicit theoretical statement, is a mere seventeen pages in length. It is as plain to see as the nose on your face and as easy to read as the Sunday paper. Why then the mystery and why the controversy? What is the problem?

The War of Ideas

Of the partisans commanding the two thought worlds, four can be singled out for mention here. On the radical side, the first in the field is Quintin Hoare, the English translator of *Selections from the Prison Notebooks of Antonio Gramsci* with its generous and well-informed introduction. This was followed some years later by Henry Giroux, a prominent disciple of Paulo Freire.

Equally notable are the captains of culture on the other side. Pride of place here belongs to Harold Entwistle, a British educator now domiciled in Canada, whose book *Antonio Gramsci: Conservative Schooling for Radical Politics* (1979) broke new ground. He was then followed by E. D. Hirsch, formerly a Professor of Literature whose *Cultural Literacy* had already made him a household word, to be followed by *The Schools We Need and Why We Don't Have Them*. Hirsch, who is also fluent in Italian, built on the work of Entwistle to make the case for Gramsci as a traditional educator. Both Entwistle and Hirsch were then duly savaged by Giroux in the once selective pages of the *Harvard Educational Review*, *Telos*, and *British Journal of Sociology of Education*. The fires in the culture war were blazing brightly.

The core of Quentin Hoare's argument is the contention that everything Gramsci says on education "must" be read in light of his revolutionary perspective as a Marxist; Gramsci's language and heresies in a more "conservative" direction were simply strategies to evade the censor. But why "must" Gramsci's thoughts "On Education" all be read in this light? Hoare offers no justification for his canon of interpretation. He simply presents it as a self-evident truth, as Higher Dogma. Gramsci might well have used certain circumlocutions to evade the censor's eye. The stock examples here are the use of Lenin, Trotsky, and Stalin's real names and the phrase "the philosophy of praxis" to stand for

"Marxism." Yet only a few essays later he refers quite openly to Proudhon and his famous book on poverty and also to "some Marxists" and so forth.[2] Once his methodological rule is questioned and Gramsci's thoughts are taken as he wrote them the Hoare case disintegrates before our eyes until there is nothing left.

Giroux has written more extensively, favoring us with three long articles and part of a book. He is a convert from Freire to Gramsci, blending them both into his own special cocktail, now made in America. Giroux's arguments are made in a blaze of passion. To a cool critic, however, they are singularly unconvincing.

Consider only a couple or so of his main arguments. Giroux makes much of Gramsci's theory of the intellectual. Much of this, such as his view that all men are "intellectuals" because they all perform some intellectual labor, is idiosyncratic and borders on the absurd. To group the local lens grinder in a class with Spinoza (or Leibniz, or Newton, not to mention Galileo) is to make nonsense of a category whose very purpose is to distinguish. More important is the category of the "transformative" intellectual with its suggestively Leninist overtones. To the extent that we simply mean leadership of a genuinely transforming power, as in Kuhn's paradigm transforming individuals, or Jaspers' paradigmatic leaders of the axial age, the Galileos and Newtons, the Bachs and Beethovens and Mozarts, the Adam Smith's and Ricardos, the Darwins, Marxes and Keynes, the Einsteins of today and tomorrow have all so far been the products of traditional culture and education. The socialist world has produced nothing to match it nor has the praxis and "the philosophy of praxis" in Gramsci, Freire, and Giroux. In fact, socialism has everywhere and at all times meant the destruction of reason and the degradation of culture. Giroux likes to think that he is "thinking like Gramsci" but this is pure illusion. Without any real competence in political theory of philosophy, Gramsci's critique of the superstructure, and hence his unique brand of Marxism, is seen through the lens of vulgar Marxism prevalent among American pseudo-intellectuals. So it comes as no surprise when he exhibits no understanding of Gramsci's thoughts "On Education." These are, however, only his most minor blemishes. In his attack on Entwistle he strikes his most characteristic pose, compounding ersatz moral indignation with bogus scholarship. Entwistle's paradoxical thesis is open to question. But this is not the way to answer it.

Giroux opens his attack on a note of lofty dismissal. He adopts the same strategy when criticizing Allan Bloom, of whose philosophy he displays no shred of comprehension, and E. D. Hirsch, whom he ranks among the "ideologues," Giroux's favorite term for "conservatives." The attack on Entwistle exceeds either or both of these in hostility and abuse. To reprint these passages is distasteful. Any interested reader can easily find them in their unlovely originals. Among a plethora of references to the secondary literature (in English) there are only three to Gramsci himself and *The Prison Notebooks*. In a passage on the skills training side of primary and secondary education, the core of the curriculum, Giroux assures us of "an array of skills" to be found in the program of instruction. To a reader of Gramsci, this is a remarkable claim. Remarkable it may be, but is it true? Giroux furnishes no documentation. When asked point-blank for the necessary documentation, Giroux is airiness itself. "It is," he assures us again, "somewhere in the Notebooks." Perhaps so, but one wonders precisely where, since no one that I know has ever noticed it. In another passage, he castigates Entwistle for likening the status of knowledge in Gramsci to the "positivism" of Karl Popper in his theory of "objective knowledge" or "epistemology without a subject."[3] In fairness, Giroux has something of a point here, though it might not be exactly the one he thinks.

For one thing, Entwistle is quite aware of his hero's Marxism. For another, we have it on Popper's own authority that, far from being a positivist, he was not admitted to the meetings of the Vienna Circle precisely because of his well-known opposition to logical positivism.[4] Such blunders would make a schoolboy blush! To castigate Entwistle, a traditional educator, for the broad similarity he sees between the traditionalist position he imputes to Gramsci and the right-wing views of E. D. Hirsch and Diane Ravitch, Chester Finn, and Charles Sykes, represents yet another form of confusion. Entwistle is not making a political alliance or even a political point. His political views, as far as I know them, are those of a British laborite or, at most, a lib-labber as they were called.

The point is that traditional education, as a form of education and teaching, is an abstract form, which can readily accommodate an extended family of opinions from the social democracy of Entwistle to the Olin scholar Sykes, and do it with no inconvenience. Giroux may have fumbled at every turn, but the question still remains. Has Entwistle made the case that Gramsci was, despite all appearances (and preconceptions) a traditional educator? Or has he pulled a rabbit out of his British hat? This is the decisive question to which we now turn.

The Hat and the Rabbit

Entwistle's hat was made in England in the mid- to late 1950s. It is not the elegant *chapeau* made in France at the *École Normale Supérieure*. Entwistle is not a Normalien. His hat is strictly British made and manufactured in the School of Education in London. The original framework was designed by a foreigner, an Austrian engineer now turned to Philosophy, named Ludwig Wittgenstein. The immediate craftsmen, however, were all British. Entwistle and his outlook are as sturdily British as John Bull and fish and chips. He has all the British virtues. He is patient, hard-working, indefatigable, knowledgeable, well informed, and full of common sense...and dead wrong. Are you surprised, dear reader? Then let me unsurprise you by sketching the profile of a British School of Ed man, in the case of Harold Entwistle vis-à-vis Antonio Gramsci. Here it is in a few steps from its plausible beginning to its paradoxical end. The fault lies not in Entwistle but in the lens provided by the School of which he is a most outstanding member. First, consider the vocabulary, the terminology through which he sees things, and which he, therefore, applies to Gramsci. There are terms like the elegant "cognitive repertoire" and the less elegant "cognitive baggage." Applied to Gramsci, these mid- and late twentieth-century Anglicisms are decidedly anachronistic.

Our second question is inevitably: Where did Entwistle develop the arcane repertoire? Where did he pick up this terminological baggage? The answer is: he was indoctrinated in it by his teachers in the School of Education. British philosophy was completing the transition from Russell to Wittgenstein, and from the Wittgenstein of the *Tractatus* to the Wittgenstein of the *Philosophical Investigations* and later the *Blue and Brown Books*. The logical positivism of the Ayer–Russell persuasion had given way to Oxford Philosophy, or analytic philosophy, or language philosophy. "Philosophy," Wittgenstein once remarked, "is the effort to keep ourselves from being hexed by language."[5]

The names which brighten Entwistle's discourse are those of Gilbert Ryle, Karl Popper, R. S. Peters, and Israel Scheffler, their most notable American counterpart. The outstanding feature of this British philosophy, like its American counterpart in the earlier philosophy of James, is the fact that it is "doing" philosophy without a subject. The psychological subject has disappeared.[6] When it is "doing" moral philosophy, it is in the language of morals and ethics in which it is most interested.[7] And when it is "doing" epistemology, it is "doing" epistemology without a subject. This is most evident in the behaviorism of Ryle in *The Concept of Mind*. The subject–act–object philosophy down to Brentano and so much a part of Catholic philosophy has long been jettisoned as outdated, and so is the subject–object dialectic of Hegelian and Marxist fame.[8] Yet, this was the tradition into which the young Gramsci was born and raised and whose great names are the early Croce and Labriola. And this is why any attempt to see him through the lens provided by linguistic behaviorism, language philosophy, and the philosophy of science, Gilbert Ryle and R. S. Peters as well as their lesser lights, is inevitably an anachronism.

Third, in reading the text Entwistle makes a crucial mistake in method. He does not attempt to understand Gramsci precisely as Gramsci understood himself. Instead he sees him, i.e., interprets him, through a haze of secondary literature. Simply said, when Entwistle looks at his hero he sees him through alien eyes. Once it is understood that Gramsci proceeds in terms of a theory of the subject, Entwistle's error is clearly seen. In focusing all attention on the object pole, on the category of content and purely content-related criteria which formed this universe, Entwistle has made a "category mistake" and given the discussion a twist in the direction of continued confusion, conformism, and sterility. The dimensions of this confusion will emerge more clearly in the critique of E. D. Hirsch, the second half of the Entwistle–Hirsch axis.

Entwistle has covered the field, not only in English but also in Italian. His vacuum cleaner takes it all in, biographies, commentaries favorable and otherwise, etc., etc. He pores over everything Gramsci has written, *The Quaderni*, *The Prison Notebooks*, the *Scritti Giovanile*, the letters to his wife about his young child, everything...and everything given about equal weight. But this is not how Gramsci wrote or wished to be read. In fact, as Entwistle well knows, he warned against it. He outlined his theory on education in its ideal form in an essay, and it is that essay which should occupy center stage and be given the spotlight. Read closely with due thought it gives us a picture as far different from the behaviorist outlook and language philosophy as the real Gramsci, the Gramsci of "On Education" from the traditional or "routine minded pedagogue" (as Dezamy called him in the first socialist critique of traditional education). Let us evaluate the traditionalist case as made by Entwistle. To wit: Entwistle points out three capital features of traditional education, all of which he insists are conspicuously featured in Gramsci. The three features are: A) the traditional curriculum, B) competitive testing, and C) discipline, backed by homework and hard work aplenty. None of this demonstrates his case. Consider the first. Entwistle repeatedly refers to "curriculum" in Gramsci. But, unless my eyes deceive me, there is no "curriculum" to be found in these pages. Can Entwistle tell us precisely what the Gramsci curriculum in, say, literature or, say, history is in fact? Of course not. Entwistle has confused a "curricular domain" with a curriculum properly speaking. Certainly Gramsci would favor the traditional curriculum in mathematics or science and also *something like it* in history and literature. But so would other critics of traditional education, such as advocates of Socratic or discovery teaching.

The latter school featuring Socratic or discovery teaching is not at all the dull, monotonous "chalk-and-talk" characteristic of traditional education. Also the chalk-and-talk *cognoscenti* are always and everywhere wedded to the textbook with its prefabricated catalog of contents. We, who use the Socratic method, range far beyond the others, and right away. Which of the two makes for better, i.e., more engaging and professionally skillful mathematics teaching and learning? And now ask yourself which of the two models is closer to the whole form and spirit of the creative school? The same can be said about testing which you can see in the form of several stiff mathematics competitions presented, in brief on several DVDs available on our website (www.institute-foractivelearning.org). In the context of discovery teaching or the "creative school," as Gramsci calls it, the entire psychological content of testing and test taking is reversed from fear learning to pleasure learning. See it for yourself in the expression of the students' reactions and those of their teachers.

Once these points are grasped, Entwistle's mistake regarding the meaning of "discipline" in Gramsci is easy to see. He has simply read his own experience into the completely different structure and horizon of Gramsci "On the Creative School," which is as different from the traditional school as cheese is from chalk.

Since I am also speaking to an audience of Latin culture, let me cite the reflections of the most outstanding critic to write in the language of Cervantes. Read the relevant passages in Ortega's *The Revolt of the Masses* (1932). Read them, ponder them, steep yourself in them, make them your own, then see how well they fit in their realism with the high aspirations articulated in "The Creative School" and how little they square with the traditional school in Spain and Italy, Europe and America, yesterday and today. The tension between Gramsci and Entwistle, of the creative school and the traditional school, emerges most clearly in their relationship to mass society and culture. In its aim and orientation, the creative school, with its rigors of discipline, tests, and sustained hard work, with its orientation toward the "select minority" (the pungent phrase is Ortega's own), stands in tension with the insistent pressures toward standardization, leveling, and deculturation. The traditional school is part and parcel of the institutional order of mass society and its culture. Nowhere is this better seen than in the vulgarization of the prepackaged textbooks, now said to be "produced" rather than written, and the indoctrination provided by the drone of the lecture. In the traditional school we witnessed the substitution of bad training for good education. Its diploma has come to be valued as a key to entry-level jobs or as a passport to a mass university or community college. Whatever its rhetoric, its actual aims are crudely utilitarian. It has nothing to do with Education understood as the culture of the mind and the formation of character and personality. Under these insistent pressures, Voegelin has written, the idea of Culture is practically dead.[9]

The Models I: The Creative School

Gramsci's contribution to the theory of Education stands or falls with his profile of "the creative school." It is the *locus classicus* of his thought and should be considered carefully by everyone, friend or foe, wishing to express an informed opinion. Yet, it is precisely this essay which has been slurred over by the iconic critics and commentators, left and right, mentioned above. Every phrase and line in it should be carefully noted and assessed for its true and proper meaning in the context of the essay as a whole. Any careful analysis will at once reveal that it is not another essay in the vein of radical ideology and journalism. It is not a partisan political polemic in simple juxtaposition to the Gentile reform. Nor is it the old traditional school now given a new label and dressed up for British or Canadian or American consumption. Quite the contrary, in these few pages Gramsci has presented a model of the ideal or best type of school, the "idea" of a school, its aim, structure, and functioning.

But first a word about the nature of a model. Simply put, a model is a mental picture of the entity or system which the model builder wishes us to see in its essential nature or structure. So, Marx gave us a model of capitalism, and Hilferding of finance capital. So again Macpherson gives us a model of Hobbesian society and society as it came to be conceived by Locke. A model, by its very nature, is an analytical or technical construction. In the large, it can be either correct or incorrect, right or wrong as an instrument of science, not of ideology. It can be useful no matter what one's political orientation. It is *a value-neutral* construction. That is why their critics can still read Marx or Macpherson with profit and pleasure, and this is how Gramsci on "The Creative School" deserves to be read.

The creative school presents a model with three moving parts: (1) the nature of the student, (2) the role of the teacher, and (3) the method by which the model is to function. The traditional school can likewise be understood as a model with three moving parts: (1) the knowing teacher, (2) the unknowing student or class, and (3) the authoritative or canonical textbook. Clearly, the polar opposition between the two models undermines the fundamental axiom at the heart of the Entwistle–Hirsch thesis. Every school has an aim, a fundamental purpose and direction which gives it its identity. The aim of the creative school is to produce those great scholars who are necessary to every civilization. Yet, Gramsci is not swept away by the flush of the romantic. His analysis is cold sober and reveals no trace of Trotsky's intoxicated "Every man an Aristotle, a Goethe, a Marx." Quite the reverse, this will be the fortune of the select few, those happy few who can find leisure and energy and diligence to develop it. To become a real craftsman, or better yet, an artist, required hard work and plenty of it, but schools alone cannot produce this. Unless he was a fool, Gramsci realized that the creative school must rest on and be the expression of a culture which really values the great in art and science, that turns its eyes upward to the true, the beautiful, and the good. The creative school is in radical tension with mass culture.

The traditional school, with its cult of skills, is fundamentally utilitarian and devoid of soul. The creative school, as a social enterprise, has a moral basis and is charged with moral energy.

The student in the creative school is the polar opposite from the student in the traditional school, docile and tractable, duly taking notes from his books and lectures, and dishing up received opinions on his exams. In the creative school the student is, above all, a discoverer of "new truths" (p. 33),[10] even if these new truths are old truths. They are new to the student, for *he* has discovered them. To the traditionalist who would say that this is simply reinventing the wheel Gramsci would answer, "You, Signor, are focusing on the wheel and not on the process of invention." What, then, is the teacher's role in this "process of invention," or "discovery?" The teacher is to act as "the friendly guide" (p. 33). There it is, the lightest touch and nothing more. What exactly does he mean? To understand Gramsci on this critical point, to grasp the range of its implications, it is necessary to circle in, to take the *via negativa*.

Let us begin by asking what a "friendly guide" is not. One thing he is not is the "routine minded pedagogue," the typically heavy-handed lecturer of "chalk-and-talk" fame. The lecturer and his lecture are incompatible with the role of the "friendly guide." The teacher here interprets the texts for the student. He tells you the right view of Marx, or of socialism, or of fascism, or of democracy, etc. He does not guide you with his critical questions to discover the truth, your truth for the moment, which can yield to a newer and better or higher truth. With the formidable figure of the lecturer (or traditional teacher) confronting you, you discover nothing for yourself.

Yet it is equally at odds with the teacher or facilitator as eunuch, as in progressive education. When the eunuch speaks, the first thing he will say is that he is a man. What he facilitates is the student's way down the sawdust trail to salvation. The progressivist facilitator, the teacher as "transformative intellectual," is an ideologue masquerading as educator. Of all this there is not a trace in Gramsci "On Education." Yet it would be a mistake to assume that there is no relationship between "the active school" and "the creative school" or that such a relationship is merely one of juxtaposition or opposition. It is not. Gramsci is clear on this point. "The creative school is the culmination of the active school" (p. 33). Why so?

For all its faults, in the theory of the active school deriving from Rousseau,[11] as handed down by Hegel and Gentile, the student was considered as subject and not as the object of instruction in the malleable world of objects which the traditionalist sees. Where the traditionalist stresses instruction almost exclusively, the Rousseau–Gentile romantic school stresses "education" and educativity, however flawed its conception and execution in fascist hands.[12] And education, the imparting of culture, comes into play when the student is treated as subject. For Culture is the world of the subject, not the object. Whatever else it has, a collection of refrigerators has no culture. It produces no music and creates no art. It has no religion because it has no soul.

The Models II: The Search for a Method

The conception of method is left implicit in Gramsci. He was not a pedagogue or teacher with experience in teaching the core subjects in primary/secondary education. We can, however, find the essentials of the method by fixing attention on the cardinal features of the creative school and asking the question: What is the method with which we realize the aim of the school? The first clue is that here the student is a discoverer. Learning for him is the discovery of "new truths" even if these be "old truths" for the teacher and for us. What then is it to discover a truth that is new for you? The answer, quite obviously, is: it is to have insight into what was originally obscure, puzzling, or confusing. "Discovery," or real learning, is in its essence insight learning. The teacher's task is to promote the conditions which make for insight into the problem at hand. Insights, if they are real, do not, of course, come a dime a dozen. But they are more frequent than has been believed, especially when the ground for them has been prepared.

The preparation is the supreme art and craft of teaching. The discovery, like the fine seducer, is never in a hurry. Hurrying to get there, to cover a preordained content, is fatal. Initially, the teacher must hold his fire and let the flow of insight come from the class. Of course, the insights or some of them might be mistaken. Here is where the stream of critical questioning, the critical fire which the teacher has held back, can come into play. This is critical cross-examination or "eristic," the quality which has given this form of teaching the name "Socratic teaching." The name is not a misnomer. All Socratic teaching is teaching conducted behind the veil of Socratic ignorance, the famous Socratic incognito. Once the student knows, or thinks he knows, the teacher's opinion, the process of discovery is short-circuited. The student has become the object of instruction, not the subject in the process of discovery. It is the most superficial of mistakes to think that Socratic or discovery teaching is against instruction, per se. It all depends on what you mean by "instruction." If you mean "instruction" as the creation of koranic mind, as a higher order variant of algorithmic or formula thinking, or indoctrination, or mental conditioning, then it is. But if you have a more elevated conception, one wide enough to include the classic model, now modernized and brought up to date, and applied to the teaching of the core subjects (with due adaptation) then of course it is not. (Again, I invite you to view our website: www.instituteforactivelearning.org). Clearly, this is the form of teaching in which the teacher functions as "friendly guide." The two terms have exactly equal weight: too "friendly" and he melts into the facilitator of the romantic school and present-day progressivism, too much the directing "guide" and he becomes the "chalk-and-talk" lecturer for whom the sonority of his words drowns out all creative energy in the student and the class. "Education," wrote Paulo Freire in his most notable line, "is suffering from narration sickness." The Socratic teacher never tells the student anything. The art of Socratic teaching is to elicit everything from the student. Here let me say that in all respects but this one, the discovery school I established in Berkeley and the creative school in the pages of Gramsci are virtually identical, this proving that Gramsci was no utopian. It can be done in the here and now and reach standards beyond the dreams of the routine minded pedagogue.

The exception, the difference between the creative school and my discovery school, is this: Gramsci comes to the table as a high-minded, convinced, and dedicated socialist. He comes as a convinced Marxist, while I come to the table from the Socratic side. From the philosophic point of view, here called Socratic, all questions are open questions since the criterion of truth is held in suspension during all conversations at "the philosopher's roundtable." Any conclusion the student comes to is his own *pro tempore* and open to correction only by him.

Gramsci opens by grounding the process, at least in the first phase, in "dynamic conformism" (p. 33). So, too, for Gramsci, I believe, the Enlightenment opened a new chapter and its truths are taken as the framework of "a new humanism." Accordingly, the creative school has an ultimate telos, an ultimate value orientation which it is to bring to fruition over time, in Gramsci's words, "...with a solid homogenous moral and social conscience."[13] My question to Gramsci, the Socratic question *par excellence*, is this: Would a school with such an ultimate telos, such a built-in orthodoxy, produce the Antonio Gramscis of tomorrow? The Einstein of only yesterday (1905), whom we may take as a model, was an academic heretic.[14]

The Models III: *The Missing Link*

Why have our previous commentators gone so terribly awry? Why have they failed to see the missing step even when the threads of the argument were in their hands? The answer is a) that they have not learned to read the text correctly, i.e., with an innocent eye and b) they have simply been looking in the wrong places: one to Gramsci's political ideology, the other to his diverse and scattered writings, and that in the context of a traditionalist schooling and paraphernalia. To understand Gramsci as he understood himself in this essay we need to supply the missing step in the move from theory to practice.

To a Latin audience it is most appropriate to begin with the name of Don Miguel de Unamuno, the most distinguished philosopher and poet to write in the language of Calderon. What a difference there is here, from the vulgar political ideology of Giroux and the dry and didactic prose of Entwistle! Don Miguel's work, *El Sentimiento Trágico de la Vida* (I refer to the English translation which is accompanied by an illuminating introduction by Salvador de Madariaga), has a place of distinction on my shelf of books. Right there in the opening pages, indeed in the very first lines, Don Miguel introduces us to the philosopher "as a man of flesh and bones." There we have it in the robust language of the Basque who became a Professor of Philosophy at Salamanca. Unamuno and Bergson are at the fountainhead of the Catholic and Mediterranean tradition into which Gramsci was born. Here we have no rigid dichotomy between mind and matter, body and soul, thought and feeling, or subject and object. Instead we begin with a fundamental unity. Socrates called it the soul. Today we might call it "intelligent subjectivity." It is this locus of "intelligent subjectivity" toward which the teacher "as friendly guide" directs all his attention, be it in the creative school as model or in the discovery school as reality. The Catholic tradition is one great source in developing the theory of the subject. The other was the Hegelian and Marxist tradition coming down to Gramsci by Croce and Labriola. Most outstanding in this tradition was the brilliant work of the early Lukács.[15] In the field of education, the situation was dramatically different. Here the names to conjure with were those of the early Russell, Whitehead, and Dewey. I invite the reader to look at Russell's writings of the time, in particular "The Study of Mathematics" and "The Functions of the Teacher." Notice the pronounced emphasis on the awakening and development of consciousness in the child, on the importance of curiosity and a sense of wonder, on figuring things out for himself and not taking old Mr. Chips' word for it, of developing an unbiased attitude and retaining a sense of healthy skepticism in the face of the authority of the teacher and the textbook, and so forth. These are all subject values and, as they are created, ideas lose their inertness and come alive. Now the vibrancy has flown into the classroom, and with it the pleasures of discovery and the ecstasy of the *eureka* experience. An even more striking *démarche* was made by Dewey in *The Child and the Curriculum*. In this little book Dewey reintroduced the dimension of experience and feeling into all learning worthy of the name. This makes him the founding father of all modern discovery teaching later developed by the National Science Foundation and its teams of scholars beginning with Jerome S. Bruner.

Russell's essays have been widely available in Britain and in the United States. So too, is the case with Whitehead, and certainly Dewey. Their names appear in every respectable reading list in the seminars at the Schools of Education. They supply all the threads of a solution which the *cognoscenti* have failed to provide.

Instead, one faction simply repeats the same old formula whose elements are all too familiar: 1) We need standards, higher standards; 2) We need a longer school day and school year; 3) We need more rigor, better texts, and more and better science equipment and, of course, computers; 4) We need more tests and more rigorous testing and, perhaps, higher salaries for the teachers and better facilities for the students. The progressivist critique is equally familiar and equally irrelevant. Into this stalemate is plunged the figure of Antonio Gramsci, who would have had as little to do with the one as with the other. As an educator he was neither a vulgar ideologue of the Giroux stripe, nor a hardened traditionalist of the Entwistle–Hirsch variety. On the contrary, he was a genuine educator with a clear and practical vision of education as a high pursuit, the best of it reserved for the select and deserving minority who were to be the "great scholars" (p. 37) on which civilization is carried to fruition now and forever, as in the days of Athenian brilliance and Roman high culture.

Prisoner of Thought World: E. D. Hirsch

A study in retrieval would be incomplete without a final word on Hirsch and the iconic Gramsci. One measure of the distance between the two is Gramsci's aim in the creative school to produce those scholars of outstanding accomplishment and culture necessary to every civilization (p. 37) in contrast to the fundamentally remedial thrust of the tradition Hirsch appeals to, holds up as a standard, and within which he operates. The word for the National Commission on Excellence in Education is: "remedial." There it is and in one word you have said it all. Ransack the Hirsch *oeuvre* (notably *The Schools We Need and Why We Don't Have Them*; Doubleday, 1996) and that of his associates and you will not find any coherent program for professional training and education designed to elevate the culture and produce the "great scholars" to whom Gramsci looked.

The blind spot at the center of Hirsch's vision of reform is his inability to appreciate the subject side in the subject–object polarity and dialectic. Yet this is precisely one of the fundamental issues in epistemology according to mainstream research, for example, as weightily expounded by James Brown in the Cromwell Lectures delivered at the University of Edinburgh (1953) and published as *Subject and Object in Modern Theology, A Study of Kierkegaard, Karl Barth, Martin Buber, and Heidegger* (1962).

Close attention to the subject pole is the distinguishing feature defining the role of the teacher in the creative school and the sizzle of insight learning in the children to be the great scholars of the future. In his fixation on the object pole, so characteristic of all his associates, he is unable to distinguish the difference between himself and Bruner, quite ignoring the great contribution Bruner and associates have made to the tradition of discovery teaching. Were it not for Hirsch's disastrous misunderstandings of the stakes in the culture war, he would not have assimilated Freire to progressive education or Kozol to liberal reform. Nor would he have mistaken his authorities, the ordinary scientists who write the ordinary books and articles in what has come to be the official literature, for the last word in "solid mainstream research." Since he has been fishing in the wrong pond, all he ever catches are the small fry of psychological research, cognitive science, and the sprightly Rita Kramer.

In another, bigger and better pond, Hirsch might have found a rich fascinating literature by mathematicians and scientists of all kinds and in various fields describing the nature and structure of insight. The subject has been analyzed from the iconic case of Archimedes to the studies of Poincare, Kerkule, Max Planck, Cannon, Graham Wallis, and many others writing on insight in mathematics, physics, chemistry, biology, etc. I plan to submit the counterevidence in a small book titled *The Timeless Way of Teaching: Handbook for Teachers and Students*. From Leibniz on down, these are among the makers of the modern world. Yet Hirsch overlooks the entire tradition in favor of the ordinary writings of "academic scribblers." Once again, there are two traditions of "mainstream research" or "solid mainstream research" and one of them is more solid than the other, if I may adapt Orwell's phrase.

Hirsch's misunderstandings are as the sands of the sea. Full treatment of them would inevitably run to encyclopedic proportions. Instead, I propose a highly condensed form stating his principle constructions or misconstructions with a brief rebuttal. Analyzing a key figure on the opposing side, Hirsch suggests (by context) that in *Savage Inequalities* Jonathan Kozol favors the equal funding of public schools. Hirsch, who is normally very free with documentation, offers none at this point. Nor could he, for there is none to be had. Hirsch phrases the case in terms of "equity" and equitable funding along, say, the lines established by the Serrano decisions ('71 and '76) and various cases mentioned in the book. This is the liberal case in school reform. Kozol, however, is not a liberal. He is an antiliberal, a socialist of Marxian flavor, who derides the liberal view as "simple minded and irrelevant." Kozol will have nothing to do with merely equal funding. Quite the contrary, "equity" in Kozol's sense means a precise reversal of the steep lines of imbalance between, e.g., the Piedmont schools and those of Oakland. Equality will not do it for these children, Kozol argues, "because their needs are greater".[16] Hirsch goes on to misconstrue Kozol's position in the politics of the culture class. He represents Kozol as an educational progressive, presumably in the romantic tradition of Kilpatrick and Colonel Parker, which flowered most colorfully in the sixties "free school" movement; in fact, Kozol is an acute critic of the romantic side of progressive education as any reader of *Free Schools* can see. Kozol says: "By their funding shall ye know them," and there is nothing romantic about that.

Hirsch contrasts the higher rank of American colleges and universities with the low estate of our schools. The higher institutions place great value on the depth, breadth, and accuracy of knowledge while the schools disparage this in accordance with the "banking theory" famously linked to the Brazilian educator Paulo Freire.

In fact there is nothing in "banking theory" to warrant a word of this. Banking theory is, strictly speaking, a cognitional theory emphasizing the student as the subject in the most active mode of thought and attention and critical reflection in the interplay of the subject–object relation. Anyone who reads Freire's small article "The Act of Study" can see that he voices no opposition to content per se. His opposition is to the narrative or third-person style of the lecture by contrast to the "I–Thou" mode of critical conversation or *dialogue*—Freire's key concept. This is also evident in the first few pages of the second chapter of *The Pedagogy of the Oppressed* where Freire contrasts the two traditions sharply as "teacher cognitive" versus "student cognitive" QED. The real problem with "banking theory" in Freire's hands is the Marxist twist he gives it at the end. The genesis of this twist is readily apparent in the essays from the early Lukács to the later Bloch (as in the former's studies of 1918 and 1923 and the latter's commentaries on the subject–object relation in Hegel.)[17]

In a startling passage Hirsch clothes himself in the authority of Jefferson. Of course Jefferson was in favor of the highest level of education, and this needed to be content based, rooted in the subject matter of history, literature, and the sciences of the time. However, his *Bill on the Diffusion of Education* was predicated on the value of rural life with a small landed aristocracy. Accordingly, Jefferson crafted one of the most selective systems in the annals of American education. "By these means," said Thomas Jefferson, "twenty of the best geniuses will be raked from the rubbish annually." The contrast with Hirsch and the promotion of mass culture could hardly be more striking. Hirsch has confused "public education" with "mass education," the "public" with the "mass": and with this the tension between democracy and education is lost.

Though he recognized the twofold nature of Jefferson's idea of education as based on talent and virtue, Hirsch focuses entirely on knowledge. Virtue, which is the moral dimension of the student as subject, has disappeared and with it the distinction between education (or culture) and training (or skills "knowledge," "core knowledge," and the like). Hirsch has given us a remedial program in training. Fair enough. But why mislabel this, calling it "education" and linking it to the name of Jefferson?

Hirsch makes favorable reference to Bruner, but fails to recognize the significance of the work associated with his name. This oversight is a clue to his method. Hirsch sees everything as falling into one or another of two camps:

factual or content-rich traditional education versus "romantic" or anticontent progressive education. The politics of this method makes for the strangest of bedfellows. Bruner would appear to be lumped with the first, along with Gramsci, whereas Kozol and Freire, along with discovery teaching, are relegated to the second.

As the *beau idéal* of traditional education Hirsch directs our eyes to "Polished Stones," a videotape of Japanese-style teaching in mathematics edited by Professor Harold Stevenson and available from the Department of Psychology at the University of Michigan, Ann Arbor. Merely to meet him point for point, I invite your attention to a homemade product, the very American "Challenge in the Classroom," a videotape available on my website (www.instituteforactivelearning.org) of Professor R. L. Moore teaching a class in mathematics via "the Moore Method," an early form of discovery teaching in mathematics. It is described in a very readable article by Paul Halmos, himself a distinguished mathematician and teacher in *Selecta: Expository Writings* now made available on my website.

As the most polished of his polished stones, Hirsch holds up a textbook for our admiration. This is an American product and not a Japanese one, homemade and Anglo-Saxon to the bone, the Protestant ethic made flesh. Its author is John Saxon, and his credentials are formidable. As an Air Force pilot he flew fifty-five missions in Korea. Turning to teaching, he was aghast at the mathematical illiteracy of his students and wrote a textbook to provide them with a no-nonsense, content-rich, back-to-basics foundation. An immediate success, it has been adopted by hundreds of schools and is popular with homeschoolers. Sequels were written, and Mr. Saxon went on to become a multimillionaire.

Place this precious stone beside a book called *Discovery in Mathematics* by Robert B. Davis (Addison-Wesley, Palo Alto 1964) or its companion volume *Explorations in Mathematics* (Addison-Wesley, 1967, 1966). While much of this is designed for a more elementary level, which of the two is superior as an orientation and approach to really fine mathematics education?[18]

To brief off his case Hirsch has consistently confused two traditions which have next to nothing in common: A) The "aristocratic" or elite tradition of Jefferson with B) the mass tradition of "core knowledge" and the basics buffs; A) Gramsci and the socialist tradition beginning with the two codes Morelley's *Code de la Nature*, 1755, and Dezamy's *Code de la Communauté*, 1842)[19] and continuing with the early Lukács and Revai down to Freire and "banking theory" with B) Bagley, Chester Finn, Diane Ravitch, and Charles

Sykes, i.e., the architects of hegemony; A) The tradition from Moore and Halmos, Bruner and Shulman, Davis, Hawkins, Stebbins and discovery teaching, strictly speaking, with B) the vagaries of progressive education, European romanticism, James Hurd, Kilpatrick, Colonel Parker, and the rest. Worst of all, he has confused a brilliant tradition, which centers on the student as subject with a movement in which the student is always and everywhere the object of instruction and propaganda dressed up as history, as classically revealed by Frances Fitzgerald in *America Revised*.

Hirsch is a gifted polemicist and his effect is overwhelming. If Hirsch has things right side up I have things upside down. Either the case for traditional education, the key function of rote learning and drill, the narrative style of the lecture, the survey style of the textbook, the teacher as oracle, the imperative for a national curriculum policed by a politburo of enlightened traditional educators, etc., etc., has been brought off with success, and the enemy, prominently including "discovery teaching" put to rout, or our flag is still flying, despite this recent advance in offensive artillery.

Gramsci as icon is the ideal entry point into the thought world of E. D. Hirsch. If Gramsci is not as I have represented him he is merely a curiosity in the museum of historical antiquities, a dull and unoriginal traditionalist hawking a baggage of facts or, worse yet, a proto-vulgarian ideologue out of business since the collapse of the Soviet Union. But if he is as I represent him in his essay "On Education" and more particularly, on the creative school, then a wholly different universe of discourse opens up in the debate on education and the nature, perfection, and destiny of America as civilization. And the analysis of Hirsch and his various misconceptions can point the way to the correct solution.

The Solution

Dewey and Russell's thoughts were presented in a paper read at a symposium on education in Halifax, Nova Scotia. In it, Professor William Hare has carefully summarized their contributions to the "philosophy of education" as the professoriate is pleased to call it. Suppose, however, that these are not regarded as matters of philosophy, consigned to some Platonic limbo and there to be debated forever. Suppose, instead, that they are regarded as cognitional activities that I, as student, perform when I am thinking. Why then, the question is: How must I, as teacher, teach so as to produce and develop these cognitional activities? How must I do this in the case of say, subtraction, exponentiation, functions and function machines, summation, imaginary and complex numbers, graphing on the complex plane, and so forth? Or, how should I do this with the equality clause of the Declaration of Independence, the free speech clause of the First Amendment, the Gettysburg Address, and so on? It is a question of *techné*, not of ideology. It follows that teaching of this form is always value-neutral. It cannot have any purely ideological axe to grind for that is the very nature of a *techné*.

This is a form of teaching I developed as a young faculty member at the University of California, Berkeley. This is also the mode of instruction developed in "the discovery school" as I here call it, which I founded and directed for twenty years in Berkeley. Or, yet, again, this is the method and style of teaching I am presenting on my website for you to see and judge for yourself. "Dynamic conformism" apart, I contend that it is at all points identical with the fundamental elements in the vision of education which inspired Antonio Gramsci in the pain-wracked solitude of his prison cell. Nor do I say this because I have the slightest desire to benefit by association with the name and legend of Gramsci. Not only is it a fact that I do not share his political outlook, but it is also a fact that discovery or Socratic teaching has, as a practical enterprise, soared far beyond anything he could have imagined. But on the crucial point we are as one, the creative school and the discovery program are identical. And we are ready to bring it out from the prison walls to the capital cities of the New World.

Notes

1. Isaiah Berlin, "The Question of Machiavelli," *The New York Review of Books*, Special Supplement, Vol. 17, No. 7, Nov. 4, 1971.
2. Quentin Hoare, *Selections from the Prison Notebooks of Antonio Gramsci*. Translated by Quentin Hoare and Geoffrey Noell-Smith, International Publishers, New York, NY, 1971, pp. 109ff.
3. Stanley Aronowitz and Henry Giroux (1988) Essay Reviews: Schooling, Culture, and Literacy in the *Age of Broken Dreams*: A Review of Bloom and Hirsch. *Harvard Educational Review*: July 1988, Vol. 58, No. 2, pp. 172–195. Henry Giroux, Schooling for Radical Politics by Harold Entwistle, *Telos*, 45 (*Fall, 1980*), "Schooling, Culture, and Literacy in the *Age of Broken Dreams*," (with Stanley Aronowitz).
4. Karl Popper, "How I See Philosophy," *The Owl of Minerva*. (Ed.) Charles J. Bontempo and S. Jack Odell, McGraw-Hill Books, Inc., New York, NY, 1975, pp. 45ff.

5. Ludwig Wittgenstein, *Philosophical Investigations/Philosophische Untersuchungen*, Third edition, New York: The Macmillan Company, 1958. The first edition is 1953: (another translation) "Philosophy is a battle against the bewitchment of our intelligence by means of language." P. 47e, §109.
6. It is precisely this point on which the issue was joined by John Dewey in "The Vanishing Subject in the Psychology of James" (*Journal of Psychology*, Vol. 37, 1940, pp. 589ff). Dewey's more general analysis in cognitional theory is presented in his earlier book *How We Think*, D. C. Heath and Co., Boston, 1910.
7. It suffices to mention the names of Toulmin, Peters, Hare, and Searle to convey the point. R. S. Peters (*Ethics in Education*, 1966) illustrated the approach to education and the debate provoked by Searle's article on the is/ought question exemplifies the general style.
8. Bertrand Russell (*My Philosophical Development*. George Allen and Unwin, London, 1959, pp. 100–101) presents an on-the-spot account of the transition from Brentano and the act–content–object analysis of sensation to the abstraction favored by the propositional function. In this abstraction, as in Wittgenstein, the "subject" is repudiated as outdated. "There is no such thing as the soul, the subject, etc., as is conceived in contemporary superficial psychology." *Tractatus* 5.5, as quoted in Russell, *My Philosophical Development*, p. 87.
9. Voegelin concludes the analysis of Helvitius in connection with Bentham and modern utilitarianism with these words: "The process of general education for the purpose of forming the useful members of society while neglecting or even deliberately destroying the life of the soul is accepted as an institution of our modern society so fully that awareness of the demonism of such interference for the life of the soul on a social mass scale and of the inevitably following destruction of the spiritual substance of society is practically dead." *From Enlightenment to Revolution*. Duke University Press, Durham, North Carolina, Third Edition, 1972, p. 70.
10. All pagination here as given in parentheses refers to the precise pages in Gramsci's essay "On Education."
11. The significance and capital importance of Rousseau in the culture clash was brought to center stage first in Italy and then in the United States. In Italy, Galvano della Volpe, writing from the left, analyzed the relationship between Rousseau and Marx in his *Rousseau e Marc e Altri Saggi di Critica Materialistica*, Editori Reuniti, Roma, 1964, subsequently available in English as *Rousseau and Marx*, Lawrence and Wishart, London, 1978. A year later, Allan Bloom published his translation of the *Émile* with its provocative introduction written from the standpoint of the Straussian right. See *Jean-Jacques Rousseau, Émile or On Education*, translated with an introduction by Allan Bloom, Basic Books, Inc., New York, NY, 1979.
12. For an account by a prominent political scientist, privileged to have interviewed Mussolini directly for the preparation of his study see Herman Finer, *Mussolini's Italy*, Grosset and Dunlap, London, 1965, pp. 461, 468, 471–472, 475 and *passim*. (The original edition was published in 1935 by Henry Holt & Co., New York, NY).
13. Gramsci, Antonio, 1971. "On Education", in *Selections from the Prison Notebooks*. Trans. and Edited by Q. Hoare and G. N. Smith. New York: International Publishers, pages 24-43; Online: https://www.marxists.org/archive/gramsci/prison_notebooks/problems/education.htm
14. The educational authority, Jacques Barzun wrote of the university: "it must always remember that the new truth almost always sounds crazy and crazier in proportion to its greatness.

It would be idiocy to keep recounting the stories of Copernicus, Galileo, and forget that the innovator was seen as hopelessly wrong and perverse as these men seemed. The cost of this freedom might be a good deal of crackpot error but nothing good goes unpaid for." Jacques Barzun, *Teacher in America*, Doubleday & Co., New York, NY, 1944, pp. 163–164.

15. Georg von Lukács, "*Die Subjekt-Objekt Beziehung in der Aesthetik*," Logos, 1918, and his legendary *Geschichte und Klassenbewusstsein*, Malik Verlag, Berlin, 1923.
16. Jonathan Kozol, *Savage Inequalities*, Harper Perennial, HarperCollins Publishers, New York, NY, 1991, pp., 204ff.
17. Ernst Bloch, *Subjekt-Objekt Erläuterungen zu Hegel*, Suhrkamp Verlag, Frankfurt-Am-Mein, 1962.
18. If the workbook style of the layout makes comparison difficult, then try Harold Jacobs, *Mathematics: A Human Endeavor*, W. H. Freeman and Co., New York, NY, 1995.
19. Morelley's *Code de la Nature*, 1755 and Dezamy's *Code de la Communauté*, 1842.

· 2 ·

"THE MAGIC OF MARXISM"

Paulo Freire Pro and Contra

> But then, if I am right, certain professors of education must be wrong when they profess to put knowledge into souls that do not possess it, like sight into the eyes of the blind. Whereas our argument shows that the soul of every man does possess the power of learning the Truth and the organ with which to behold it; and that, just as the eye was unable to turn from darkness to light without the whole body, so too must the instrument of knowledge be the movement of the whole soul turning away from this world of Becoming toward the real world of Being until its eye can bear to contemplate Reality and the vision of that supreme splendor which we have called the Good.[1]

* * *

The educational philosophy of Paulo Freire can be cut in two with a methodological stroke. On the one side is his political philosophy which is substantially Marxist. On the other is his cognitional theory which is substantially Hegelian. The former, the political philosophy, is sociological and names or describes, or explains the universe of objects: classes, class society, exploitation, inequality, oppression, etc., and looks to the future, the classless society, which is its obverse. The latter, his cognitional theory, is very different: It is not a sociological theory but, on the contrary, a theory of the *subject*, that is to say, a radically individualist theory deriving from Hegel, the early Lukács, and the later Bloch. To be sure, these are intimately connected in Freire's mind. Analytically speaking, however, they are entirely different. And failure to see this difference is at the root of the confusion alike among his friends and followers and, on the other hand, his critics from Harold Entwistle to Sol Stern.

Freire's theory of the subject is unquestionably his most distinguished contribution to the philosophy of education. It is not an idiosyncratic or eccentric statement but part of a long tradition which began with Plato and the Platonic Socrates and one to which the Church Fathers such as Abelard and St. Thomas, Hegel and his followers down to Lucien Goldmann, Dewey, Bruner, and associates have all contributed in one way or another.[2] The tradition incorporates Protestant, Catholic, and Jew with names like Soren Kierkegaard, E. F. Schumacher, and Martin Buber. Yet its contributions to the theory of consciousness and the mind of the student as subject have been totally overlooked. A rich and diverse tradition in philosophy, and with Kierkegaard and certain of the Church Fathers, in philosophical theology, has been overlooked in favor of modern physics and cognitive science. The debate surrounding the name of Paulo Freire is an example of this in the domain of educational philosophy. For Freire's lasting contribution is solely in the domain of cognitional theory understood as part of a long and unfolding tradition. To confuse this with his political philosophy as friends and foes of his critique of "banking theory" have done is only to produce confusion and division along purely ideological lines. Freire's central term was "dialogue." So let me enter into the problem in the form of a dialogue or critical conversation with Sol Stern, his most recent critic.[3]

To work my way into the problem and confront the central issue I will proceed conversationally responding to Sol Stern point by point precisely as he makes his case. He begins by recognizing Freire's prestige and "near iconic status" in the educational world. In American edition the *Pedagogy* has sold nearly a million copies, and its author was invited to a Visiting Professorship at Harvard. But, Sol Stern complains, the book does not treat much or any of the standard fare in Ed School literature (testing, standards, curriculum, the role of parents, school organization, etc.)

Response: Of course not! If it had, would it have sold a million copies and fired the imagination of young and old, students and teachers? Would you expect a Brazilian writing in Portuguese after work with peasants in Recife to be treating these topics in a School of Ed handbook? As its title suggests it is a work of political philosophy, of consciousness-raising among the "oppressed" represented by the peasants and workers of Brazil. And it is precisely as such that it makes its impact on the American Left. As such, it has next to nothing to do with US schools, curriculum, and teaching. And Harvard, like Sol Stern, has missed the point.

* * *

Next, Stern makes the point that *Pedagogy* is in essence "a utopian political tract" for the times. Quite so. Why, then, does he go right on to argue that none of the great names in European and American educational philosophy are to be found in its pages, not Rousseau, not Piaget, not Dewey, not Horace Mann, not Maria Montessori!

Response: Why would one expect a work on adult literacy to be dealing with the Émile and Piaget, and Maria Montessori? Why would a Brazilian be dealing with Horace Mann and how does Dewey fit in to the project of Marxist consciousness-raising? Freire's project is "emancipation" via the creation of a conscious vanguard composed of revolutionary men like himself and driven by students and teachers on the Left.[4] Freire's prime purpose is political, and he makes that clear. Hence his retinue of authorities: Marx, Lenin, Mao, Fidel, and Che, but it is also moral and ontological (Lukács, Marcuse, and Sartre, Frantz Fanon, and Regis Debray). And here is where the issue in philosophy could be joined. But Sol Stern to our regret does not do so. Nor is he alone. If Harvard wished to favor Freire with a Lectureship, it should have been in the Department of Government with Harvey Mansfield and Louis Hartz and an invitation to Paul Heidelberg and Gerhart Niemeyer. A few such guests at the table and the conversation would really brighten up. Make no mistake, Freire has posed a fundamental challenge, and it has taken fire. But it is an issue in political philosophy, not in the standard School of Ed superficialities. And that is where it should be confronted.

To say that Freire's language is "metaphysical and vague" and that he operates with a two-factor "oppressor–oppressed" theory is not to say too much. Metaphysical language is to be expected in a work in political philosophy. And metaphysical language does not come with scientific precision. But here again is where the issue could profitably be joined. But, again, Sol Stern does not do so. Freire has given us the clearest and most elegant definition of Education as "the process by which knowledge, first received on the level of the *doxa*, is transformed into true knowledge now comprehended on the level of the *logos*." This ranks far beyond Chester Finn and the Fordham Institute, Sol Stern and the Manhattan Institute, and the retinue of traditional education, skills-oriented rhetoric from the Gardner Commission on down to E.D.

Hirsch and Diane Ravitch. Indeed, I know no better definition. Does Sol Stern disagree? Freire's definition is concise and elegant. But as a Marxist, as a believer in dialectical materialism, what right has he to invoke the *logos*, notably a term of classical and Christian vintage? Surely this is a touch of Christian or, rather, Catholic socialism.

    I would not be as hard on Freire for employing a two-factor theory of "oppressor and oppressed" because we can say that he is working with a simplified model as indeed was Marx himself with his Capitalist–Proletariat model. A two-man board game is a permissible simplification when one's main objective is to cast light on the fundamentals of exploitation and surplus value, be it among the workers and peasants of Brazil or elsewhere. Freire is working with a general or universal model and the complaint that you cannot verify it by reference to peasants here or workers there is beside the point. What is not misguided is Stern's further point, namely that the case rests on Marx's theory of the eventual classless society toward which all history is inevitably moving. Marx makes this as a flat empirical or historical prediction. And here he, and Freire following him, is completely mistaken. The entire theory is complex mythology.[5] The myth is neatly caught up in Engels' famous dictum of "the withering away of the state" following the socialist revolution. In fact what we have seen everywhere is the precise opposite, namely the strain toward totalitarianism. And this points to the fundamental moral inversion at the heart of Marxism prominently displayed by Lenin in *The State and Revolution*. More: with this doctrine Marx has condemned all of history to the pale status of "pre-history," with real history, a history never to be written, as real history. This is the case Sol Stern *should* have made but did not. Recast in evangelical and moving terms it is the source of the appeal of Freire in Catholic Latin America and among the secularized Left in this country conveyed to perfection in Herbert Kohl's obituary article on the death of Paulo Freire.[6]

    In an uncharacteristically ungenerous moment Stern displays contempt for Freire, calling him a "derivative and unscholarly" thinker. What he means by this I do not know. He submits no evidence and no argument to back up this judgment. Perhaps unlike Sol Stern I knew Freire and spent a long evening conversing with him at the Julia Morgan Theater on the occasion of his visit to Berkeley. And I must say that I found him one of the two most open-minded thinkers I have encountered on the Left. (The other was Ivan Illich.) Paulo listened to all my criticisms with the closest and most friendly attention. And he responded to each and every one of them fair-mindedly and with precise reference to the texts in Marx and Lukács, Sartre and Marcuse, etc., etc. The disciples surrounding him were becoming increasingly upset. But Paulo silenced them saying "No no! I think this is very interesting, very important." He really meant what he said about "dialogue."

The more important point about this little sketch is the light it casts on the failure of Sol Stern to communicate. This failure occurs on two levels: First he fails to grasp the existential context. And second, he fails equally to understand the philosophical context in any depth whatsoever. A word about each is in order. Fidel and Che are certainly among the two most popular men in Latin America (circa 1970). What's more natural than that he should refer to them and not give us a purely abstract treatise, a play without characters. And in a work on consciousness-raising the names of Regis Debray and Franz Fanon are not entirely inappropriate. Fidel and Che had made a successful revolution, and Regis Debray and Franz Fanon had broadcast the gospel to "the wretched of the earth." It's all perfectly understandable.

What all this calls for is philosophical critique. But this is precisely what Sol Stern does not make. Two examples: Freire mentions the concept of "love" and its critical importance in developing the movement, and he cites Che precisely in this regard.[7] What exactly does he mean? It will not do to characterize Che as the (brutal) executioner of hundreds, perhaps thousands, of people. In much of Latin America to those familiar with the brutalities at the close of the Batista regime, the execution of counter revolutionaries will not cut much ice even if alas! the executions were often summary justice. The significant question is: Why does Freire consider it important, consider it of critical significance to introduce the dimension of "love?"

The answer, I contend is simply this: The dimension of love, or more precisely "the politics of friendship" marks the dividing line between bourgeois society or the commercial world in its icy impersonality, its ice-cold purely contractual relations, and the premodern world from Greece and Rome and all through the Middle Ages. And this in its later incarnation was a Catholic and precommercial culture, the culture into which Freire (and Fidel and Che) was born. The politics of friendship is characterized by trust and built on camaraderie. The politics of the commercial world or bourgeois society is "the politics of distrust." A socialism, Paulo is saying, built on anything but "love" is a socialism in name only for it will reproduce the alienation of bourgeois or market society and the commercial world.

But the problem of understanding runs deeper still. Once "the politics of friendship" is perceived as the fundamental and dividing line, the question arises: Who is on the side of friendship, and who on the side of "the politics of distrust?" The answer to the latter is obvious: It is Sol Stern and the Manhattan Institute, Chester Finn and the Fordham Institute, etc., etc. And this is what the politics of the culture war in education is all about. The answer to the former, however, is more subtle and infinitely more complex. Its complexity only reveals itself when we study the actual history of the culture clash and develop a familiarity with the *dramatis personae* in their strangeness to an audience on either side of the border. In the culture war as it was actually fought out we have not two but three and maybe four main actors. The first two on our board game are familiar as progressive education (and Dewey) soon followed by the American Left (and Freire), while on the other side we have traditional education from Entwistle on Gramsci to Sol Stern on Freire. This, then, is the war between liberal or market society and its critics coming from the postmodern or Marxist world of postcontractual relations predicated on the vague idea of Equality. But there is a third and possibly fourth actor. The next actor to enter the stage is a somewhat strange and recluse figure. And it is with him that we are first introduced to Aristotle and the politics of friendship in the premodern and classical world. His name is Leo Strauss, and he made his impact felt in two waves.[8] With his Walgreen lectures, published as *Natural Right and History*,[9] and especially his sharp critique of Locke, Strauss became instantly controversial as *the* major voice from the Right. The second wave came in the form of a series of books and articles by his students on various major figures forming the modern understanding of politics and society, education and culture. They presented a new understanding of Machiavelli and Rousseau (or Hagel, or Marx), Hobbes and Locke, Montesquieu and Bacon, the American founding, the Civil War, and the meaning of politics and the American republic. All this was in sharp criticism of modernity and the commercial world favored by Locke and liberal political theory.

The flat opposition between Strauss and Marx, the classics and the moderns, Plato and Aristotle versus Machiavelli and Rousseau (or Hegel and Marx), accounts for the resumption of mutual hostilities. But this should not blind us to a certain similarity: Both take what we may call "the Lockean world" as the object of criticism, one from a premodern and the other from a postmodern standpoint. The Strauss critique of Locke in *Natural Right and History* has a certain kinship to Macpherson's critique in *The Political Theory of Possessive Individualism*, and earlier in "Locke on Capitalist Appropriation." Phrased differently, the politics of friendship so prominent in Aristotle (or Sophocles, or Homer) is the other side of the coin called Marx on alienation or estrangement, the central problem at the heart of market society with its

Leibnizian Universe of windowless monads. Friendship or "the American Regime?" that is the central question posed by the Left and the Right, Strauss and Macpherson or, if you wish, Freire.

When posed in these starkly naked terms a fourth and most unlikely actor steps to the center of the stage. Unlike Strauss he is not a recluse but the most famous actor in our two hemispheres and known to one and all. On screen he was played by Marlon Brando with whom I spent a long afternoon and evening in California. He, too, was a foreigner…and Catholic. He is known to the world as Don Vito Corleone, and his disquisition on friendship and the value of acquiring "real friends" made to Amerigo Buonasera (or Good Night America) is the single most significant dialogue in film history. When Puzo's novel, stripped of the extraneous sex and violence, is read with an innocent eye, it can be seen as nothing short of a treatise on politics and the nature and dynamics of political power in the premodern world of The Five Families. Amerigo Buonasera is the epitome of the modern world: "America," he declares, "has made my fortune." He wanted and tried to live like a good American. And dutifully he went to the Court for justice when his daughter, the light of his life, was cruelly beaten. But the Judge was bought and the Court did not give him justice. For justice, he says to his wife, "we must go to Don Corleone." But he does not come with respect: He comes, good American as he is, as a contractor prepared to pay a fee for a service and retain his superior and independent status. He is unwilling to give his friendship and swear his fealty, his first loyalty to the Don. "If you had come to me," says Don Corleone, "your enemies would be my enemies and they would fear you." And, "my purse would have been your purse." Such is the value of "real friends" and such "the politics of friendship." The impact of *The Godfather* with its saga of community is the secret of success behind Puzo's novel, Coppola's brilliant film, and Freire's hymn to love and comradeship. And Sol Stern has missed it all!

Stern's failure to meet Freire on any proper philosophical level is matched by an equal if not total failure to understand him on the level of cognitional theory, a totally neutral domain of analysis. In cognitional analysis one is either correct or incorrect as a neutral or purely technical fact. Of course, any given writer's cognitional analysis will likely be linked to his broader philosophy: Kierkegaard to Lutheranism and fideism, Marx and Lukács to socialism, Dewey to democratic education, Schumacher to the small and local, Buber to one's neighbors and the kibbutz, etc. But the two are different in nature, and this difference must be kept in mind in all valid analysis. Stern, on the contrary, blends all into one. He blends progressive education (and Ed School) with Freire and Marxism, and divides the sides into two, teacher cognitive and child centered, as if there were no third. The result is a logical disaster. Consider this point by point.

1. According to Stern, Freire rejects the teaching of "any academic content." Is this true? Stern cites no evidence, and I do not believe that Freire rejects the teaching of mathematics and science in the schools.[10]
2. Secondly, he cites Freire correctly on his opposition to textbook teaching as "official knowledge." In light of Frances Fitzgerald's classic 1979 study *America Revised*,[11] how wrong is Freire? Is the conventional version of Columbus, traditionally taught over many generations, right or wrong? How likely is the traditional teacher's lecture to be correct, whether liberal or conservative, in the light of recent scholarship? The point at issue is deeper and more complex than Stern allows with his simple dichotomy. He attacks Freire's critique of "banking theory," but offers no genuine critique. To cite E.D. Hirsch and the "Core Knowledge Program" will not do. Has Stern tested the students to see whether or not they have any real knowledge and understanding of, say, the equality clause in the Declaration of Independence, the free speech clause in the First Amendment, or, say, Federalist Ten and a variety of the Federalist Papers, or, again, Lincoln's Gettysburg Address? If he has not, it will not do, and multiple choice tests provide no answer. Finally, does Hirsch himself demonstrate the least understanding of Gramsci whom he links to Bagley as the twin icons of the traditionalist approach?

The real issue is this: Freire says that schooling "is never neutral." On the facts, is he right or wrong? In mathematics and science, it necessarily is, and to that extent he is mistaken. But he is speaking of history and the liberal arts. And strictly speaking he has a point and a reasonable one (*pace* Frances FitzGerald and James Loewen). But is he right in theory, in principle? I contend that he is not, and that the key to his error lies in his failure to follow up the results of his celebrated critique of "banking theory."

Brief as it is Freire's contribution to cognitional theory is his outstanding contribution to the philosophy of education. It is his lasting contribution and stands in sharp contrast to his political philosophy which lies outside the American tradition and has nothing to offer to the American school system. Nor was this his intention. The Pedagogy is addressed to the landless and the poor and powerless in Brazil and Latin America. It has nothing to say to the improvement of curriculum and the raising of standards in the United States.

The significance of his work lies in another, misunderstood and totally overlooked, dimension. And this can be readily seen when placed in its proper historical context. But first we must remove an enduring misunderstanding deriving from his equivocal use of language. His use of the term *logos* in the example cited earlier is one case of this. But there are many more. He consistently uses terms like "emancipation" and "transformation," and many others deriving from his Christian and Catholic background and heritage, and gives them a consistently Marxist twist. This accounts for his appeal especially to the young. But he has no right to it.[12] This use of ambiguous and equivocal language blending two traditions, the progressive and the Christian, into one has a long history. It was originated by the progressive literary critic Vissarion Belinsky and nailed down with precision by Dostoyevsky after his break with Belinsky and the progressive movement and Russian populism. But none of this is to be found in Freire's cognitional theory which, as theory, is free from all such disfigurements.

Freire's pure theory comes to us in two parts, the first negative and the second positive. The negative is his critique of "banking theory" and the lecture or *narration as an art form*. This is not in the primary sense a political statement, though it has obvious political implications in our concrete historical context. It is pure cognitional theory and, technically speaking, it is either right or wrong on its merits. I contend that it is right, though not in as sweeping a sense as Freire presents it. But to assess its rightness or wrongness it must be considered together with his positive statement presented in "The Act of Study," a tiny four-page contribution to the field, curiously overlooked by the critics. "The Act of Study" presents a model of "student cognitive" learning. It presents the student as the active agent in the creation and recreation of ideas. It is too brief and too simply and lucidly written to require summary here. Read it for yourself and make up your mind. You don't need me as "friendly guide."[13]

"Friendly guide," the phrase recalls Gramsci and his characterization of the teacher, not as lecturer and authority but as a "friendly guide." Lay the texts down side by side and we see that Freire is precisely, on the level of cognitional theory, in the tradition of Gramsci. Nor should this occasion be of any surprise. For they were both heirs to the subject side of the subject–object polarity, dialectic, and unity cast into prominence by Hegel and celebrated by the early Lukács and the later Bloch.[14] On the subject side of the distinction some of the great names are those of Kierkegaard, E. F. Schumacher, and Martin Buber, to name Protestant, Catholic, and Jew. But the tradition itself is far more ancient. Indeed, it goes back to Plato and the Platonic Socrates who, in our opening quote, says: "But, then, if I am right certain professors (of education) must be wrong...." Question: Which professors? Answer: The Sophists, or traditional professors of "official knowledge." Question: Why "must" they be wrong? Answer: Because they profess to put knowledge into the minds of the young (as if they were empty heads). Question: And why is this wrong? Why is it wrong to transmit such knowledge, the holdings of the culture? Answer: Because knowledge (of the essential things, moral and metaphysical knowledge) is always a self-appropriation and not contained in books or lectures. When I question them, says Socrates, of the books he has consulted, they do not answer back. Knowledge is the result of dialogue, of question and answer, of the matching of argument and counterargument. But the books are mute, and the lecture (like the one by Protagoras) can fill the hour: The teacher talks, the student listens, etc., etc. The first great critic of "banking theory" was Plato himself and the Platonic or historical Socrates who drew the dividing line between the sophists (and official knowledge) and himself. And this line continues to divide us to this day. For, make no mistake, the other side has equally great names from Hume and Russell, to Wittgenstein, Ryle and linguistic behaviorism, E.D. Hirsch and the core knowledge program. Question: Is Sol Stern prepared to defend linguistic behaviorism and E.D. Hirsch? If so, let's hear the defense.

Knowledge is a self-appropriation. This is the core and essence of Freire's position, and on this he is either right or wrong. I contend that he is right. For, if knowledge is not a self-appropriation, then it is the result of advocacy and persuasion, rhetoric and indoctrination. This danger, always present, is built into traditional education as a form of teaching. On the level of cognitional theory Freire has overturned this as is plain to see when the negative and the positive, the critique of "banking theory" and "The Act of Study," are fitted together and seen as a whole, as one. This is his real achievement, and it fits right into Gramsci's sketch of "the Creative School." Taken together they present the socialist tradition at its best and most progressive. But two points remain to be argued: Freire's theory has been orchestrated from the level of the individual pupil to the level of the school once it is fitted in to Gramsci's sketch of the creative school. But A) how can this actually work, in the case of the individual subjects in the school curriculum? Will it in fact give us superior standards coupled with high motivation? And B) Can such schooling, however desirable, be neutral?

Take the last question first: Freire has himself provided the answer to this question. For if the sketch he lays down in "The Act of Study" is rigorously followed and knowledge is self-appropriation, then I do not see how it can be anything but neutral. And this is also precisely the burden of Gramsci's sketch in his article "On Education." Nor is the reason difficult to see once it is understood that cognitional theory is itself, as a *techné*, perfectly neutral. It can be fitted into an overarching socialist philosophy as with Freire and Gramsci, or into a liberal and democratic philosophy as with Dewey. But in and of itself it is as neutral as, say, the procedure for training retinal surgeons whatever their overall medical philosophy and religion. Education is in its innermost essence the pure and free play of the mind in its search for truth. Accordingly, Socratic knowledge is famously "knowledge of ignorance," of how little we know in the light of the whole. Consequently, it questions all official knowledge. Its movement is not from left to right or right to left but from below to above. It is an ascent from opinion to knowledge.

Finally, can it develop far higher standards of learning coupled with motivation raised to fever pitch? My answer to this question is placed on our website for all to see and judge. I offer it as my final word to say more would be inappropriate. Judge for yourself.

Summing up: There are *two* major dimensions in Freire's educational philosophy, and not just one, though these are intimately blended in his mind with the slogan "to make the political pedagogical, and the pedagogical political." These are his cognitional theory flowing from Hegel, and his political philosophy deriving from Marx. The former has been misunderstood where it has not been totally overlooked by his disciples and critics alike. The former is of inestimable value. The latter is purely mythological, the source of his appeal to the Left and confusion to the Right. The appeal is readily understandable. The confusion then and now is not. Yet it is there: Harvard, whose School of Education was once presided over by Patricia A. Graham, invited him to be a visiting Lecturer. Professor Graham was also President of the Spencer Foundation which only recently made an award of three hundred thousand dollars to a Freire follower, Ron Glass. The use to which this is put, according to Ron Glass over our local radio station, would make one laugh. More laughable still is the two million awarded another follower, Herbert R. Kohl, by the Carnegie Foundation to stage some "happenings."[15] Yet in a way none of this is surprising: Freire's followers have come up with nothing because there is nothing there to come up with. Simply said, begin with a theory of the subject as with Gramsci and Freire, Bruner and associates and you open the way to a theory of instruction and an engaging craft of teaching. *Per contra*, where the student is visualized as object the teacher naturally assumes the role of a transmitter of information and the road to a viable craft of teaching is closed.

In the culture war in education Freire's significance is entirely different. He is iconic of the first of three waves against modernity in its Lockean capitalist or market society liberal democratic formation. This view from Marx to Marcuse is postmodern and rooted in the anarchist utopia of the future. But there are two other waves, one Athenian and classical, the other Italian and rooted in medieval and feudal culture. The first revolves around the name of Leo Strauss now well-known with his "secret writing" and "hidden truths." The second is the yet more famous name of Don Vito Corleone and the eulogy on "friendship" with which Puzo opens his novel and Coppola still more brilliantly opens his film.[16] The perspective of both is *pre*modern, and the link between them is friendship, celebrated by Aristotle and the ancients and discarded by the moderns from Machiavelli to Montaigne and Bacon.[17] But there is also a second side to Don Corleone, and this is overlooked in the controversy about *The Godfather*. Stripped of the sex and violence *The Godfather* is a treatise on political power, its nature, structure, and dynamics. Before Tip O'Neill *The Godfather* understood that "all politics is local" and built on community and friendship. Unlike Marx he was a realist who understood the need for organization on the local or community level. He was the Prince of Organization.[18]

In the novel the theory of organization is presented in seven steps. Taken together they form a *model* of organizational theory standing in sharp contrast to the postmodern model followed by the radical critics. The steps are these: 1) Quality Over Quantity: The motley, undisciplined assortment is trimmed down to become a select and disciplined regime of soldiers divided into two "superbly organized" regimes each headed by a Capo, Clemenza and Tessio. 2) The two regimes were separated to minimize the opportunity for collusion and conspiracy against the Don. Now well-trained, smooth lines of communication leading to the *Consigliori* were developed for action within the regime and stretching outward to other cities like San Francisco, Detroit, and Chicago. 3) Each family was autonomous. 4) But the families as a whole were linked together in something like a federal structure. 5) Since "all politics is local" (*pace* Eric Cantor) no request was ever turned down. In return the Don could deliver votes *en bloc* to Congressmen and "the Senator." 6) The Don laid the greatest value on this interconnection between the family and the outside world of law and politics, lubricating the wheels with "the mother's milk of politics," generous infusions of cash. 7) But his supreme gift was manifested in his choice of Michael to succeed him as Head of Family with Rocco Lampone to back him up with a secret regime trained to strike when the time was ripe. This last reveals the Don as a *Menschenkenner* who could read men because of his own self-understanding beginning with Fanucci and ending with Barzini and Phillip Tattaglia and the preemptive strike.

As a model of organization this premodern model stands in striking contrast to the postmodern model favored by Freire and the radical critics. They, too, operate out of a model, and it is one whose main lines are clearly visible. 1) Instead of organization they place their faith in ideology. 2) As literary intellectuals, mostly historians, journalists, and publicists, they place their faith in the Word and its transforming power. The magic of Marxism worked for Freire, so why should it not for them?[19] 3) The result is an academic tempest, an endless stream of books and articles, talks over the radio and conferences rebroadcast over the radio. 4) Is always the same: Here is a blemish or problem, usually a very real one in market society, or capitalism, or liberal democracy. But this will magically disappear under socialism, or communism, or rather anarchism when all good things will at last be yours. 5) No Marxist thinker beginning with Marx himself has shown that this is remotely possible. And, in the absence of organization the message of the radical critics in education is condemned to impotence. And the model tells us why. Concretely speaking, the model reveals three faults: A) the goal on which it is fixated, action on the Federal level, is too vast, especially in view of their puny resources and lack of organization. An example is Kozol's *Illiterate America* with its "Plan for Action" funded by Rockefeller and Guggenheim. The description of school inequality was well done and quite moving. But the "plan" was no *plan* at all. As a proposal to a conservative Congress (and President) to appropriate two hundred billion it was no more than an exercise in fantasy. The votes were just not there, and writing a Marxist book in the tradition of Freire was not going to create them. B) Kozol and Kohl, Giroux and Aronowicz return time and again to their two heroes, Gramsci and Freire. But they have misunderstood them both. Gramsci spoke of the need to develop "those scholars who in their thousands, or hundreds, or even dozens are necessary for every great civilization." But the radical critics have inverted the emphasis and neglect the problem of the best and brightest in favor of a hopeless attempt to "bring up the bottom half." The American tradition of "radical" critique is a complete inversion of its European past. C) As a bureaucracy the school system is notoriously resistant to change. In the great heartland, i.e., between Berkeley and New York, to approach it in terms of Freire's political philosophy is to try to make a sea change with a lot of hot air. Freire's contribution was to cognitional theory in the tradition of Gramsci and, dare I say it, and Bruner alike. But this is precisely what the radical critics have consistently neglected and overlooked. So let's place it on the table for them.

"The best way to learn is to do. The worst way to teach is to talk." So writes Paul Halmos in his fine article on "The Problem of Learning to Teach," a write-up of his talk to teachers of mathematics.[20] By "talk" he is clearly referring to the lecture method favored by traditional education. Why, in the view of this distinguished mathematician, is the lecture "the worst way to teach." The answer can readily be found in the model presented by Freire in the opening pages of the second chapter of the *Pedagogy of the Oppressed* and known as the critique of the banking theory. Professor Halmos was, of course, no Marxist. And this shows that the critique is not intrinsic or unique to Marxism. From the Oxford tutorial to Freire, Dewey, Bruner, and associates the opinion is shared by the most enlightened thinkers. And the model to operationalize this was first sketched by Antonio Gramsci.

"The best way to learn is to do". Question: Do what? Answer: Since he is addressing teachers of mathematics it cannot be referring to doing anything in the external or physical world. It must, therefore, be referring to thinking, to cognitional activities which occur in the mind of the student. Examples of these cognitional activities are familiarly noticing, paying attention, marshalling the data, making a conjecture or forming a judgment, searching for a weak point or rebutting a counterargument, verifying the proof or structure of argument, etc. All this is relatively familiar to the teacher, especially when the student is transformed into a subject. But the best place to study the model of this transformation, the *locus classicus*, is Freire's brief article "The Act of Study" which forms the positive complement to his critique of the lecture system which is "the worst way to teach" because it converts the student into an object, a passive or receptive "banker" of knowledge and information. And this is likewise the transformation toward which Gramsci is aiming in his sketch of the creative school in his essay "On Education" which began the modern tradition in discovery or Socratic teaching. Here Gramsci and Halmos or Moore are at one.

In this tradition how best could we as an Institute proceed in our outreach program to a Latin country across the border? On the level of organization theory the method favored by the radical critics (aiming at change on a national level) was immediately discarded as useless, as ineffective moralizing to no purpose. The postmodern alternative was dead on arrival. So, what about the premodern alternative of community organization outlined in model form by Mario Puzo in his novel? We were not a mafia family and I was no mafia Don. Nevertheless, I saw that it could be well adapted by making a few critical amendments. The *locus classicus* of the new approach was founded in friendship (and not in contract or market morality). But it was friendship of a new and different kind. To wit: Don Corleone famously said "Why do you fear to give your first allegiance to me?" We, on the contrary, expect our colleagues to continue to give their first allegiance to *their* country and *their community*. We are an educational and philanthropic organization and ask for nothing in return. Nor do our donors! This said, we ask only that A) they form a responsible Committee and open a bank account for the transmission of funds. B) Organize a Competition to which a number of students, teachers, and schools could be invited. C) Learn to create genuine mathematical problems for the Competition. D) Invite the parents, leading citizens, and media to attend. E) Videotape the proceeds and place them on a website for complete transparency. And, finally, form a Leadership Team to enroll other cities in neighboring states for a finale to Havana. And this, I submit, is the true gift of Freire and Gramsci before him to the capital cities of the New World.

Notes

1. Socrates, in Plato's "The Allegory of the Cave," *The Republic*, Book VII, pp. 376–377: http://www.idph.net/conteudos/ebooks/republic.pdf.
2. "Dialectic," says Abelard "is the soul's way to truth."
3. "The Pedagogy of the Oppressor," *City Journal*, Spring (March) 2009, Vol. 19, No. 2, pp., 19–20.
4. His aim he says clearly and openly is "to make the Political Pedagogical and the Pedagogical Political."
5. For three different perspectives on the problem see: (1) Stanley Aronowitz, *The Crisis in Historical Materialism*, University of Minnesota Press, First Edition, Minneapolis, MN, 1990. (2) Robert Tucker, *Philosophy and Myth in Karl Marx*, Transaction Publishers, Third Edition, New Brunswick, NJ, 2000 and (3) More generally M.M. Bober, *Karl Marx's Interpretation of History*, W.W. Norton & Company, Second Edition, revised and enlarged edition, New York, NY, 1965.
6. Herbert Kohl, "Paulo Freire: Liberation Pedagogy," *The Nation*, May 26, 1997.
7. The reader will recall the dimension of *eros* prominent in Allan Bloom's *The Closing of The American Mind*.
8. His tenure at *The New School* where he edited *Social Research* and published *Persecution and the Art of Writing* might be considered the first small wave or wavelet.
9. Leo Strauss, *Natural Right and History*, University of Chicago Press, 1953.

10. I do not believe that Paulo would oppose the teaching of mathematics and science in the schools. The distinction he makes is clear and precise: He opposes teaching via the lecture system as an art form because of its inherently narrative quality which transforms the students into an object. The form of teaching he advocates is in his words "problem posing" education typically starting bursting with problems which a teacher is invited to introduce with a question. For evidence and illustration, I invited you to look at our website. Paulo's signal limitation as an educator was his inability to see his Marxism itself as posing a problem.
11. Frances Fitzgerald, *America Revised*. This is a textbook genre dated 1979.
12. "Electricity," said the more consistent Lenin in his debate with Krassin, "will take the place of God," Dimitri Volkogonov, *Lenin: A New Biography*, Free Press, New York, 1994, p. 373. The electrification of theology was Lenin's distinctive contribution to politics, "socialism," he said on another occasion, "equals Soviets plus electrification."
13. Paulo Freire, *The Politics of Education: Culture, Power, and Liberation*. Intro. by Henry Giroux, tr. by Donaldo Macedo, Westport, CT: Bergin and Garvey, 1985, pp. 1–6.
14. Georg Lukács, "Die Subjekt-Objekt Beziehung in der Aesthetik," *Logos*, 1918, pp. 1–40. Ernst Bloch, *Subjekt-Object: Erläuterungen Zu Hegel*, Suhrkamp Verlag, Frankfurt am Main, 1971.
15. In the first happening, as Kohl describes it, one set of students was required to paint a wide strip down a highway, after which a second set was required to erase it. In the second happening the students were required to watch a large block of ice dissolving slowly in the noon day sun.
16. "Friendship is everything," he declares to Johnny Fontane in a later seen. "Friendship is more than talent. It is more than government. It is almost the equal of family never forget that."
17. For a fuller account see the fascinating and very learned study "Don Vito Corleone: Friendship and the American Regime" by Paul A. Rahe in *Reinventing the American People: Unity and Diversity* (Ed.) Robert Royal, Ethics and Public Policy Center, Washington, D.C., 1995, pp. 115–135. The difference in our two approaches turns on two related points. Firstly, friendship in Aristotle and classical culture is personal and social and is predicated on equality between the friends. In the feudal culture of Don Corleone, however, it has become radically transformed into hierarchical requiring fealty to the Don. In brief: friendship has become political friendship within the compass of the family circle. Secondly, and more importantly, Professor Rahe and his friends remain on the level of political philosophy and the higher learning, "the great conversation," while I proceed to enter the academic market place, the schools and teachers, of action on the ground which is the real stuff of politics and the transformation of political culture.
18. Notice the fine organization, strategy, and tactics in the war with the rival Don Salvatore Maranzano with victory leading to his development as a great Don.
19. See Michael Polanyi, "The Magic of Marxism," *Encounter VII*, December 1956, pages 5–17. For my application of the idea see my article "How Myths are Made" part one.
20. Paul Halmos, "The Problem of Learning to Teach," *American Mathematical Monthly*, May 1975, Vol. 82, No. 5, pp. 466–470, See also Jones F. Burton, "The Moore Method," *American Mathematical Monthly*, April 1977, Vol. 84, No. 4, pp. 273–277.

· 3 ·

THE TWO CODES

Origins and Meaning of the Culture War in Education

"Wastelands" as Symbolic Form

Perhaps the most intriguing fact about Arthur F. Bestor's classic work *Educational Wastelands* was its title. For it could as easily have been the title of a book by Neil Postman or Herbert Kohl, Henry Giroux, or Stanley Aronowitz. When the iconic figures of either side, progressive or traditional, survey the landscape what they see is an educational wasteland perceived by the other. We are, it would seem, looking at two entirely different wastelands; one characterized by race and class inequities, unmotivated students lacking any curiosity and sense of wonder, and a stultifying curriculum patrolled by administrative policemen, etc.; the other sees a collapse of standards, falling SAT scores, a farcical curriculum produced by the Ed school follies, the threat to business and government, and America's low ranking in every international survey. In the polemical exchanges, now known as the "culture wars," the protagonists continue to talk past one another in tones of rising frustration and anger. They do not engage. Neither side really understands the other. This much is clear. But does either really understand itself? This is the question, the question of self-understanding, to which I invite your attention as the key to the puzzle posed by Bestor's title, now understood as a symbol in the conflict.

Since the twenties, certainly since the sixties, the Left has traveled a distance from the vision which originally inspired it. The modifications and adjustments, changes of emphasis and priorities made step by small step suggested continuous development and enrichment over time. In fact, it has created a wholly new tradition, part socialist and part progressive, compounded of Marxism and Dewey. Today all is seen and studied within the context of a new horizon whose catalogue of contents, readily available in any of our educational journals, guarantees a small readership mostly restricted to the schools of education which have themselves been demoted to the basement of the academy and cut off from the professional faculty in mathematics and sciences, philosophy and the liberal caricature to Marx and Dewey. When the canonical texts of the movement are set down and considered as a whole (from the Postman of *Subversive Activity* and "The Politics of Reading" to the Kohl of *The Open Classroom* and the Freire obituary, or the Kozol of *Savage Inequalities, Illiterate America*, and *The Nation* article) they add up to a picture of moralistic and utopian thinking derided by Marx and to the distortion of Dewey's ideas as he himself reported. How did this all come about, and where do the points of inflection lie? Once we know where to look and pin this down, a comparison with the originals from Dezamy and Marx, Lukács, Gramsci, and Freire will reveal the path beyond a shadow of doubt.

To take the debate at face value, namely, as a discussion about the merits of phonics vs. look-say is to miss the point and mistake the epiphenomena for the real thing, the thing-in-itself. Men of Kohl's caliber are not just shooting at gnats. This is readily seen in *Basic Skills* and *Discipline of Hope* where the trouble in Turin, his symbolic city, soon moves far beyond phonics. Phonics and the curriculum are symbolic forms. They are two of the symbolic forms of oppression, suppression, and repression in the regime of capitalist exploitation and enslavement. The repair work in the basic skills as advanced by the opposing side is, in Giroux's derisive words, to produce a "culture of yuppies." What is needed is a new culture. Some leave us to guess what the new culture would be, others are more candid. It would be a socialist culture, distinctively American and, of course, post-Stalin, with some variety of progressive education paving the way. The teacher is to be much more than a specialist in his field. He is to be an "intellectual," nay more a "transformative intellectual" in the footsteps of Gramsci and Freire. And with this the scene is set.

With this, we also come to the critical points of inflection where the path taken by the reformers changes direction and moves further and further away from the classical writings. In the betrayal of the classical tradition (be it in socialism or in Dewey), three features stand out amidst a host of others. The outstanding features are these: (1) The promotion of equality, now dressed up as "equity" in a special sense. (2) The attack on the canon and with it the disparagement of the drive toward the highest achievement, now denounced as "elitism." (3) The lack of interest and wonder in the child.

Yet, the development of a cognitional theory to serve as a basis for the development of curiosity and wonder was the signal achievement of Gramsci and Freire alike. Indeed, Gramsci went so far as to speak of those "great scholars in their thousands, or hundreds, or even dozens which are necessary to every civilization." And, neither Marx, nor Lenin, nor Trotsky attacked the canon *per se*. In the classical writings, socialism stood for a culture that would surpass the heights of bourgeois culture. It would reach heights beyond Balzac and Stendhal, Thomas Mann and Hölderlin, beyond even Goethe, to produce those great scholars....[1] "which are necessary to every civilization." The new horizon contents itself with drop-outs and the rising tide of illiterates in *Illiterate America* with the structureless class in the attack on discipline, with the teacher as facilitator and the need to hear "student voices" talking about their concerns, and with curricular offerings readily parodied by the conservative Olin scholar Charles Sykes. The door to the conservative backlash was flung open.

Education and Indoctrination

Of the captains of culture on the Right special mention should be made of Diane Ravitch alike for the professional and personal qualities displayed in her work. As a professional historian, she writes with clarity and a command of her materials. More than once, she provokes interest by bringing fresh research to enliven a tired field. More important still, she presents her case with an objectivity which is wholly admirable. Her account of Dewey, coming as it is from the traditional side, is a model of impartiality. She presents Dewey's criticisms of the vulgarization of his thought without flinching. And all who have fallen sway to the blandishments of progressive educations mentioned above should return to these pages for a refresher course. More interesting still, she mentions a class she visited and found engaging and effective. The students were involved. They were learning. The class was alive. It was, she tells us, a class in Socratic teaching! But the mention is casual, and Professor Ravitch does not go on to investigate the anomaly. It remains a strange beast, a curious animal in the garden of letters. Why so? Answer: for all her many virtues, Professor Ravitch remains trapped within the horizon of the professional historian. They constitute a *terra incognita*, a dark wood into which those few who stray might never be seen again. It never occurs to her that Socratic teaching can be schematized into a fully developed craft of teaching. So she goes right on with her story. The result is the partial and, therefore, misleading history and theory which vitiates the traditionalist case in education at its most critical point. Here, two of the outstanding names are those of Chester Finn and William F. Buckley Jr. The former on the primary and secondary level, the latter the scourge of Yale and Liberalism. We can drive straight to the point with the former. But it is only with the latter that the disastrous mind-set reveals itself.

"Facts are to thought," Finn tells us, "as bricks are to mortar."[2] Finn writes as a man who knows the "facts," who has all the answers and need not, therefore, ask any of the questions. In particular, he does not ask Carl Becker's question: "What Are Historical Facts?" "Facts," to his mind, are what is substantial, what is solid, what is real in building the house of intellect. (Question to Chester Finn: When was oxygen discovered? And who discovered it?) But facts, as Norwood Hanson tells us, are richly impregnated with theory: fact is theory-laden. Collingwood invited attention to the "fact" that "The Battle of Hastings was fought in 1066," and showed immediately the myriad facts, each of which could again be subdivided, out of which it was composed. Differently phrased, Collingwood, like Becker, reverses the emphasis in Chester Finn stressing the priority of the cognitional over the brute facticity of the "facts." The interesting point in this little *esquisse* is the fetishism of the fact and the mindset it reveals. It explains the overemphasis on the curriculum as a catalogue of contents over the craft of teaching, and it explains the misunderstanding of Gramsci by Entwistle, and his misappropriation by Hirsch who joins him to Bagley as the Siamese twins to whom he dedicates his book. And, most interesting of all, it explains the consistent confusion of teaching with advocacy in the teaching of history and literature. To the conservative mind the facts are clear. It remains only to indoctrinate our students in them. This is revealed in its most glaring form in the case of Mr. Conservative himself, William F. Buckley Jr., gadfly in a world forgotten by God.

Buckley crashed into fame and notoriety with *God and Man at Yale*.[3] He presents a lawyerly case, arguing that education, rightly understood and responsibly administered, has been undermined at Yale and subverted by the culture of Liberalism. It has been turned from God and the free market to a culture of atheism, materialism, and skepticism, in ethics, morality, and religion, and to Keynesianism, collectivism, and socialism in economics and politics. And this in clear contravention of the tradition and beliefs of alumni whose pride and generosity endows the institution. *God and Man* is a lightweight text and easily read. Casual reading can, however, convey the wrong impression. A casual reader might infer that the wrong values were, generally speaking, being taught in philosophy and religion, economics and politics, and that right values should be (taught, that is). But this is only half the point, and perhaps the lesser half. His larger point is the nature of teaching itself, and what in his subtitle he calls "the superstitions of academic freedom." In Buckley, we come the whole way from the advocacy, latent but always present in the textbooks, to "values inculcation" and candid, straightforward indoctrination. In fact, Buckley cannot see any difference between teaching, good teaching, teaching at its best, and indoctrination. For Buckley they are one and the same thing. Good teaching is inevitably proper and successful indoctrination. This theme is developed explicitly in his next, more mature work, *Up From Liberalism*.[4]

To dramatize the case, Buckley holds up the figures of three teachers as iconic. The iconic figures are Lenin, Adam Smith, and Socrates! Into what myth or belief system Socrates was indoctrinating the men of Athens is a secret Buckley carried with him to his grave. The Platonic Socrates denied this twice, once famously in the *Theaetetus* comparing himself to a midwife, herself barren, who brings forth what lies pregnant in others, and, again, more famously yet in the *Apology* where he speaks of mission as dedicated to philosophy, question and answer, and the improvement of the soul. All this is familiar. More interesting is the mindset, the frame of mind and horizon that produces this curious misperception in Buckley.

The problem, as Buckley sees it, is the pejorative connotation that clings to the word "indoctrination." Really, we ought to get over that. After all, as he explains, it is the result of a liberal hangover. "The result of a false antithesis between education and indoctrination cultivated by the liberals themselves." After all, he points out in his suave, most teacherly tone "… education is largely indoctrination any way you look at it" (p. 81). Well, one way to look at it is in terms of Socratic teaching as a rigorous, developed, modern form of teaching which centers exclusively on the critique of the counterposition, whatever it be, radical, liberal, or conservative. In answer to Buckley, taken as iconic of the conservative mind set, I am placing a DVD on our website of myself teaching a workshop on *The Gettysburg Address* for a score of teachers in our public schools. And I challenge the conservative mind at its best, Chester Finn, Diane Ravitch, or M. D. Eshelman, for example, to find any trace of indoctrination in it.

The halfway house between education and indoctrination is education understood as *advocacy*. Education accepted as advocacy is, especially in the liberal arts, the door through which the teacher passes from advocacy, now widely accepted, to indoctrination with the make-over skillfully provided by Buckley. The transition, made with the suave ease of a diplomat, is barely noticed and has never been repudiated by the conservative elite. The reason is simple: Once teaching is understood as the simple transmission of a series of *contents*, in Arnold's phrase "the best that has been thought and written in the past," the lecture with its transmission of contents emerges as the natural, i.e., the ideal and most efficient form of teaching. The good teacher is the good lecturer, clear and concise with the right touch of humor at the right time, a storyteller with a tale to tell, whose story never fails to rivet the attention of the class. When the authority of the lecturer is backed up by the authority of the textbook, always chosen by the teacher as lecturer, the cards are stacked against the student. The landscape becomes one of dull conformity. Only the rare exceptional student goes against the grain to emerge as a critical mind, and educated man. Few have described this better than Buckley himself. So the reader can turn to his pages for enlightenment on the point.

Buckley is dismayed by the *contents*, which are Liberal. He does not question the form which is that of narration and not of critical questioning, the form which made Socrates an iconic symbol in the literature of philosophy and the Platonic dialogues a vast mark of interrogation. Socrates is not an indoctrinator, but the inquiring mind personified: "Come," he seems to be saying, "let us think together. Let us inquire. Let us investigate."

The source of the error in Buckley and the conservative elite in education lies in the fact that they are unable to see the student as *subject*. This is the *scotoma* or blind spot at the very center of their vision. They only see him as the *object* of instruction in which the lecture slides into advocacy and finally indoctrination. So it is that—what the conservative takes to be "real" learning in history—is seen as largely bunk by the liberal-left. In time, the bunk has been debunked classically in Frances Fitzgerald's *America Revised* and more recently by James Loewen in *Lies My Teacher Told Me*. The left has broken with the content: This is its virtue. But it has not broken with the form: That is its problem. Failure to break with the form is the heel of Achilles in the body of left-wing literature in Britain and the United States. Two rival sets of propaganda, two bodyguards of lies, confront one another in the culture clash. And neither is really Education, understood as the free play of the mind in the formation of a culture of citizenry worthy of the name. What they *have* produced is a looking glass war in which Kohl, Kozol, and the company function as the mirror opposites of Buckley, Chester Finn, and company, with education, properly understood, going to the dogs.

When what is presented by the Right, is viewed as an *ensemble,* it can be seen as a code, a rule, a canon of interpretation, a lens through which all things are seen. Facts are judged as relevant or irrelevant, and given their due weight and importance. Things are set in place in their right and proper context. And all is again well in the world. To the Left, this augurs in a regime of conformist monotony, the night in which all cows are black. But, the contemporary Left has its code, too. It is one with which Charles Sykes can make easy sport. And E. D. Hirsch can, as professors do, target it the "critique of a thought world." The culture clash today can be understood as the clash between the two codes. Two souls, traditionalist and progressive, are striving for mastery over culture and the body politic. While this is true in a real sense it does not take us very far. The clue to the problem is Buckley's radical misunderstanding of Socrates taken as a symbol for all true and proper education and culture. Buckley has misunderstood his own tradition at its best and finest.

Precisely the same can be said of the Left today. Step by step, the American Left has strayed so far from the compact experience and vision of its founders and key figures whose work as an ensemble constitutes a more elevated and certainly very different tradition. The source of the tradition was the French Enlightenment. But the tradition really begins, at least in education, with the two codes of Morelly's *Code de la Nature* (1755) and, more particularly, Theodore Dezamy's *Code de la Communauté* (1842) which, taking Morelly's title as symbolic now focused on society and became the first significant socialist work to devote an entire chapter to education. To read Dezamy on education is to enter close to the compact experience and understand the vision in something like its pristine purity. The first shock is that here in its compact form we find no war against the canon. On the contrary, Dezamy is steeped in culture in its classical sense and may be said to embrace the canon. He calls for a study of the earth and the stars or what we would today call physics, optics, and astronomy, geology, and the earth sciences. More: he is interested in history, in high culture of Rome, and the brilliance of Athens. Yet, he is far from being a traditional educator: Under socialism we would finally rid ourselves of "the routine-minded pedagogue" and the sterile discipline bordering on violence to the child and his psyche. And, while he does not quite say this, he is close to presenting the student as subject, the theme taken up by Gramsci and Lukács in education and philosophy, that is to say, in culture. This tradition becomes precise in Gramsci, and is brilliantly developed in Lukács and later in Freire.

The decisive step was taken by Gramsci in his sketch of "the creative school" where the discovery in learning and, therefore, *discovery* or Socratic teaching, is the hallmark and distinguishing feature of the school. Nor, again, does Gramsci attack the canon and traditional curriculum in essence. On the contrary, he would have broadened it, bursting the rigid and narrow confines of the textbook to make way for the enterprising student to discover the classics of literature and history, to enter into a dialogue, albeit still on the child's level, with the great minds of the past from the Enlightenment and the Renaissance to Roman high culture and the dazzle of Athenian brilliance. Nor, yet again, did he orient education in the direction of remediation. The creative school in his hands was oriented to produce those "great scholars in their thousands, or hundreds, or even dozens which are necessary to every civilization." And he provided a structure, a university-like seminar setting for dialogue, for conversation, with the teacher as "friendly guide" to ensure it. In present-day parlance, Gramsci was an "elitist" to his fingertips. And, while this could not quite be said of Trotsky, who aspired to have it for "every man," at least down the line, his embrace of high culture is unforgettable in the line with which he chose to conclude *Literature and Revolution*. "Every man an Aristotle, a Goethe, a Marx."

But by far the most significant contribution was the dialectical philosophy of the early Lukács made between 1918 and 1923.[5] The origin of these ideas lay in the philosophy of Hegel, and particularly in the *Phenomenology* where in the "Foreword," Hegel announces "the turn from substance to subject" and shapes all modern dialectical thought on the Left from the early Lukács and Adorno to the later Lucien Goldmann and *The Hidden God* on through to his *Recherchés Dialectique*. Its impress is clearly visible in Freire's *Pedagogy of the Oppressed*, especially in the critical second chapter which presents the students as *subjects* and that makes a powerful critique of the lecture as an art form which makes the student the object of regular communiqués in class after class.

Insight and Oversight: The Looking Glass War

In overlooking this line of thought the Left has produced a looking glass war. Its partner in the enterprise, its mirror image, is the conventional Right. Together they produce the looking glass war with education as the first casualty. Buckley is only the most prominent name to stand for the retinue of conservative and traditional educators who have lost touch with the best and most interesting thought in their own tradition. He calls us back to religion with his first book. But he overlooks entirely the contribution that religious thinkers, Protestant, Catholic, and Jewish, have made to cognitional theory and the theory of the subject. In the breakup of the Hegelian tradition the most significant name here is that of Soren Kierkegaard and the *Concluding Unscientific Postscript*. Equally significant in the Jewish tradition is the name of Buber whose *I and Thou* has passed into the language. As a Catholic, Buckley must know the work of Jacques Maritain, whose "Knowledge Through Connaturality" presses us hard in this direction.[6] And, so again, does E. F. Schumacher in the central two chapters (*Adaequatio* One and Two) of *A Guide for the Perplexed*,[7] also the author of *Small Is Beautiful*. The political and sociological dimensions of the theory were developed by Max Scheler and in his country by Manfred Frings, two scholars without whose work the psychology and politics of the Left is not fully comprehensible.[8] In Britain, Collingwood made the question the central thrust in all real teaching. "The question," he said, "is the gas that explodes in the cylinders and fires the pistons." In this context, Buckley and associates would have come to genuine appreciation of Dewey, and he would have dropped the disastrous conflation of education and indoctrination. For, discovery teaching always respects the moral sovereignty of the subject. It is the antithesis of indoctrination and propaganda.

The looking glass war is conducted in terms of a number of assumptions taken as axiomatic by both sides. In my view, these assumptions are flatly mistaken. But that is only *my* view. At the very least, they deserve to be more widely debated than ever they have been. The critical assumptions are these: Axiom 1. The culture clash began in the 1960s, or in greater historical perspective, in the 1920s with Dewey and Kilpatrick. Axiom 2. Our culture war is essentially our own, as American as it can be and waged in an essentially autonomous America. Axiom 3. The key figure here is John Dewey, the Dewey of progressive education and *Schools of Tomorrow*. Axiom 4. The apple of discord plucked from the tree of knowledge can only be cut in two. On the Right, is traditional education; on the Left, progressive education: there is no third tradition. Axiom 5. In writing its history, therefore, the Russian connection can be entirely overlooked and with this the French connection disappears from sight. American history is exceptional. Axiom 6. There is not one war, beginning in Europe and extending over two hundred and fifty years since the birth of modernity. Those wars were merely local and historical skirmishes, battles, or revolutions. They have little or no connection with our war. The appropriate unit of time is seventy-five years, and not two hundred and fifty.

The axioms stated above are themselves the result of a still more fundamental assumption which we can call "the grand axiom." The grand axiom states that there is *one* logic, one single logic that guides all rational and scientific inquiry. In Karl Popper's magic phrase, this is "the logic of scientific research," the title of his celebrated work *Logik der Forschung*. It is unable to recognize the most salient fact of all philosophy and science: the fact that there are two logics: the logic of demonstration or proof, and the logic of creation or discovery, the logic of insight. The one is abstractly logical, scientific, cerebral, and ratiocinative: The logic of the scientist, historian, social scientist, or political theorist engaged in his normal or everyday work. The other is psychological: the logic or psycho-dynamic of the creative thinker or theorist as subject in the moment of insight dramatized by Archimedes in the *Eureka!* experience.

We can think of these as "the cold current" and "the warm current." The one is distinguished by logical analysis, by scientific or purely empirical investigation. It asks Joe Friday's question "What are the facts?" and understands the "facts" to be the facts of purely external experience, and elevates the truth of impersonal or interpersonal validity into the true and only test of knowledge: knowledge is scientific knowledge, positivistically understood. Knowledge is knowledge of the objects of consciousness. All else is noncognitive. And, so, philosophy becomes the handmaiden of science. As Russell tells us, when you have finished analyzing the nature of justice or the good, all you have made is a linguistic discovery, not a discovery in ethics.

The result has been a violent distortion of the classical texts, and with it of the two traditions of discourse. This, in turn, has come about in two ways, the second of which is more subtle and less easy to detect than the first. The first is to marginalize certain writings, or place them entirely outside the professional writer's field of vision. I have called attention to some of the most prominent. But, a hundred others could as easily be cited. More subtle is the mental phenomenon, sometimes known as foreground and background, by which one line of thought is cast into bold relief, front-burnered as we might say, and anther back-burnered, marginalized, and overlooked. The writer's political orientation hogs the footlights; his cognitional theory vanishes into the dark. The analyses of Gramsci and Freire, not to mention Dewey, are three conspicuous examples of this phenomenon.

In terms of analysis, Gramsci's sketch "On Education" can be divided into two parts: one is value-neutral; the other is value-oriented. The two parts are interrelated, but they are distinct. The first is his picture or model of "the creative school" featuring the student as subject, as the discoverer of "new truths" (with the teacher as "friendly guide"). This is located ultimately within the context of socialism. Gramsci alludes to it as a "new humanism," which provides its political or value-orientation. But both are present, and the one is not the other. By focusing entirely on the latter, the Left misunderstands Gramsci as a creative thinker of rank in the field of education. So, too, the traditional educator who, like Entwistle and Hirsch, focuses entirely on the canon, discipline and self-discipline, homework, hard work, and tests, misses the dimension of subjectivity, of the student as subject, which sets it apart from all traditional and conservative schooling in our time. The two sides highlight two very different effects. But, they are based on the same misunderstanding. This is seen even more sharply in the case of Paulo Freire who presented his cognitional theory, first sketched in the *Pedagogy*, in clear, separate, and distinct form in a little article called "The Act of Study."[9] Generally overlooked by both sides, Left and Right alike, it represents the most notable contribution to cognitional theory on the Left since Gramsci. And this, again, is value-neutral cognitional analysis. But both sides focus on Freire's Marxism or Socialism, his value-orientation!

The error outlined above leads to a signal misunderstanding of the tradition. The Strauss-Cropsey *History of Political Philosophy* closes with the impressive figure of Martin Heidegger. And Allan Bloom closes his tract on the culture clash with a chapter "From Socrates' *Apology* to Heidegger's *Rektoratsrede*." While this can pass muster on the purely philosophical level, it is widely off the mark as an analysis of the American clash in the culture war. The Russian hand, the hand of the *Narodnik*, well known to political actors as different as Dwight McDonald and Whittaker Chambers, not to mention Richard M. Nixon and Eldridge Cleaver, is overlooked and with it the crucial dimension of history.

So, again, in a work ranked among the "American Classics in Education," James Jarrett likens Socratic teaching to "programmed learning," thus missing the fact that Plato was the dramatist of the life of reason, in a drama requiring the constant and continuous interplay and mutual transformation of subject and object, the very theme of Freire and Gramsci alike. Dialogue in Plato cannot be likened to the craft of the programmer, no matter how skillful and artistic. And the value-orientation of a Freire and Gramsci, the Marxian Lukács and the Hegelian Lukács, should not be confused with their value-neutral analyses in cognitional theory. Of course, these are interrelated, one is the other inside-out, as it were. One focuses on the individual as subject and is, therefore, distributed on the individual or micro-level. The other is political, and distributed on the general or sociological plane. They are intimately interrelated, but they are not the same. And their continued confusion is the source of the trouble emanating from the grand axiom.

Philosophy and Education: Identity and Difference

It ought to be obvious, but obviously it isn't. A political philosophy is, in essence, nothing more than an educational philosophy writ large precisely as an educational philosophy is nothing more than a political philosophy writ small. *The Republic of Plato* can be read as the first and grandest statement of political philosophy or as the cornerstone of *paideia*, the educational ideals of Greek culture. Nettleship reads it one way, Jaeger another, and both are right.[10] The Rousseau who wrote *The Social Contract* was the same Rousseau who wrote the Émile. Meiklejohn's *Education Between Two Worlds* becomes more fully comprehensible as we come to understand its grounding in the political philosophy of Rousseau and of Kant, without which his house of intellect is a structure without a foundation.[11] Dewey's *Schools of Tomorrow* is the educational expression of the social and political philosophy of Instrumentalism, quite as Tolstoy's pedagogy at Krasnaya Polyana fits neatly into his philosophy of anarchism. The child-centered class in Holdt and Kohl follow *The Radicalizing of a Guest Teacher at Berkeley* and the impetus of the Teachers' College at Columbia. Kozol and Giroux are domesticated variants of Freire and Gramsci. Political philosophy and the philosophy of education are identical in structure and intention, however much they differ in scale and application. The one is the other inside out. They move on two different planes and, therefore, have two different goals. The aim of political philosophy is Justice, understood as the health or overall development of the body politic. The aim of education is culture, understood as the unity and perfection of the intellectual, moral, and aesthetic in the soul of man and citizen. Political philosophy and the philosophy of education are, then, two aspects of one and the same identity. This evident truth has vanished before our eyes: Today we confront two rigidly separated compartments, a School of Education largely innocent of political philosophy and a Department of Political Science which has in every University abandoned the cause and vocation of education to become a mechanistic and technocratic caricature of what it once had been. To recover a sense of that original unity of which Plato remains the classic example, we should return for a moment to Dezamy, a minor writer, in whom the insight was still fresh before the overspecialization of the modern age would produce its characteristic *déformation professionelle*.

Paradigm Shift: The Move from "Plato" to "Socrates"

In a remarkably perceptive article, Hans Meyerhoff describes "The Move from 'Plato' to 'Socrates'," where "Plato"[12] is a metaphor for discursive thought most suitably conveyed in the form of the lecture, review, or communiqué, the book, the learned monograph, the summa, or encyclopedia; and "Socrates" for the inquiring mind, the questioning stance, and the critical interrogation. The two forms typically coexist in society. In times of stability, in the long decades, centuries, millennia of massive consensus "Plato" naturally dominates the scene. In times of transition, however, in moments of breakdown when the consensus itself is in question, the stage is set for "Socrates," and the "move from 'Plato' to 'Socrates'" constitutes the decisive element in the paradigm shift.

The case of William F. Buckley, Jr., now taken as model for "Plato," illuminates the central problem at the heart of the culture clash in education. Buckley is merely the most candid of the protagonists, Right and Left, to make the case for education as advocacy and, finally, indoctrination. Against this, two lines of argument can be advanced. The first is highly damaging to his case, but not decisive. So I note it here for your consideration and best judgment. Buckley's teacher at Yale was the brilliant political theorist Willmoore Kendall, later a Senior Editor at *National Review*. Coincidentally, he was also my teacher in "Classics in Political Thought," the graduate seminar in political theory at Yale. In that intensely dialectical experience, I can say flatly, I noticed no indoctrination and, what is more, no advocacy. Either the leopard had changed its spots or Buckley missed the most interesting fact about his teacher's teaching: For Kendall was a consummate master of Socratic teaching in the sense here advocated. His most well-known work as a political scientist was on *Democracy and the American Party System*, coauthored with Austin Ranney.[13] In the Preface to this work, perhaps the best on the party system (circa the mid-fifties), Kendall points out that this is a work of collaboration between two scholars, one a conservative and other a liberal, working together on the plane of value-neutral scholarship. Kendall's analyses were characteristically value-neutral, though off at the end, value-oriented.

But, Buckley was not merely a student of Kendall. The mature Buckley was also the reviewer of *The Conservative Affirmation*. In his glowing review, Buckley misses a salient fact. Once more, in his Preface (pp. XXXIII and 6), Kendall makes the point that this book is intended to *identify* the conservative position rather than to affirm it, to situate it correctly in the landscape of American politics rather than to win more converts for it. To be sure, there are passages that may do the latter, but that is not why they are there: that is not their aim. The form of the essays ("What is Conservatism?", "The Two Majorities in American Politics," the essay on McCarthyism, and the review of de Jouvenel's *Sovereignty*) demonstrates this to the hilt. Yet Buckley has missed it all. Why so? If this were merely a personal failing it would not be interesting. But viewed as an iconic failure it becomes more significant. And this is revealed by my second line of argument which is decisive. On this the case of the iconic Buckley stands or falls.

The iconic Buckley presented his case with a skill that made it plausible to the conservative mind. However, the case was compounded of two very different criteria. The first was a truth claim: The Liberal as indoctrinator suppressed the work of Von Misses, Hayek, Wilhelm Roepke, Frank Knight, etc., etc., and these made for wise and good public policy. It made for as sound a public policy as could be established by unassisted reason. The second was very different. This could be called "producers sovereignty," or the right of consensus. The trustees and major donors have the right to call the turns on matters of religion and public policy because they provide the endowment and funding. A playful thought experiment suggests the precariousness of this view in a time of transition. Suppose over time there occurs a gradual influx of Indian, Chinese, and Saudi multimillionaires. Should the professoriate be required to "teach" (i.e., indoctrinate) the students in polytheistic Hinduism, atheistic Buddhism, and Wahhabi Islam? But these, according to Buckley and Catholicism, are false religions. Nor is the stance on public policy much clearer, and less dangerous. Buckley (and associates) famously favored McCarthy whom his hero, Whittaker Chambers, called "a raven of disaster," and favored a policy of "liberation" (as against "containment") despite the risk of precipitating World War III. Should these, too, be included in the teaching of political science as indoctrination? Kendall, who also favored these policies, called for "discussion," Buckley for "values inculcation" or "indoctrination." And there's the difference, and the rub. Discussion we should have, especially as Kendall presented it in his article on McCarthyism and in his vigorous Introduction to Alfredo Rossi's *A Communist Party in Action*, but indoctrination in a school or university, never.

The iconic Buckley, Left and Right, feels that indoctrination is unavoidable. All teaching is, in the last analysis, indoctrination. This belief is obviously false, and would have reduced Yale to the status of a mediocre Christian college after a predictable faculty revolt. More interesting is the question why Buckley as iconic form was unable to see it. Why was he blind to it? In the literature on insight this phenomenon is known as "the *scotosis* of the dramatic subject." And this blindness leads us to the crux of the theoretical or knock-down argument against it. In the culture clash Buckley is forever "Plato," never "Socrates." All he can see is the universe of objects, never the student as subject. And this despite the fact that he was taught by Willmoore Kendall whose teaching was purely Socratic and for whom the student was always subject, never object.

Buckley makes reference to Kendall's insight into the asymptotic nature of the liberal's theory of truth. For the liberal truth is always one jump ahead. We are always and forever pursuing it, never grasping it. But this is an epistemological theory, not a cognitional theory. A cognitional theory answers the question: "What am I doing when I am thinking?" While an epistemological theory answers the very different question: "Why does the result constitute knowledge (*epistém*)?" The former is on the side of the subject, the latter on the side of the object. As his student, Kendall forced me to think even more critically. And, while his value-orientation as a conservative was always clear, he never forced his opinions on me. In true Socratic style he elicited my counterarguments from me, always respecting my sovereignty as moral subject. And this is precisely the move from "Plato" to "Socrates."

"In the hands of the skillful indoctrinator," writes Buckley, "the average student not only thinks what the indoctrinator wants him to think...but is altogether positive that he has arrived at his position by independent intellectual exertion."[14] His entire argument with its many examples presupposes the figure of the teacher as lecturer. Once we move to the seminar setting his model begins to break down. When we take the next step to the seminar, now conducted in terms of Socratic teaching, his model collapses completely. Here, teaching is not purely critical questioning, except for certain passages occasionally favored for dramatic effect. Second, the Socratic teacher is carefully trained never to express an opinion either by word or tone. This is the famous Socratic incognito, the mask which fell away only with death. Third, to insure the absence of influence, Socratic teaching favors the "intentional error" or "deliberate mistake" as it is sometimes called. "Where you have the intentional error," Professor Drake once said, "you have Socratic teaching. Where you do not have the deliberate mistake, you do not have Socratic teaching." This might be a trifle extreme, but you take the point. The move from "Platonic" to "Socratic" teaching is the knockout punch to the iconic Buckley and his alter ego on the left. Buckley once said something like this: "Sit me down in the middle of a crowded cocktail party. Blindfold me, spin me around, and I will always find the nearest liberal standing there on my left." He was a man very sure of himself. He could always tell left from right. He just couldn't tell up from down.

In the culture war with which we are cursed, two great sets of antagonists have fired at one another and fought to a standstill. One result is the contemporary impasse in education and the degradation of culture. The other is the breakdown of rational discourse and comity in the public and even in the academy. Allan Bloom writes of "Our Listless Universities," by which he means morally adrift. And Sheldon Wolin refers to Bloom's book as "erudition gone slightly bonkers," i.e., as somewhat insane. What the two sides disagree upon in the resulting "educational wastelands" is plain enough and hotly contested. What they agree upon is the lecture form and advocacy, or what in our metaphor we have called "Plato." This might by now be unchangeable in our universities with their research orientation. But in primary and secondary education it can still be reversed. "Plato" as metaphor might well have been suited to a time of tranquility, of agreement on the fundamentals of the good life and good society, of consensus in education, culture, and public life. In a time of transition, marked by widespread alienation, dissatisfaction, resentment, anger, and disruption, it is markedly out of sync, and it is high time we make the paradigm shift and move from "Plato" to "Socrates." I ask you: "What is the nature of the time through which we are living?" Is it a time of reassuring stability and peace? Or is it a time of protracted transition, of breakdown and change? I put the question to you as the ultimate Joe Friday question: "What are the facts?"

Notes

1. For an appreciation of this signally important point, see the excellent article
   "The Mirror of Reality," *Times Literary Supplement*, Sep. 22, 1950, pp. 591–595. For an example in philosophy see Karl Korsch, *Marxismus and Philosophie*, C. L. Hirschfeld, Leipzig, 1923, and in *Literature and Philosophy* the Contemporaneous articles by Georg Lukács, *Die Rote Fahne*, Berlin, 1920–1923.
2. Chester Finn, Jr., *We Must Take Charge*, New York: The Free Press, a Division of Macmillan, Inc., 1991, p. 209: "*Facts* are to thinking as *bricks* are to *mortar*."
3. William F. Bucklley Jr., *God and Man at Yale*, Chicago: Henry Regnery Company. 1951.
4. William F. Bucklley Jr., *Up from Liberalism*. Lanham, Maryland: Rowman & Littlefield Publishers. 1961.

5. The first was specifically in cognitional theory titled "Die Subjekt-Objekt Beziehung in der Aesthetik" (*Logos*, 1918, pp. 1–40). The second was his brilliant *The Theory of the Novel* where he returned to the topic (see pp. 50ff.), now in the context of literature. And third, of course, was in the legendary *Geschichte und Klassenbewusstsein* (Malik Verlag, Berlin, 1923) which developed the theme, now from a Marxist perspective.
6. Jacques Maritain in *The Review of Metaphysics*, Vol. 4, No. 4 (Jun., 1951), pp. 473–481.
7. E. F. Schumacher, *A Guide for the Perplexed*, New York: Harper & Row Publishers, 1977.
8. Church history tells much the same story down through the ages. "Dialectic," said Abelard in *Sic Et Non*, "is the soul's way to truth."
9. Paulo Freire, "The Act of Study," in *The Politics of Education: Culture, Power, and Liberation*. Intro. by Henry Giroux, tr. by Donaldo Macedo, Westport, CT: Bergin and Garvey, 1985, pp. 1–6.
10. R.L. Nettleship, *Lectures on the Republic of Plato*, R. West, Philadelphia, PA, 1976. Werner Jaeger, *Paideia: The Ideals of Greek Culture*, Oxford University Press, Oxford, UK, 1986.
11. Alexander Meiklejohn, *Education Between Two Worlds*, Atherton Press, New York, NY, 1966.
12. Hans Meyerhoff in Karl-Heinz Wolff and Barrington Moore, eds., *The Critical Spirit: Essays in Honor of Herbert Marcuse*, Boston: Beacon Press, 1967.
13. Austin Ranney and Willmoore Kendall, *Democracy and the American Party System*. New York City, Harcourt, Brace and Company, 1956.
14. William F. Buckley Jr., *Up from Liberalism*, New York: McDowell, Obolensky, 1959, p. 83.

· 4 ·

THE TRADITIONAL MISTAKE OF THE TRADITIONAL EDUCATOR

Substance and Subject: The Dividing Line

"Truth," said Hegel in the Foreword to the *Phenomenology*, "must be understood and expressed not only as substance but also as subject." This insightful comment, expressed in compact form, marks the real dividing line between two very different traditions of educational philosophy and, accordingly, of curricular reform and the reform of teaching. One tradition, by far the more ancient, fixes attention on the *subject* in the subject–object distinction, dialectic, and identity. It is an *identity* theory focusing attention on the interplay of opposites, of subject and object.[1] The other, a more modern theory, fixes all attention on the object of knowledge on the substance of things, and rejects the critical significance of the *subject* in learning and educational philosophy. It is, therefore, not an identity theory but, on the contrary, a *perception* theory in which the scholar or critic, teacher or student confronts the objects of knowledge, the substance of things whether these be the "facts" of history or the formulas and problems of mathematics and science. The emphasis in the first is on the theory of instruction or craft of teaching and the promotion of insight in the *student*. The second is engaged purely with the curriculum and the standards it is designed to reach. The watchword of the first is insight or the *Eureka!* flash, or thought *thinking*, a subject term. The watchword of the second is "intellectual capital" or thought *thought*, or pre-thought thought, an object term, and the discipline required to reach it. The great names in the first tradition are Plato, Aristotle, and Hegel. The great names in the second are Hume, Locke, and British empiricism, Helvetius, Comte and French positivism. The first is discursive in the philosophical Platonic, Aristotelian, or Hegelian mode and is predicated on a theory of the subject. The second is positivist, empiricist, or behaviorist and is predicated on the "findings" of the social and behavioral sciences. The clash between them plays out the drama of the "culture war" in our time.

In our time, the conventional wisdom divides the two camps very differently. On the right we have conservative or traditional education, and the names which adorn this register are names such as Lynn Cheney and William J. Bennett, Chester Finn, Diane Ravitch, and E. D. Hirsch Jr. Their books range from *The Book of Virtues* to *The Schools We Need: And Why We Don't Have Them* via *We Must Take Charge* and *Left Back: A Century of Failed School Reform*. While on the left we have the many works of Neil Postman, Herbert Kohl, Jonathan Kozol, Henry Giroux, and Stanley Aronowitz, the last four presided over by the figure of Paulo Freire, and later Antonio Gramsci.

But this is to make a superficial, misleading, and purely ideological division which leads to endless confusion on the level of theory. Of course, the ideological content of one side is the polar opposite of the other and this leads to "the looking glass war" conducted as a dialectical exchange between the advocates of Wonderfulism and those of Awfulism: Everything would (again) be wonderful except for Dewey and Kilpatrick, relativism and the ravages of progressive education and, of course, the American Left. Contrariwise: Everything has been awful (at least since the end of the New Deal) from Bush One to Bush Two, what with war, the economy, unemployment, continued poverty and differential wages for equal work, corporations and banks, the rich and the super-rich, the elite and the media, racism, sexism, and homophobia (fill in the rest) except for the promise of progressive education, equality, equity, and social justice, harmony, and the brotherhood of man in a world now colored Green: Chester Finn meets Pedro Noguera. Structurally speaking, both sides today are based on the same premise: the denial of the subject and the consequent focus on the ideological contents of knowledge. In terms of deep structure Kozol and Kohl, Giroux and Aronowitz are simply the mirror opposites of Buckley and William Bennett, Chester Finn, Diane Ravitch, till she changed her mind, and E. D. Hirsch. One is the other with the ideological sign reversed. Ideologies apart, both are forms of "traditional" education, one conservative and the other progressive.

The true dividing line is the line which divides this false dichotomy from its genuine alternative and opposite, a theory based on the learner as subject, as the active subject of the knowing process. This tradition, too, has two main roots or sources. One is the classical tradition founded by Socrates, dramatized by Plato, and perfected by Aristotle. Via Aristotle and St. Thomas, the most outstanding work in cognitional theory or the theory of the subject comes from a school of Jesuit thinkers known as "the transcendental school" or "movement" and is presented by Otto Muck in his study *The Transcendental Method* (Herder & Herder, New York, 1968). In part, their work derives from Maréchal's *Le Pointe de Départ de la Métaphysique*. But in large part it is brilliantly original and creative, showing none of the marks of the schoolmen of old. In modern times, the second source was the philosophy of Hegel, particularly the *Phenomenology*, and the distinguished names which make up the Hegelian tradition in our time. In philosophy, the most celebrated names are those of Croce and Labriola, not to mention Gentile, the early Lukács, Korsch, Revai, and Deborin, and more recently Ernst Bloch and Lucien Goldmann.[2] In his *Philosophical Notebooks* (circa 1916) Lenin returned to Hegel, making Hegel's *Logic* the key to the correct understanding of Marx's *Das Kapital* beginning with chapter one. In Leningrad, the young Andrei Zhdanov wrote his dissertation on *Socrates as Pedagogue*. In Moscow, a generation later, W. Lektorski wrote his dissertation and published it in East Berlin under the title *Das Subjekt-Objekt Problem in der klassischen und modernen bürgerlichen Philosophie*. In education, the two names coming immediately to mind are those of Gramsci and Paulo Freire. Gramsci was born into a Catholic family, as was Freire, and both turned later to Marxism. But in each case it was a Marxism of a special kind: Marxism with a pronounced Hegelian dimension, though a subject-centered tradition is not limited to these names. In our time, it extends to Dewey and the movement in educational reform called Discovery or Socratic teaching associated with the name of Jerome S. Bruner and his colleagues extending from the National Science Foundation to Berkeley. Failure to understand the dichotomy between the subject- and object-centered traditions is the fundamental failure of the traditional educator as the voice of authority in educational philosophy. The many facets of this mistake, readily seen wherever we turn, demonstrate this beyond a shadow of a doubt.

Scribes and Pharisees versus the Sadducees

The literature of the culture clash in education can be divided into the clash between two sects, the Scribes and the Pharisees versus the Sadducees. If the left are the Scribes and Pharisees excoriating the sins of a fallen world, the right are the Sadducees grounded uncritically in the tradition or, as with Lynn Cheney, Bennett, and Buckley, expatiating forever on its virtues. A small sample, beginning with Harold Entwistle and his book on Gramsci, will illustrate the point at issue. Entwistle's approach shows all the merits of this form of investigation. It also reveals its characteristic defect. The merits are obvious. It is the product of much learning, detailed, thorough, and based on original archival research at the *Istituto* Gramsci. It is a painstaking, somewhat pedantic and tedious slog through the trenches, not a page turner but a learned account by a conventional academic. Books of this kind have been appearing with increasing frequency as the academic mind becomes more like the mass mind in the transformation foretold by Ortega in *The Revolt of the Masses* (1933). Such works bear all the stigmata of the mass mind now elevated to academic rank and status. They are uniformly atheoretical and devoid of genuine culture and learning with nothing new, or enlightening, or even interesting to say. Unlike Ortega, to mention only one example, they are monotonously repetitious, one building on another in explicating the same simple paradigm whose rightness or validity is taken for granted, or else dogmatically affirmed. In Thomas Kuhn's sense of the word, they are the "ordinary" books of the tradition. In the name of education, they function as the paradigm enforcers of mass culture. Theirs is the craft of the uncritical Scribe, a second-hand commentator, not the "messenger" with new light on an old and traditional problem. Unlike the messenger, such a scribe himself has nothing to say.

Paradox and the Traditional Educator

Entwistle's study of Gramsci is the *beau idéal* of the traditionalist educator as scholar, investigator, researcher, and authority. Both E. D. Hirsch and Dante Germino base their views of Gramsci on his study. Entwistle subtitles his book on Antonio Gramsci *Conservative Schooling for Radical Politics*.[3] And he concedes right away that this is surely a "paradox." He does not stop to ask whether the paradox is really in his own mind or in Gramsci's. The conclusion

THE TRADITIONAL MISTAKE OF THE TRADITIONAL EDUCATOR 65

toward which the "facts" drive him is the "fact" that Gramsci was a "conservative" or traditional educator, and for Entwistle that's that. It never occurs to him to ask whether the "paradox," and a host of other problems, might be the result of his own methodology and interpretation of the facts or, in a word, of the horizon he takes for granted.

His presentation of Gramsci on education, as distinct from his life and politics, ranges across nearly two-thirds of the book and defies simple summary. The main structural elements are, however, clear and can be stated in compact form. Compactly stated, Gramsci has all the earmarks of the traditional or "conservative" educator: He favors homework and hard work, discipline and self-discipline, tests and competitive testing. Indeed, he is not even averse to drudgery. As a socialist, he is "for" the traditional conception of equality of opportunity. But, in the scheme of things this inclines toward the development of a meritocracy (pp. 54ff.) etc. Does this apparently solid demonstration prove the case? Not a bit! Entwistle's case is that Gramsci was, in the final analysis, a "conservative" educator, but his evidence does not prove that at all. If Entwistle's conclusion is mistaken, where does the error lie? What precisely is the dividing line between Gramsci and the traditional or conservative educator?

Look at it this way: What Entwistle has laid out is, broadly speaking, the *phenomenology* of the serious or good school, whether it be purely traditional or otherwise. What he has overlooked is the characteristic feature or defining essence; what learned folk call the *differentia specifica* of "the creative school" in Gramsci's model of the ideal school in his essay "On Education." Here, in his final, most explicit, and extended statement, Gramsci defines the student as "the discoverer of new truths," even if these be "old truths" for the teacher. Correlatively, he characterizes the teacher as a "friendly guide," and not as a transmitter of information, or knowledge, or the uncritical holdings of tradition. Equality of opportunity we must have, whether as socialists or as democrats. But "the creative school" in Gramsci is also oriented toward the production of those scholars who "in their thousands, or hundreds, or even dozens are necessary for every great civilization." In this respect, Gramsci like Jefferson and every Enlightenment thinker was an "elitist" to his fingertips. The contrast between him and Entwistle or Hirsch could not be more striking.

When the student is defined as "the discoverer of new truths" we are in the presence of discovery in learning and, therefore, Discovery or Socratic teaching in which the teacher acts as "friendly guide." In Discovery teaching, the student is immediately transformed into the *subject* in the knowing process just as he is transformed into the object, the passive or receptive audience, as in the lecture. In following the lecture he is still thinking. But this activity is minimal when compared with his activity as subject in the critical analysis, creation and recreation of ideas and argument. The first form is acutely focused on him as subject, a partner, albeit a junior partner, in the development and criticism of ideas. In the second, however, he is primarily receptive to the flow of ideas in the lecture and the transmission of knowledge and information from the teacher and the textbook, the supplementary article and now the Internet. Entwistle's cardinal mistake is to overlook this distinction, the *differentia specifica* of Gramsci's theory, and to treat the phenomenology itself as the defining essence of Gramsci's thought as expressed in his most mature and final statement.

His mistake leads to a host of errors of which the following are merely the most crucial. His procedure, or if you wish, methodology, is all backward. Instead of "beginning" with an insight into the core of Gramsci's thought precisely as Gramsci understood it, and scrutinizing its merits as philosopher of education, he begins with his birth and early years and scrutinizes every piece of juvenilia, early writings, letters to his wife, etc., and the comments of various and sundry second-hand writers from Broccoli to Zabaglione. The myriad pieces of this jigsaw puzzle are then fitted together to give us a picture of a "conservative" educator who looks like an idealized image of Entwistle himself. The question Entwistle addresses is, in Rousseau's phrase, *"une question mal posée."* The question is not whether Gramsci was a progressive or conservative educator, the two alternatives Entwistle confronts steadfastly throughout his book as if there were no third. The question *bien posée* is: What did Gramsci actually say in his final, so to speak, death-bed statement? This test provides another paradox. Assuming for a moment Entwistle's thesis is correct, what might we expect Gramsci to say? Surely, he would say something like this: "The creative school is the culmination of the traditional school." Why then—an impish sense of humor aside—did he say the exact opposite: "The creative school is the culmination of the active school" (p. 33). The main connection between the two is the fact that in each the student is the active subject and not the comparatively passive object of instruction. Entwistle makes much of the naturalistic difference between flying and swimming, on the one hand, and thinking, on the other. But the logic and dynamic of insight in the discovery of new truths is as much a defining fact in the student as "discoverer of new truths" as it is in *Homo sapiens*, or man as a rational animal.⁴ The oversight of insight, of the interplay between the *knower* and the known, is the besetting sin of the traditional educator from Entwistle and our galaxy of stars to the recent article by Caitlin Flanagan in the Atlantic Monthly.⁵

Entwistle's work is iconic of the species. It is unusually thorough and careful, painstaking and attentive to the facts, learned, scholarly, and erudite. And yet, it is markedly atheoretical. Of theory, understood as self-clarification and understanding, of critical reflection on the deep structure of the argument, there is not a whisper. The ways in which the traditional educator takes the mind out of matter will become more evident with our next few witnesses. But they all spring from the cardinal error dramatized by Plato, pinpointed by Hegel and remedied by Dewey and Bruner.

Change and the Traditional Educator

"*La donna e mobile.*" Woman is famously changeable. And a few months ago, Dr. Diane Ravitch famously changed her mind. In the galaxy of stars this makes her unique. The traditional educator is never wrong. How could he be when, like Chester Finn, he is guided by the facts or, like E. D. Hirsch, by the "findings" of mainstream science or solid mainstream science published in peer-reviewed journals. His frame of mind is dogmatic, not zetetic: the stance of inquiry, search, or investigation caught in the metaphor of the detective. For him there is no search in the Socratic sense, no insight into a puzzling fact or tormenting problem. No judgment or decision to be made with "fear and trembling." For him, the facts are always clear. It is not he who speaks, but history or science that speaks through him.⁶

Not so Professor Ravitch, who has looked again and changed her mind. The facts, she announced to the public, were otherwise. Question: What facts?⁷ Answer: The facts on testing and choice, multiple choice test, charter schools, and the voucher plan. So much for Chester Finn, the Fordham Institute, and National Review.

Left Back, her most recent history is iconic in the genre and the best of her works. It is very clearly written and betrays no partisanship. It is thoroughly researched, balanced, and informative without slipping into excessive detail. Above all, it is admirably, almost marvelously, objective. So, too, in *The Troubled Crusade* her sketch of the Free Speech Movement in Berkeley is a model of objectivity in style, tone, and detail.

Still, one comes away from this account without understanding any of the complex of issues, the Civil Rights Movement, Free Speech on the campus, the increasing radicalization of the University, and Clark Kerr's nakedly pragmatic plans for the uses of the University, which tore apart the University and still divide the nation. Is the University a better place for the Free Speech Movement? Is America and American education any better or worse? What were the issues down deep, and the contrasting visions of the best thinkers on the two sides? Strangely enough, the reader will not learn much from her brief account of this dramatic episode. He will not come away much enlightened by it and much else in the book. In the work Professor Ravitch does show some discernment. What is missing, what is woefully absent, is *judgment*, and the rationale on which it is based and which makes it more than mere opinion.

This is not history in the sense of Gibbon or Macauley, Carlyle, Trevelyan, Namier, Collingwood, Harrod's *Life of Keynes*, or Deutscher's magnificent biography of Trotsky, Trotsky's *History of the Russian Revolution*, Soloviev, Vernadsky and Karpovich, or Karamzin, Klyuchevsky, or Weber, Dierke, Troeltsch and a galaxy of contemporary German historians from Droysen to Meinecke. It is chronicle, but it is not quite history. Or, if it is history it is history of a special kind: history without the play of mind to enliven it and make it significant. An example will illustrate the point of this curiously atheoretical historiography.

Professor Ravitch concludes her history with an epilogue,[8] which is, I take it, the moral of the tale. The moral is the same old scheme of traditional education. But does this really follow from the tale? She presents no theoretical analysis to demonstrate any organic connection. It's just tacked on as if to say "If you like my tale you'll buy my epilogue." She makes a powerful case against progressive education in all its vagaries, fits, and starts. But that *per se* does not prove the case for traditional education. Like Entwistle, she too subscribes to the dogma that these are the only two choices,[9] so in demolishing the claims of the first, she has proved the case for the second. But this in a theorist and educational philosopher and historian, is pure legerdemain. As history, it borders on the delusional.

Where did the ideas of Mario Savio, Suzanne Goldberg, and the key FSM leaders and sympathizers (some names coming immediately to mind, and merely to illustrate the point, are: Art Goldberg and Jack Weinberg, Peter Frank, Michael Rossman, and Lenny Glaser, Bettina Aptheker and William Marx Mendel, Suzanne Goldberg and, of course, Mario Savio) come from? The few liberals apart, they were mostly deracinated Jews and Catholics deeply influenced by the *Narodnik* and the rise of Russian radicalism and Marxism and later by Marcuse and the Frankfurt school.[10] And, where, in turn, did these ideas come from? They came, beyond a shadow of a doubt, from Paris, the French Revolution, and the French Enlightenment. As a historian, Professor Ravitch is myopic, her unit of historical time (a mere seventy-five years) too short.

She laments the decline of foreign languages in the teaching in our schools, and rightly so. But a critic will need an eagle eye to spot the influence of foreign literature in her work, even when it would have benefited the most, namely in the domain of philosophy and history, i.e., of theory in the deepest sense. Example: Her text is adorned by the names of three heroes, William C. Bagley, Michael J. Demiashkevitch, and Isaac L. Kandel. And very fine heroes they are. Consider the first two whom she treats in quick succession, and the problem that this coupling raises. She quotes Bagley as saying that the one quality the teacher (!) needs most is *insight*. More: she goes on to quote him as saying that if he had by some miracle a choice between Socrates and the freshly produced teacher from Teachers College with all this new-fangled methods and equipment, he would choose Socrates hands down. She then praises Mashkevitch for his grasp of foreign languages, philosophical scholarship, and easy familiarity with the great writing of the past. His orientation, she tells us, was grounded in the philosophy of Comte. And she sees no problem! To begin with, the fact that Bagley has it exactly wrong on Socrates escapes her notice. More: if the view of the Platonic Socrates is right, then the view of the positivist Comte is pure sophistry. Conversely, if the scientific positivism of Comte is right, then the transcendental orientation of Socrates with its focus on the centrality of the soul and moral knowledge is pure moonshine. Philosophy and morals or science and sociology, Socrates or Comte, you can't have it both ways.[11] Nor will it do to say that they, Bagley and Mashkevitch, were both critics of progressive education and favored the traditional position. This amounts to saying that as long as you favor traditional education it doesn't much matter what philosophical view you ground it in. As educational philosophy this is a scandal, papered over by the atheoretical narrative of an historian acting as mythmaker.

Here, as everywhere, the traditional educator poses as the defender of tradition. The boast of the traditionalist, strident in Lynn Cheney and Bennett, Chester Finn and Buckley, is hollow, and its hollowness is revealed the moment we ask the question: "Which tradition?" It is certainly not the classical tradition which begins with Plato and dialogue, the matching of argument and counterargument, the dramatic form of Socratic teaching as opposed to a curriculum or catalog of contents frozen in a book and unable to answer back. Is it, then, the tradition of teaching going back to Britain since the Reformation? Again, a round "No" or at best, a hesitant and a very uncertain "Yes" in light of its most representative spokesman, John Milton: "A wise man can gather gold out of the drossiest volume...." Milton wrote, "A fool remains a fool with the best book" (Milton, *Areopagitica*, Sabine Edition para. 30). In historical terms, the tradition to which the traditional educator has given his loyalty is the new tradition of mass education and mass indoctrination in latter-day mainstream American values, conservative and American or progressive and European or Russian: And this is "the culture war" in a nutshell.

Meta-Critique and the Traditional Educator

The traditional educator does not really dispose of a theory. Indeed, theoretical analysis of any kind is entirely foreign to his mind. Instead, what he disposes of is a meta-theory which, by definition, takes care of all his problems. Ask point blank how they would teach something simple yet important, they confess either that they do not know, or that they would leave this critical question to the teacher, the very person they criticized as "miseducated" and incompetent. Another dodge is to aver that since there are several different ways of teaching the writer will not take sides or even discuss the issue but... leave it to the teacher to decide. Some quick examples: 1) After I had done four workshops on "The Gettysburg Address," I read a fine essay criticizing Dewey by M. D. Eschelman, a Professor of Education at Boston and Geneva. In an e-mail replying to my question "How would you instruct the teacher how to *teach* 'The Gettysburg Address'?" Professor Eschelman said he did not know, and advised me to check with Chester Finn and The Fordham Institute. 2) I put the same question to Professor Diane Ravitch who e-mailed back saying "I don't know. I'm not a teacher" (I quote from memory). 3) On reading an excellent article by Professor William Hare of the University of Halifax, Nova Scotia, I telephoned him to ask how he would train teachers to teach the elementary mathematics taught in primary school. He, too, said he did not know because (in his words) he did not feel "competent" to do so. His article was on Russell, Whitehead, and Dewey! 4) In her book, *Sustain Our Schools*, Professor Patricia L. Graham, Dean of the Harvard School of Education, employs the dodge that there are various and sundry ways of teaching and goes on smoothly to her next topic on the various and sundry ways of sustaining our schools! Think of a Professor of Medicine who hadn't a clue as to what to do with a patient with a severe stomachache and possible appendicitis, or even a simple headache! The meta-theory is defined as the structure and functioning of the traditional classroom as the mechanism for transmitting the orthodoxy of the canon. This meta-theory is seldom avowed explicitly, and never defended on the level of articulate theory. But it is always there in latent form and surfaces occasionally as in Diane Ravitch's "Epilogue" or Hirsch's reply to Walter Feinberg's extended criticism of *The Schools We Need and Why We Don't Have Them*.

The meta-theory dictates a strategy of attack which takes three forms. The first is the strategy of The Trojan Horse, and is best seen in Caitlin Flanagan's attack on Alice Waters and the school gardens project (*Atlantic Monthly*, January/February, 2010). The meta-theory never surfaces to be defended. The impression left is that if Waters is all wet, then the meta-theory must be right. The latent assumption is, here and everywhere, that there are only two positions, and if the first can be shown to be absurd and wrong, then the second must be right. The second defines the strategic form of the traditionalist movement and is readily visible in the most prominent names associated with it: Chester Finn, Diane Ravitch, Charles Sykes, and E. D. Hirsch, and can be called "The Critique of a Thought World" strategy, to borrow a phrase from its distinguished creator, E. D. Hirsch. The third is the *form* of this body of literature. They vary in detail and presentation, but their underlying form is always the same. In a word, these are "theses books" in which the authors already know the answer contained in the meta-theory, before they completed or even began their "research." They are prosecutorial briefs presented as disinterested research. Their claim to academic neutrality is as authentic as Grandma Moses' store-bought teeth. Except for Diane Ravitch, this is evident anywhere you look.

Entwistle commends the quality of disinterestedness in Gramsci. But his own book is a sustained polemic refashioning of Gramsci into that dullest of creatures, a traditional schoolman. Hirsch professes neutrality. But the two main authorities, on whom he relies, Rita Kramer and James Koerner, are both situated far on the right. Koerner's research was funded by the Relm Foundation, perhaps the most conservative foundation of its time. Rita Kramer expresses her gratitude to Midge Dechter, whose right-wing credentials are impeccable. But politics aside, how useful or reliable are his authorities? Koerner, a historian, has nothing useful to say on the craft of teaching either in history, or in mathematics and the sciences. And, in her sprightly polemic against progressive education, Rita Kramer mistakes Shulman's book, *Learning by Discovery*, for a variety of progressive education in the Kilpatrick tradition. Shulman, of course, was a student of Bruner and the book is solidly in that tradition. One wonders whether Hirsch or his authority (Rita Kramer) ever opened the book. Perhaps they did not consider it necessary. One tactic pursued by the traditional educator is to focus attention away from themselves and on to a very different problem called the "Why Johnnie can't read, do math, or think" problem. And the reason is obvious: Johnnie can't read, do math, think, tie his shoelaces, or button his shirt because of the ravages of progressive education. Specifically, what he lacks is "cognitive baggage" in Entwistle's phrase or "intellectual capital" in Hirsch's phrase. "Intellectual capital," Hirsch contends, is "the tool of tools." With "intellectual capital" at his disposal Johnnie can become a millionaire of the mind. In the debate on education, the scholars who come to the table with "intellectual capital" are the traditional educations like Chester Finn and Hirsch himself. This, in a way, is the core of the traditionalist case for "capital" or "substance" over process in teaching and the student as subject. So let's test this bold hypothesis. But let's first be clear about one point. Substance we must always have, as in Socratic or Discovery teaching. As Maritain famously observed "We don't eat eating. We eat bread."

All Discovery teaching in the strict sense is based on content, topic by topic, chapter by chapter, class after class. Content and process are like the two blades of a scissor, and one needs both to cut. The Socratic turn, if I may so put it, is in stressing the priority of the cognitional, and so of process over the substance or content to be learned or mastered. Look at it this way: if you are to benefit, really benefit, by Alice Water's books of recipes, you must (1) already know something about cooking and (2) you must learn how to use the recipes with *discernment*. And that discernment is what makes for the art and craft of the chef. But no one, least of all Alice Waters, denies that you need fish and meat, vegetables and fruit, and a little of California wine.

The obsession with "content" over discernment, analysis, critical interpretation, and judgment results in a curious form of blindness in the traditional educator as critic. He is incapable of understanding the text before him precisely as the author means it. This is remarkable in the case of the author of *Validity in Interpretation*,[12] though he is not alone. Hirsch criticizes "banking theory" in Freire as a variety of typically contentless progressive education. Following him, Sol Stern makes the exact same mistake in his recent article on "The Pedagogy of the Oppressor" in City Journal (March 2009, pp. 19–20).

"Banking theory" is, of course, devoid of "content." It is a cognitional theory sketching the cognitional mode and activity of the student as the active subject engaged in the process of knowing. This is the proper stance and activity if the student is to become "the discoverer of new truths." Freire is here (see "The Act of Study") in the precise line of development from Lukács and Gramsci to Lucien Goldmann, i.e., the Marxian tradition with a pronounced Hegelian accent. To absorb this into a variety of progressive education American styles is to make a category mistake of the most fundamental kind. It is bad theory and worse history.

The cognitional error which prompts this mistake is expressed most crudely by Chester Finn. In Finn's opinion "facts are to thought as bricks are to mortar." Finn is blind to the interpenetration of fact and thought or theory. A moment's reflection would reveal the fact that the question: "When did the Cold War begin, and who began it?" cannot be answered without a substantial interpenetration of fact and theory: The American critic has one view, Professor Blackett, a Defense expert and Nobel laureate in physics, another in *Fear, War and the Bomb*.

The traditional educator is a master of legerdemain with an authoritative style of delivery. His catalog of contents is delivered *ex cathedra* from the government, the think tanks, and *National Review*. Few have mastered this style better than William F. Buckley Jr., the founder, editor, and pundit of *National Review*. Yet, when we descend from airy abstractions to concrete facts, Buckley is no better than the rest. Typically, the traditional educator is a literary intellectual, for the most part a historian without any direct classroom experience. Though he regularly speaks of the 3 R's, he seldom evinces anything more than a casual acquaintance with mathematics and the sciences. This can make for a disconcerting gaffe. In *Up from Liberalism*, Buckley assures us that you cannot take the square root of a negative number. But, of course you can, as any high school student can tell you. The square root of minus sixteen is four "i," where "i" is defined as the square root of minus one. How the fact checkers at Arlington House, his publisher, allowed this to pass is anyone's guess. Buckley's grasp of education, which he confuses with indoctrination, is even shakier than his grasp of square roots.

Traditional education plays well in Peoria. But that is because Peoria is only Peoria, not Athens or Rome, Paris, London, or St. Petersburg, and does not aspire to be. The traditional educator is a venerable man, part of a venerable tradition. It is like the tradition of Ptolemy before the Copernican revolution. He is the last of the Ptolemaic wise men and the transcendental turn, from the primacy of "substance" to "subject" has passed him by, leaving him with nothing to say—and all the time to say it.

Notes

1. So, in the Hegelian tradition Marx famously characterized the proletariat as "the identical subject-object of the historical process." And Lukács defined historical materialism as "the self-knowledge of the proletariat." In his study *Lenin: Studie über den Zusammenhang seiner Gedanken*, Malik Verlag, Berlin, 1924, opening line.
2. See particularly "Die Subjekt-Objekt Beziehungen der Aesthetik," *Logos*, 1918, pp. 1–40, as also Ernst Bloch, *Subjekt-Objekt: Erläuterungen Zu Hagel*, Suhrkamp Verlag, Frankfurt am Main, 1951.
3. Harold Entwistle, *Antonio Gramsci: Conservative Schooling for Radical Politics*. New York: Routledge, 1979.
4. Strauss makes the point neatly when he says that "nature is a term of distinction." Entwistle, as a positivist, is of course employing the idea as a term of inclusion. His thinking in this respect is indebted to Karl Popper's "epistemology without a subject."
5. Caitlin Flanagan, "The Ivy Delusion", *The Atlantic Monthly*, April, 2011, issue.
6. This self-conception and form of address was, I believe, created by Fustel de Coulanges who in *La Cité Antique* wrote: "It is not I who speak but history that speaks through me."
7. The facts about standardized testing have been public knowledge since at least Linda Darling-Hammonds' article "Mad Hatter Test of Teaching," *New York Times* educational survey, January 18, 1984.
8. Diane Ravitch, "Conclusion," in *Left Back: A Century of Failed School Reforms*, New York: Simon & Schuster, 2000, pp. 453–468.
9. See, for example, her extended, lucid, but somewhat superficial discussion in chapter 7 of *The Troubled Crusade* where the work of Bruner and Davis is briefly mentioned in the course of her litany without any real analysis of its fundamental methodological difference from traditional education and marked advance over it. Diane Ravitch, *The Troubled Crusade: American Education 1945–1980*. New York: Basic Books, 1983.
10. While a direct acquaintance with the primary sources from Chaadayev and Radischev on down to the rise of Russian radicalism and Marxism is all but indispensable, the lay reader can nonetheless begin to grasp their significance by looking at E.H. Carr's very readable *Studies in Revolution*, Macmillan, London, 1950 or, more compendiously, Avrahm Yarmolinsky, *Road to Revolution*, Cassel, London, 1957, or still more compendiously, Franco Venturi, *The Roots of Revolution* (with an Introduction by Sir Isaiah Berlin), Weidenfeld and Nicolson, London, 1960.
11. For a strikingly different picture of Comte as evangelist see Eric Voegelin, *From Enlightenment to Revolution*, Third Edition, Duke University Press, Durham, NC, pp. 136ff.
12. E. D. Hirsch, *Validity in Interpretation*, New Haven, CN: Yale University Press, 1973.

… 5 …

HOW MYTHS ARE MADE

The Mythic Power of Marxism

Educational Reform and Community Organization

> "If you want to promote Druid culture you must begin by growing trees, there is simply no other way."
>
> William Arrowsmith

In an age of science the most striking fact is the prevalence of myth. In the technological rationality which has invaded all spheres of life the foundations of knowledge and communication have become wholly mythologized. The most outstanding case of this has been the mythic quality of Marxism and the myth of socialism before and after Khrushchev's secret speech. Yet even so a number of academics, publications, and radio stations continue to preach it, and a number of radical educators continue to propound it as the answer to the nation's educational predicament and the progressive deterioration of culture. The problem is not limited to the Left or to politics. Indeed, it has become so all pervasive as to become invisible. Like the air we breathe it is all around us and we do not see it, contaminated and we do not diagnose the contamination. What is the "democracy" for which we say we stand? And what is the "education" which is to redeem us as a democratic republic and heir to the standards of Western Civilization at its best? In the few pages of the previous chapter I took William F. Buckley Jr. as iconic of the problem in its widest and most fundamental sense because he began his career by taking precisely this as his problem and announcing his solution in all its controversial polemic to a skeptical readership in the academy and the world of letters. In other words, here I took Buckley not as a whipping boy but as a prism through which we can see, even as through a glass darkly, the problem of understanding and communication in the domain of culture and education by pursuing the argument to its highest levels in the English speaking world from political sociology to political philosophy, from the Oxford don to the American educator, and from the President to the US Secretary of Education. In a word, I shall contend that the arguments with which the *literati* make their case derive their plausibility by the mythological character with which the problem has been redefined and which makes their wisdom a sham wisdom and their policy proposals "dead on arrival."

The magic of Marxism has worked its wonders by disguising its message as science. But its appeal has from the first been the appeal of myth. The essentially mythological character of Marxism emerges most clearly when its scientific discoveries and predictions are viewed as an *ensemble*. Consider only a brief list: The historical dialectic with its five stages leading inevitably from utopia to science and from capitalism to communism, the historical inevitability of the historical process viewed as science, the rise of the proletariat as *the* agent of change in the advanced capitalist countries, the international structure of the change in "the permanent revolution," the philosophy of Freedom and the promise of Equality, the slogan of "Bread-Peace-and Land" and the strain toward totalitarianism, and the boast to overtake the West only to be followed by economic and political collapse, and the implosion of the whole structure. Nothing has worked as intended, yet the radical critics from Bowles and Gintis, Kohl and Kozol, to Giroux and Aronowitz continue to hawk their message even as it produces no traction on the ground, the real ground of schools and teachers, curriculum and the craft of teaching. The case of William F. Buckley is strikingly similar when viewed as iconic now on the higher ground of the higher learning in America and the English speaking world.

In retrospect it now seems that Joseph Campbell's study of *The Hero with a Thousand Faces* was too narrow to illuminate the structure and function of myth in our time. With the decay of organized religion in the secular world man's search for meaning has entered into the developing worlds of science and politics, and thus into education. To Max Eastman's question *Marxism: Is It a Science?* the now indisputable answer is clearly "no." In *Washington Witch Hunt* Bert Andrews concludes his narrative with a revealing statement by William Z. Foster, then head of the Communist Party, on Marxism as a rational and scientific analysis of US capitalism versus Soviet socialism.[1] Less than a decade later in Khrushchev's secret speech the Soviet Premier himself exploded the entire analysis as pure mythology resting on deception and the credulity of its followers. And the CP (USA) was finally dissolved. Khrushchev had accomplished in a stroke what decades of scholarship in America had been unable to do. The history of such mythmaking in American education is sketched in outline form by Diane Ravitch in her *esquisse* of the Frontier Thinkers in *Left Back: A Century of Failed School Reform*[2] and forms an introduction to our understanding of Buckley and the problem of conservative education. For once seen in this light, namely the light of actual history, the iconic figure of Buckley and the problem of traditional education of which the Frontier Thinkers were one wing and Buckley the other takes on new meaning in the culture wars and the way through them to a genuine, that is totally nonpolitical or ideological process of education.

In *This is My Story* Louis F. Budenz,[3] once managing editor of *The Daily Worker*, presents his narrative of "wishful thinking" among his comrades, the pattern of their mental inversions, and his final break with the Party. The pattern is now familiar and no longer contested. But to understand its true meaning it should be taken with three reservations. First off, it was not simply "wishful thinking," but a structural part of an elaborate structure of myth and mythmaking. More importantly, it was not purely mental: the mental inversions narrated were themselves the product of a prior and more fundamental *moral* inversion.[4] And, most important of all, this fundamental moral inversion, first manifested in Bakunin and Marx, emerges most clearly when the list is seen not as a series of disconnected particulars or individual items but as an *ensemble* or interconnected whole forming an elaborate secular mythology of political reform.[5] The way in which this first entered into the debate on education is revealed by the sketch of the Frontier Thinkers, their crusade and inevitable disillusionment. Of the many who composed this movement two deserve special mention here, Harold Rugg and George S. Counts.

"No point of view once expressed" wrote Sir Alexander Grey, "ever seems wholly to die. And in times of transition like the present our ears are filled with the whisperings of dead men." The "Frontier Thinkers" are from this point of view more than merely antiquarian interest. The whisperings of German philosophy which they breathed across the land can still be heard in the radical critics from Berkeley to New York, in Berkeley in the work of Richard Lichtman, a philosopher, and in New York in the work of Richard Wolff, an economist. Two salient features in the activity of the Frontier Thinkers dramatize the continuity of the message and the innermost appeal to their followers past and present. The first of these is the pronounced strain toward utopianism in theory and practice as measured by the distance between their ends, visualized as the classless, stateless, lawless, familyless, structureless…association, and the method and means at their disposal to bring about this end.

Lichtman, a retired professor of philosophy, sets about it in a tribute to the Word. His style is all word, words, words without any attention to political organization and strategy; so let's attend to the words. Valiantly he continues to teach two small private classes at the Northbrae Community Church in Berkeley, address the Public Affairs Forum in Alameda, and speak over our local radio station. He does not seek allies but likes to go it alone in the face of the disparity between ends and means. In the Marxist tradition out of which he speaks his prime emphasis is not on the "base," i.e., the economy and its movement through rise and fall but on the "superstructure" or culture, ideas, and philosophy marked by the great names of Lukács, Gramsci, and Marcuse, Adorno, and the Frankfurt School. As in all Marxist writing the fundamental emotion he appeals to, the tap root of the message is *ressentiment* or the sense of *moral* outrage at the crimes of capitalist society from Columbus to Newtown and the morning paper. What he sees at the heart of American society as the paradigm of capitalism is corruption. And he titles his talk "Cry, the Corrupted Country." In a well-wrought presentation he makes this plausible to his Eastbay audience by sharpening the contrast between capitalism or the economic system and democracy or the political and social structure, and the rising inequality which has marked the process, economic and political, from the beginning to its present staggering proportions. And in his own terms, in terms of "the universe of discourse" as he defines it, he is unquestionably right. But is this relevant to the American tradition as it is lived, and the men who made it? "Equality," the fundamental value in Lichtman's concept of democracy, does not appear in the Constitution to which the president, the Congress, the Court, and the people are pledged. The most celebrated definition of democracy or a democratic republic is Lincoln's "government of the people, by the people, for the people." And this, quite obviously, is a purely *procedural* definition. Democracy is defined by a procedure which is compatible with virtually any degree of inequality, economic, social, and political. To replace the Madisonian or Lincolnian or American tradition with a species of European and Anarchist tradition, unknown to the framers and alien to the tradition, and produce the impression of "corruption" Lichtman has with a sleight of hand replaced a procedural understanding with a *substantive* definition going back to Marx and before him to Babeuf and Buonarroti, Condorcet and the Enlightenment.[6]

The strain toward mythmaking began early with Marx himself and the Communards. In a passage unfortunately too long to be quoted, Edmund Wilson cites his mythologizing account of the Commune and the heroism of the Communards (*To the Finland Station*).[7] A similar mythmaking tendency can be seen from Lichtman to Wolff and back to the Frontier Thinkers. For example, Lichtman speaks of "the destruction of Indian culture" by the British. In fact the actual record is more mixed on both sides. After some initial accommodation to the culture the British outlawed the traditional practice of *suttee*, named after the goddess Sati, by which a widow was burned alive on the funeral pyre of her husband. Later in the century Lord Curzon, the Viceroy, initiated extensive reforms in education, modern irrigation in the village areas, development of a police system, the army, and administration resulting in the formation of the Indian Civil Service, a model civil service. On the other hand, according to a prominent historian, Mohandas Gandhi paid "a respectful visit to Mussolini in 1932."[8] Later in the decade Mr. Gandhi wrote to Winston Churchill recommending nonviolence and the laying down of arms during the Blitzkrieg and Britain's mortal struggle with Nazi Germany. More extreme still were the fascist sympathies of Subhash Chandra Bose, the much celebrated leader in Bengal, who traveled to Germany and met Hitler in 1942, set up the Indian Legion some three thousand strong to stab Britain in the back in the extremity of her predicament after the fall of Singapore, and died of third-degree burns when his plane caught fire on the island of Formosa *en route* to Tokyo to enlist Japanese support. He did not die in Burma as legend has it but in Taiwan. And speaking as one who was born and raised in India and was right there in Calcutta when the news broke, I must say that the British had nothing to do with it.

With Wolff, a Professor of Economics at the New School, we turn from the superstructure to the base, from philosophy to economics. But the mythmaking and utopian strains implicit in Lichtman become explicit to a degree that is breathtaking. First off we see the same game played with the concept of democracy normally understood as characterized by four features: popular sovereignty, political equality (one man one vote), majority rule, and popular consultation, understood as applying to government on the Federal and State level. Wolff, on the other hand, advances the notion of coops or democracy in the workplace, to salvage the failure of the movement on the Federal and even the State levels. So, in a recent talk he advocates the reorganization of Boeing as a cooperatively run enterprise. Well, if Boeing, why not Lockheed, Airbus, etc.? And if the aircraft companies why not the automobile, the pharmaceutical companies, etc.? And how would the workers amass the capital to manage the takeover? In Wolff's proposal they should receive it from the Federal and State government! Has Wolff developed an organization or at least a following to make this remotely possible even in the future? Has he even given the problem of political organization any thought? Not as far as we know, and this is the key to his dream world or utopian fantasy. Wolff has mistaken his problem which lies "out there" in social and political reality, in the consciousness of the American people in their generality, and the American economic and political tradition. And this cannot be changed by books and articles and singing to the choir every Friday.

A second example: The main area where the present unsatisfactory system is possibly, just possibly, open to change is education. But this is precisely what Wolff is skeptical of and rejects. He cites the well-known case of Mississippi at the bottom of the barrel and the characteristic extremes of economic inequality in the state. His solution: since performance in education shows a high correlation with wealth or poverty the solution is to equalize wealth or income in the State of Mississippi. Once more, what forces in terms of organization can he bring to bear to equalize conditions in Mississippi? And again, the answer would appear to be "nothing." Wolff's conviction that "education," (by which he means "training,") cannot result in equal performance in the face of inequality in society – obviously flows from historical fact. Schools in wealthy areas have always had the privilege of better education than schools in areas wracked by poverty. The fact of inequality in human intelligence remains and we need to distinguish the political problem from the educational problem. In the face of inequality, the Socratic method of teaching will give children in poor schools the best advantage.

In the sixties and seventies I observed a number of classes conducted by teachers trained in Socratic or discovery teaching in Oakland, Berkeley, and Richmond in National Science Foundation-sponsored programs in minority education and I am witness to the fact that the classes all performed at grade level and beyond. Such programs were conducted in scores and even hundreds of schools, and I am sure the records are there in the National Science Foundation (NSF) archives and will give the lie to Wolff and the radical critics who divert attention to the fruitless endeavor to achieve equality in Mississippi and let a thousand coops bloom through the land.

Summing up: If the solution of the radical critics does not lie here on earth, in the native soil of the American tradition, where is it to be found? The answer was famously given by Judy Garland in a radical song called "Somewhere Over the Rainbow," which famously transports us to a region "where troubles melt like lemon drops" and is located not here in *Terra Firma*, but "way up above the chimney tops." This dream, wistful in its fantasy, is the source of the appeal and its fundamental message. And, once seen in this light its pathos and tragic appeal is evident.

"The true descendant of the theory of natural law" wrote Tawney, "is the labor theory of value. The last of the schoolmen was Karl Marx."[9] Why, then, do Wolff and Lichtman continue to cling to it almost a century after Jevons and its near universal repudiation in the world of economic theory from Vienna to Oxford and Cambridge, Berkeley and New York? To the consistent Marxist its failure as a theory of price is not the salient point: What the labor theory of value does is to supply him with *an* objective, i.e., scientific theory of surplus value and, therefore, of exploitation by the capitalist. In the labor theory of value and exploitation we see the blending of the scientific and the moral, and the repression of the moral (which is radically subjective) by the iron hand of science, objective and impersonal. But the moral must be out and it emerges in the form of the message propagated tirelessly by the radical as evangelist and, like all evangels, immune to fact and argument. "We are not the doctors," said a disillusioned Herzen, "We are the disease." In a recent broadcast Wolff speaks of "the demonization of the Left." But he fails to note the origins of this demonization. Its origins lie in a celebrated novel by Dostoyevsky appropriately called *The Devil's* or *The Demons* and more generally known as *The Possessed*. In it, Shigalev, the icy logician of totalitarianism, presents his program in compact form: "My premiss: complete freedom. My conclusion: Complete dictatorship." Here we have it in a nutshell from Marxism to Leninism and Stalinism and the East European satellite states not to mention Mao, the Cultural Revolution, and the further millions dead. The Russians have a saying "Stavrogin in the clothes of Rudin—the fascist streak."[10] In the radical program spelled out by Lichtman and Wolff, and earlier by the Frontier Thinkers, we see the two sides: the Rubenesque critique of society in its *ressentiment*-laden message and the strain toward nihilism, symbolized by the figure of Stavrogin, concealed within it.

Wolff makes no attempt to engage the other side, his critics at their best, liberal or conservative. One searches in vain for any serious engagement with Buber, Berlin or Wolin, or Dahl, Kennan, or Morgenthau, Strauss, or Voegelin, or Kendall, Jaspers, Löwith, Guardini, and De Lubac. As a result his talks are one-dimensional and verge on propaganda and not inquiry or theory in the best and highest sense. Of that wonder (and open-mindedness) which Aristotle says is at the heart of all philosophical engagement there is not a trace.[11]

At its core and in its innermost essence the appeal is that of an evangelist. "The critique of religion," said Marx early in his career, "is the alpha and omega of all critique." "The problem of socialism," wrote Dostoyevsky "is not an economic problem. The problem of socialism is the problem of Atheism." This theme of transcendence, of religion and redemption marks the culmination of Berdyaev's study of *The Origins of Russian Communism*, one of the three best books ever written on the subject.[12] And Whittaker Chambers makes the point that Marx closed his analysis in *Das Kapital* with the words taken from Dante. "And so we emerged once again to see the stars." With the radical critics at their best we are talking about nothing less than human destiny and the meaning and purpose of life itself, and not the day-to-day sometimes brilliant, too-often superficial, and even trivial work of a political scientist. But our recent critics from the Frontier Thinkers to the present have lost their footing. With the decline of the labor movement and the disappearance of the proletariat as *the* agent of change and transformation they have no *locus standi* in the theoretical sense. And with the implosion of the Soviet Union and its satellites they have lost it in the political sense as well. Nor can they look to a liberalized China and a liberalizing Cuba as evident from Raoul's willingness to admit mistakes in the past and look to a brighter future and, perhaps, even better U.S. relations after President Obama's lifting of the embargo. And it is with this in mind that I should like to round out my critique of this way of delusion and present a contrasting view featuring our work in Mexico with its finale in Havana as a mode of "constructive engagement" for schools to follow…and for a future president to lead.

Notes

1. Bert Andrews, *Washington Witch Hunt*, New York: Random House, 1948, pp. 162–205.
2. Diane Ravitch, *Left Back: A Century of Failed School Reform*, New York: Simon & Schuster, 2000. Some titles of the same book read: *Left Back: A Century of Battles Over School Reform*.

3. In tracing the Communist course on religion, we are confronted with the same deep-dyed deception that stamps their other activities. Duplicity was created, it is true, long before the Communists came upon the scene. Its history is long and lugubrious. In the case of the Communists though, it has been elevated to the importance of a first principle. "Democracy" is their term for dictatorship, "elections" are the imposition of hand-picked slates on nations and peoples, "defense" is aggrandizement by the Soviet Union, but air bases for the United States' security is "imperialist aggression," and democracy is "fascism." Louis F. Budenz, *This is My Story*, McGraw-Hill, Book Company, 1947. (p. 363).
4. For a very perceptive analysis of the phenomenon of moral inversion in politics see Michael Polanyi, "The Magic of Marxism," *Encounter*, Dec. 1956, pp. 5–17.
5. On Bakunin's moral inversion and turn toward demonic see his frank self-portrait in Mikhail A. Bakunin, *God and the State*, (1872) Dover Paperback edition, 1970), pp. 3ff.
6. For a couple of sharply contrasting views of equality, liberal, and conservative, see the fine article by Isaiah Berlin and Richard Wollheim, "Equality," *Proceedings of the Aristotelian Society*, 1955–1956, Vol. 56, pp. 281–326. And the similarly provocative article by Willmoore Kendall, "Equality and the American Political Tradition," *Willmoore Kendall Contra Mundum*, Arlington House, New Rochelle, NY, 1971.
7. Edmund Wilson, *To the Finland Station*, New York: Farrar, Strauss, and Giroux, 1972, pp. 282–283. Originally Published by Macmillan in London, 1940.
8. R.J.B. Bosworth, *Mussolini*, Oxford University Press, Arnold, NY, 2002.
9. R. H. Tawny, *Religion and the Rise of Capitalism*, New Brunswick, NJ: Transaction Publishers, 1998, p. 36. Originally published by Harcourt, Brace and Company, Inc., New York, 1926. Verbatim: "The true descendant of the doctrines of Aquinas" wrote Tawney, "is the labor theory of value. The last of the schoolmen was Karl Marx." (The natural law is of course one of his doctrines.)
10. Stavrogin, the charismatic antihero of *The Possessed* was fashioned after Nicolai Speshnev whom Dostoyevsky called "a Mephistopheles of my own." Rudin is the hero of the celebrated novella by that name, whom Ivan Turgenev fashioned after the character and personality of Bakunin.
11. On the development of Kitsch to an art form in mass society see the provocative article by Susan Sontag, "Notes on Camp," *Partisan Review*, Fall 1964, Vol. 31, No. 4, pp. 515–530.
12. The other two surely George Lukács' *History and Class Consciousness* and Hendrik Deman's *Socialism*.

· 6 ·

TRUTHS, HALF TRUTHS, AND ONE AND A HALF TRUTHS

From Diane Ravitch to Sheldon S. Wolin

The wit and wisdom of Diane Ravitch can be summed up in a sentence: She favors liberal education and the teaching of the traditional subjects, mathematics and science, history and literature, and foreign languages. This said, the content of her positive contribution is substantially exhausted. To favor the teaching of the traditional subjects makes for good common sense. Indeed it is refreshing in a culture war marked by the ravages of progressive education and the emergence of the radical critiques. But it is not quite enough to fill a book, an article, or an academic tea cup. So, when Professor Ravitch took pen in hand and set to the writing of history she turned to the culture wars in a set of three famous books *The Great School Wars*, *The Troubled Crusade*, and *Left Back: A Century of Failed School Reform*. And, again inevitably, this always found her on the side of the angels. It also found her in some dubious company. In time she teamed up with Chester Finn *et al.* and was invited to the White House to advise the first President Bush and his top advisors in the counteroffensive called "the back to basics movement."

Then one afternoon while reviewing her old notes she suddenly discovered that the whole conservative case, the voucher program, charter schools, high-stakes testing, accountability, and the business model were all dead wrong. One disaster had followed another in San Diego and in New York after funding to the tune of seventy-five million dollars a piece by "The Billionaire Boys Club." To her eternal credit she resigned from the Fordham Institute, abandoned the professional company of Chester Finn, the Fordham Institute, and the high and mighty in the billionaire boys club. *The Death and Life of the Great American School System*, her latest history, documented these latter-day follies and made her a darling of the left speaking to a packed house in wicked, wicked Berkeley. With the about face from right to left Professor Ravitch as philosopher of education has repudiated the political and moral of her past work, the work on which her reputation was based. These works were presented with a couple of curious titles such as *The Troubled Crusade* and *Left Back: A Century of Failed School Reform*. Such titles were iconic of the genre: They affect a bored, supercilious treatment of the history of school reform as uniformly utopian, naive, misplaced, and destined to failure. A typical title is her Stanford colleagues David Tyack's *Tinkering Toward Utopia*, published (with his co-author, Larry Cuban) by Harvard University Press,[1] and Richard Elmore's *Getting to Scale with Good Educational Practice*, published by the Harvard Education Review.[2] The right and good is lumped along with the foolish and destructive, discovery or Socratic teaching is not distinguished from the varieties of child-centered progressive education, and all reform is flushed down the same drain. This is Professor Ravitch's failure as a genuine or paradigmatic historian of rank in the tradition of Frederick Jackson Turner, Bancroft, and Beard, Carr, Collingwood, and Namier, Sir Henry Sumner Maine, Marc Bloch, and Pirenne. But this should not blind us to her merit as one who simply tells us what happened, namely, a programmatic historian, albeit of more minor rank. Her programmatic account or chronicle of what happened is always well researched and lucidly presented without partisanship and any evident bias. They are all models of objective chronicle. And among them none is better than her picture of the Frontier Thinkers and especially the last two, Harold Rugg and George S. Counts, who marked the transition to the extreme left and ushered in the radical critique and its first great disillusionment in the middle to late thirties. And it is to this we now turn as a preface to our sampling of the academic critique from Plato to the present or at least the recent past.

    According to Diane Ravitch, whose readable account we follow, "The Frontier Thinkers" took their name from Harold Rugg at a dinner party in 1927 for leading progressive educators including Dewey himself. They were a sprightly group of reformers vigorously reacting to the impersonality, rigidity, and boredom of school understood as a reflection of society itself. By 1934 they had developed to the extent of forming a journal *The Social Frontier* with a readership of near ten thousand to broadcast their views to schools and professors in the Schools of Education. Following the lead provided by Dewey in his Schools of Tomorrow and Kilpatrick in The Project Method they attacked the authoritative role of the teacher, the traditional academic curriculum, and the distinction and separation of school from society. Instead, they championed the child-centered class, a *laissez faire* role for the teacher, a catering to students' immediate interests, and a blending of school activities with society and the home. In a word, education was not for culture and rigorous training, education was for life! And this is precisely the resurgence, so natively American, we see again in the sixties in Allen Graubard and more famously in the early Postman and Herbert R. Kohl. And, of course, it provoked the traditionalist reply from William C. Bagley and I.M. Kandel precisely as it did later from Diane Ravitch and Chester Finn in their now well-known books and articles. The debate conceals a problem which comes to light when the historiography of the traditionalist reply is examined more closely.

Depression Decade: As the depression decade developed "progressive education" (I place it in quotes because it was neither progressive nor education) began divided into two irreconcilable camps: One was the original group still favoring child-centered education. The other led by Rugg and Counts marked the turn toward radicalism in the form of socialism in the image of the Soviet Union where the works of Dewey and Kilpatrick had been well received by Lunacharsky and Soviet reformers.

The turn to the Left came in a daring question by Counts: "Dare Progressive Education Be Progressive?" Progressive education was running into criticism first from Dewey himself, and then at length by Counts. Counts had visited the Soviet Union and published a book on The Soviet Challenge to America. He now attacked the pure activities theory central to Kilpatrick and the movement, calling instead for "activities with a purpose." And this "purpose" was the subordination of education to the reform of society in the Soviet image. Kilpatrick and others had pointed to the large dimension of indoctrination in Soviet schooling with Lenin's widow, Nadya Krupskaya, in charge of political education. But Counts was undaunted by this. In fact he wanted to remove "the groundless fear of indoctrination." "Indoctrination," he said by way of a counter, "goes on anyway." And these are all precisely the controversies that erupted again in the sixties and seventies. But my concern here is not with content but with historiography.

Any reader of her clear and readable account will come away with a radically misleading impression. She criticizes the Dewey Laboratory School and the later Lincoln School as unrepresentative of the problems confronting the public schools: The Lincoln School, for example, had students of high quality with parents from the elite, top-quality teachers, a well-endowed facility: all such criticism is quite irrelevant. The schools were models. And it is the function of a model to abstract from reality, singling out certain essential features for analysis and application to (social) reality with the necessary critical amendments. Example: A) Highly qualified graduate students can be obtained from the University, B) inexpensive science units such as the Stebbins module on natural selection or the NSF module on *Life in a Drop of Water* were readily available, C) a specific unit, for example in mathematics, can be simplified and made readily accessible, etc., etc. Professor Ravitch, a historian of the middle range, has failed to understand the nature of a model in theories of the highest range.

The historiographic defect flows from her otherwise handling of the Counts case. The reader will almost certainly receive the impression that indoctrination as favored by Counts is unique to socialism and the left. But this is precisely not the case. It is precisely indoctrination that is advocated by Counts' mirror opposite on the right, William F. Buckley Jr. in his controversial *God and Man at Yale* and then again in *UP From Liberalism*. And the real question then is: How is it that Counts on the far left and Buckley on the far right are as one on this crucial issue?

The issue in the writing, and therefore the reading and teaching of history was concisely made by her colleague, Chester Finn. "Facts are to thought," Finn writes "as bricks are to mortar." The "bricks" and the "mortar" are distinct and different and do not interpenetrate. History is objective, a solid wall of facts held together by the "mortar" or thought which makes it a coherent narrative. And this is precisely the view of Diane Ravitch and the theorists of the middle-range histories of traditionalist cast. But it has been questioned, criticized and rejected as an oversimplification by Carl Becker and Charles Beard, E.H. Carr and R.G. Collingwood, namely by historians of the first rank in the United States and Britain. Simple narrative history (or programmatic history as I shall call it) misses the significance of the facts which only emerges when the facts themselves are subjected to analysis in the most intimate intermingling of fact and theory, "bricks" and "mortar." How is it that a dozen years or so after Counts' bold advocacy, the most prominent conservative publicist was championing the very same thing? What interconnections might it point to between the extreme left and right? Buckley and Burnham went on to support McCarthy and McCarthyism. And Kendall wrote a remarkable article on McCarthyism as "the *Pons Asinorum* of Conservatism," defending it as a form of heresy hunting and thought control. Buckley and the early Counts are at one in their opposition to liberalism and the free play of the mind in the school classroom and the higher learning. Where they differed was on the *content* of the political indoctrination: free market capitalist and Soviet socialist. Counts went on to change his mind and Professor Ravitch has famously changed hers. The policies she advocated (and on which her reputation was built) were dead wrong and proved to be destructive. She has turned on them, but not on her simple prescriptions and the roots of the theory on which they were based. The business of this essay, therefore, is to uncover these roots, the *fundamentals* of the conservative position in the main and *confront* them with a genuine alternative as the way to real standards beyond the deadlock of the culture wars.

The eruption of the culture wars of the sixties can be bracketed by two sets of works: those by R.S. Peters on the right and Bowles and Gintis on the left. One is the exact mirror opposite of the other much as Bagley and Kandel were to Rugg and Counts. The personnel have changed but the issues remain the same. In a paper called "Education as Initiation" Peters presented his view in the Inaugural Lecture at the University of London's Institute of Education in December 1963 and it was subsequently published by George Harrup and Company in 1964. He comes to the table from the school of analytic philosophy and his lecture introduces us to the mind and contribution of that distinguished school. Analytic philosophy dedicates itself to the analysis and clarification of language and is also known as Oxford or language philosophy. In his lecture Peters devotes himself to the analysis of the concept of education to clarify much that was obscure. His approach is dialectical and he spends the first thirty-five pages out of forty-six on the confusions of the two main positions he rejects before coming to his view of education as initiation.

Rousseau, he reminds his audience, regarded education as coming from nature. But this is too broad: Anything can be included as "natural," such as "visiting a brothel perhaps." The point is that there are no aims external to education: the metaphor of aiming is itself the problem, suggesting as it does a target external to itself. To say that a man has been educated but that the change was in no way desirable would be a violent paradox. It would be as paradoxical as saying that a man had been reformed but that this "made no change for the better." The case of Heidegger, of Gentile and various

Communist intellectuals on the left, suggests an immediate problem. All were highly educated, but developed a pronounced totalitarian cast of mind. The aim of education is the development of culture, aesthetic, moral, and metaphysical. To say that a man has been educated but is devoid of culture would indeed be a striking paradox, a contradiction in terms.

A closer look reveals the conservative bias behind the apparent neutrality in linguistic analysis à la Peters and Passmore. "Initiation" into what? a critic might wonder. Peters' ready answer is into "a form of life…", and "a public and differentiated mode of thought." And that seems neutral enough. But this "mode of thought" is, as his reference to Oakeshott reminds us, the expression of a prevailing culture.

To the question "initiation into what?" Peters' second answer is the neutral "into the processes and activities" which constitute the prevailing body of knowledge and "content without criticism," he tells us, "is blind." But equally "criticism without content is empty." This is Chester Finn's bricks and mortar analogy, and misses the point completely. The question is where does the emphasis fall? Where does the priority lie? To this Whitehead and Dewey Bruner, Halmos, and Moore offer a radically different answer. Peters cites Whitehead's remark that "a merely well informed man is the most useless bore on God's earth." But he adds immediately that reading encyclopedias is among his favorite occupations. The problem lies in the fact that Peters (like Passmore after him) comes to the table as a language philosopher who pays no attention to what scientists and mathematicians of rank have to say. In his celebrated lecture "On a Piece of Chalk," a minor classic in discovery teaching, T.H. Huxley graphically demonstrates the priority of the cognitional, of thought or criticism over raw content, and the intimate interpenetration of "bricks" and "mortar." And this is precisely the Socratic or discovery tradition from Galileo to Polanyi as you can see by visiting our websites.

Another way to put it is this: In periods of scientific revolution upon whose side would Peters be—on the professors of the prevailing body of knowledge or Copernicus, the Catholic Church and the Pope or Galileo? Would he have joined "certain professors of education" and voted Socrates guilty? And finally, does he, as his reference to Oakeshott suggests, require that the teacher's job is to transmit the wisdom and goodness of the prevailing culture that lies behind the prevailing body of knowledge? And what if the prevailing culture is radically divided, as in all times of transition it is. Would he demand that the teacher's job is still to transmit the prevailing body of knowledge and culture only to switch sides when in time Galileo finally wins and the Copernican revolution is an accomplished fact? The empty "criticism without content" is the bogey of progressive education. But on the radical side of the culture war the case is well made by Bowles and Gintis who stand out as the mirror opposite of Peters and Oakeshott.

At the very moment that R.S. Peters was delivering his inaugural lecture on the virtues of encyclopedic knowledge, of content over process and bricks over mortar, the revolution in education was exploding all around him. In mathematics education this was launched by Davis in the pioneering Madison Project in Syracuse NY funded by the National Science Foundation in response to Sputnik and the condition of American education. In physics and biology Davis's work, published as *Discovery in Mathematics*, was complemented by the work of David Hawkins and Robert Stebbins, all three of whom I invited to speak at The Lincoln Conference sponsored by then Governor Bob Kerrey. In psychology (or cognitional theory as I prefer to call it) this side of the case was presented by Jerome S. Bruner in his widely read *Toward a Theory of Instruction* (Harvard, 1966) and Lee Shulman in *Learning By Discovery* (Rand McNally 1966). A graphic presentation of discovery teaching in mathematics featuring the distinguished mathematician and teacher R.L. Moore can also be seen by visiting our website under the title "Challenge in the Classroom." And this was followed up by a second eminent mathematician, Paul R. Halmos, in his talk to teachers of mathematics and published as "The Problem of Learning How to Teach," also available on our website. But there were also two countercurrents dominating popular culture. The first of these was progressive education now linked to the names of Neil Postman and Herbert Kohl. The second was the turn to the radical left and linked to the names of Jonathan Kozol, the later Kohl, and Giroux and Aronowitz. The major theoretical study which emerged from the Marxist left was a book by Bowles and Gintis called *Schooling in Capitalist America*[3] with a mirror opposite case to present to Peters and Oakeshott.

Bowles and Gintis take up where the reforming Rugg and Counts left off. They subtitle their book "Educational Reform and the Contradictions of Economic Life." But this should really have been the title since it expresses the central intention of the work. Educational reform is fundamentally impossible within the constraints of capitalism and economic life. The aim of education is (equals, should be) to develop democracy, real democracy in which the freedom of each (and his self-development) is the condition for the freedom of all.[4] They cite the early Dewey to this effect but they ignore his major statements precisely on cognitional theory or psychology and the curriculum and craft of teaching leading to the work of Bruner and associates mentioned above. The revolution in discovery teaching, the most significant advance in American education, is simply ignored. For Bowles and Gintis it simply does not exist. On real classroom teaching they have nothing to say. The problem for them is the problem of equality understood in the Marxist sense of complete equality in the classless or communist state of anarchy where even society is dissolved into a free "association." Critics of the book, they complain in a new Introduction, talk about the bad things that happened in the Soviet Union.

But, they add wistfully, there were also good things in the Soviet Union. A decade and a half later the implosion of the Soviet Union exploded this threadbare argument and the radical derailment of reform in the classroom.

Peters' inaugural lecture reveals the mind and perspective of the analytic or language philosopher. But to move from perspective to procedure, i.e., classroom procedure and curriculum, we must stop in our flight through time to interrogate two more philosophers who address the problem of teaching, of education, and the culture war. The first is John R. Searle, Professor of Philosophy at Berkeley, and the second is John Passmore whose detailed study of *The Philosophy of Teaching* takes us straight to the heart of the matter.[5]

As a Rhodes scholar Searle was trained in Oxford philosophy and his many and very readable contributions to the philosophy of language, intentionality, and the study of consciousness all flow from this school and the later Wittgenstein. In the debate on consciousness his main adversaries are materialism and the computational model of mind and the universe. In the United States this has a long history going back to William James' fateful question "Does Consciousness Exist?" to which James returned a very large and round no! Consciousness was merely the fleeting ghost of a metaphysical or religious substance or entity called the soul. In the American culture war this, i.e., *The Principles of Psychology*,[6] was immediately answered by John Dewey in an article called "The Vanishing Subject in the Psychology of James" which (together with his book *How We Think*) forms the philosophical foundation of his theory of instruction and the later work in discovery teaching by Bruner and associates, Moore and Halmos. In the theory of consciousness the critical issue on which the schools divide is simply this: Is consciousness to be understood in terms of a theory of the subject or is it best understood in positivist, or materialist, or scientific terms as in present-day cognitive science, artificial intelligence, programmed learning, and online teaching? In Britain this second view reaches back to Hume, Russell, and Wittgenstein of the *Tractatus*.

In the *Tractatus* Wittgenstein flatly said "There is no such thing as the soul or subject as is conceived in contemporary popular philosophy" (*Tractatus* 5.5). Hume's theory led to a number of paradoxes which he faced unflinching: He famously rejected induction, denied there was anything such as causality, and the notion of personal identity and the self. When he looked into himself, Hume declared, he could see nothing, no object like a self. In the debate on consciousness Searle ranges himself on the side of subjectivity and against the forces of pure materialism, artificial intelligence, and, by implication, the vogue of programmed learning.

In his reply to David Chalmers Searle sides with the human and not the machine or mechanical conception of mind or the brain as a high-grade computer. He reminds us "that the brain is a biological organ like any other and consciousness is a biological process like digestion or photosynthesis."[7] I would venture to make a small amendment: consciousness is not a biological process but a state of mind which is the result of a biological process. And in this, I believe, it is quite unlike digestion and photosynthesis for here a biological process has somehow created something mental, and the mystery remains. A step toward the solution of the mystery can be taken if we formulate the question in slightly different terms, namely: Is consciousness radically a form of perception or is it radically a form of experience (on the part of a subject)? All views of discovery or Socratic teaching from Dewey to Bruner *et al.* flow from a view of the student as subject (with a very different conception of understanding. And all theories of lecturing, programmed learning, and online teaching depend *per contra* on a conception of consciousness as perception. Once you decide which side of this distinction you are on all the rest flows alike for education as for philosophy. And there is no third way.

Insight and Oversight: Searle's contribution to our problem, made in a lecture to a distinguished California audience, is interesting in telling us what a philosopher sees and does not see, notices and does not notice when he looks out of his office window.

What he sees is remarkable. What he does not see is even more remarkable. Like Isaiah Berlin, Searle comes to the table as an heir to the tradition of the Enlightenment in the footsteps of John Stuart Mill and Bertrand Russell. And in the crisis of liberal democracy he takes the new left, identity politics, ultrafeminism, and women's studies, etc., as his adversaries in the culture war in education.

His counterstatement is introduced in the form of a thought experiment. Suppose it is discovered that a classic work such as Plato's *Republic* or Aristotle's

Politics (or *Ethics* or *Rhetoric*) were written not by Plato and Aristotle but by Mrs. Plato and Mrs. Aristotle. What would be the likely result to one side or the other, traditional education and its critics? To the traditional educator it would merely be an interesting but small fact, a tiny piece of biographical detail. In feminist politics and women's studies it would likely cause a minor revolution. So, what to do? Searle's solution is to amend (slightly) the curriculum. To Hawthorne, Melville, and Mark Twain, Hemingway, and Faulkner let's add *The Color Purple* and *To Kill A Mockingbird*, and business can proceed as usual. In a word, Searles' solution is to look "out there" at the curriculum and not "in here" at the mind of the student. And this is all the more remarkable because the switch in perspective from "out there" to "in here" was first proposed by the Oxford philosopher R.G. Collingwood in his celebrated study *The Idea of History*.[8] What escapes Searle's notice as an educator is the contemporary work by Bruner and Shulman, with the latter going on to serve as president of the Carnegie Foundation for the Advancement of Teaching right here in Menlo Park. More remarkable still is the fact that he fails to notice the substantial work being done around him in the classroom in Berkeley, Oakland, and Richmond by Bill Rupley in the CTF program in Richmond and Bill Johntz and associates in Berkeley. And the late Bill Johntz lived on Keith Street, a block or two from my house and just a few blocks from Searle's on Yosemite Street in Berkeley. "What's going on?" as Searle likes to say. Why this strange oversight? The answer is simple enough: The problem is not a problem in philosophy (or political philosophy or ideology) at all, but a problem in cognitional theory or the psychology of the student as learner. And this is why Dewey and Bruner, a psychologist, could address it with such notable success. And this is also why Passmore, the third of our three philosophers, fails so completely to engage. The wheels spin, but they spin in the air. There is no real engagement with real work and real progress.

With Passmore we come to a direct engagement between Oxford philosophy and Bruner or discovery teaching in the sense advocated here. If Passmore is right then Bruner is wrong and the movement he developed can be discarded as part of "a century of failed school reforms." The subject–object distinction (on which the argument turns) "is a linguistic distinction." This view, flowing from Russell and Wittgenstein, destroys the experiential base of Learning by Discovery in the style developed by Bruner and Shulman, Davis, Hawkins, and Stebbins, and practiced with outstanding success by R.L. Moore.

Bruner's central thesis is placed right on the table: "The school boy is a physicist and it is easier for him to learn physics behaving like a physicist than doing something else." Passmore's reply is crisp and to the point: "The notion that a young child can discover for himself what it took physics centuries to discover is manifest nonsense." But this is not in the least what Bruner is contending. The difference between the child and the mature physicist is obvious. The student is not a physicist or mathematician but behaving "like" a physicist or mathematician, i.e., learning by steps to think mathematically or like a scientist. In the case of young children you can see this displayed on our website. And in the case of young adults you can see Moore practicing it on the DVD "Challenge in the Classroom" also available on our website. Passmore is certain it can't be done ("he cannot ... even learn his physics in this way," he writes in *The Philosophy of Teaching*.[9])

But Moore on one level and Davis on another can show it being done every day. So what's wrong? Where precisely is the problem in the philosopher's argument?

The problem in all such arguments is cast into bold relief by the very title of Passmore's book: *The Philosophy of Teaching*. For teaching is a learned activity, a pure activity whose success depends on the appropriate cognitional activity. And it makes no sense to talk about a philosophy of teaching just as it makes no sense to talk about a philosophy of retinal surgery. Passmoore's confusion can now be pinpointed with precision. He has confused cognitional theory as in Dewey and Bruner with philosophy. In fact coming to the table as an Oxford philosopher he is blind to the nature of cognitional theory and its function in discovery teaching. This leads to a host of errors of which the following are merely the most crucial. This "attitude of mind," he says in his critique of Dewey, is called "scientism." And he cites the names of Hayek and Popper as his main authorities. But in fact there is nothing in either Dewey or Bruner that can properly be called scientism. In Hayek's brief criticism Dewey is not accused of scientism or the misapplication of the methods of science to the study of man but rather of a power-oriented philosophy. And there is nothing in the development of this work by Davis, Hawkins, and Stebbins that is in any way open to this charge.

The point is worth repeating: Passmore has quoted Bruner, "The school boy is a physicist and it is easier for him to learn physics behaving like a physicist than doing something else." To this Passmore rejoined: "The notion that a child can discover for himself what it took physicists centuries to discover, is manifest nonsense." But Bruner does not mean that at all. He does not mean that the child will like Heisenberg be working at the frontiers of science and discovering the principle of indeterminacy but that the student will be behaving "like" a physicist, or scientist, or mathematician, i.e., modeling scientific and mathematical thinking in pursuing the analysis of a problem. To test the feasibility of the method the reader should turn to the pages of Davis' book, *Discovery in Mathematics*, or Stebbins' book on the teaching of natural selection, or visit our website for contemporary examples and illustrations including one of a child of four working with imaginary numbers and graphing on the complex plane. The notion that this cannot be done is to borrow Passmore's phrase, "manifest nonsense." Passmore has simply confused "the end point," imaginary numbers and the complex plane, natural selection, etc., with the "entry point" or where the student stands at the time and the cognitional steps in progressive understanding which will lead him to the *eureka* flash of final insight. To learn to accomplish this and do it with regular success is the key problem in professional education and teacher training for success in our schools. To this none of our philosophers have anything to contribute because it is not a philosophical problem but a problem in cognitional theory to which, however, philosophers and sociologists of the first rank have entered serious objections. These flow from the subject–object distinct and the debate surrounding two simple words "I think" as in the famous Cartesian "*Cogito*" or better yet "I understand," and the question whether there is an "I" at all to do the thinking or special form of understanding. So let's turn to it.

Three otherwise unrelated events form the background to our presentation and analysis of the object side of the subject/object debate on the level of the higher learning and theorist of first rank. The first of these is the celebrated Turing test and the development of artificial intelligence, cognitive science, and the computational theory of the mind and universe. The second, serving to pinpoint the debate, is Karl Popper's study of "Epistemology Without a Knowing Subject". And the third is James Jarrett's study of *The Educational Theories of the Sophists*. Place the three together and we travel the distance from the first computers to the anticipation of programmed learning via the elimination of the subject in epistemology and learning or teaching. In them the phrase "I think" or "I understand" assumes the contemporary meaning which rides high in the universities, schools, and the expanding universe of online teaching. The earliest presentation of the attack is the very able article by Theodore Abel titled "The Operation Called *Verstehen*."[10]

In "The Operation Called *Verstehen*" Abel drives to the heart of the matter by exploding the concept of *Verstehen*. Taken literally *Verstehen* simply means understanding. But Abel rightly prefers to use the German term because *Verstehen* as a technical term means a special kind of understanding which we may call "sympathetic understanding" or understanding based on a certain degree of empathy with the state of mind of the subject studied. Writing from a behaviorist or stimulus–response point of view Abel rejects the idea of *Verstehen* completely and totally: And thus the lines are drawn. Simply stated, are we to understand society and men in society, students and teachers in terms of an I–Thou relationship or in terms of an I–It relationship? Should we as teachers relate to the student as subject or object in an array of objects called a class? If Abel is right (and there is no such thing as *Verstehen* or understanding as a subject) then there is nothing in principle wrong with scientific sociology, the textbook, and the purely objective exam, programmed learning, online teaching, and mass testing. In a word, mass education is education in the only right and proper sense of the word.

Abel claims that the "operation" has never been analyzed and presented in rigorous or philosophically respectable form. But, of course, it has both from the side of science and philosophy as in Michael Polanyi's *Personal Knowledge* and Bernard Lonergan's *Insight: A Study of Human Understanding*. We see it displayed in Dostoevsky's novels and many and true to life characters from Ivan Karamazov to Stavrogin, in the dramas of Shakespeare, the dialogues of Plato, and the epics. Without it great art would be impossible. Abel opens with a dichotomy, the split between physical and social science.

But the deeper divide between the two sides is the divide between two views of human consciousness: Is consciousness fundamentally and primarily the result of perception or of experience in the human subject? Is there really such a phenomenon as insight? Do we in fact as human subjects have a sense of awareness, a subject state? Do we have common sense in a field of social intersubjectivity? Is our universally shared sense of self simply a shared delusion? From Hume and Russell to James, Abel, and Skinner the two sides answer our question differently and in the most radical sense. In the case of the *eureka* phenomenon the name of Archimedes is known to all. But you can also see it happening right before your eyes with a girl of six or seven in a mathematics class called "Beyond the Three R's" placed on our web site, and read about it in an article called "The *Eureka* Phenomenon" by Isaac Asimov on the case of Kekule and the benzene molecule. Teaching for understanding in this sense is developed by Davis in *Discovery in Mathematics* and Stebbins in his module on natural selection. They represent understanding and, therefore, learning of a radically different kind and accordingly a different form of curricular development, irreducible to Abel's stimulus–response theory and behaviorism, textbook teaching, the lecture, and the test. In its larger implications the destruction of *Verstehen* erases the distinction between the Cartesian *Cogito* and the computer, the human self and the machine. The clear and most forceful case for this was made by Bertrand Russell in his widely read *History of Western Philosophy*.

The climate of opinion out of which Russell's history is a distillate was marked by the three unrelated events mentioned earlier. In the Turing test a respondent is placed on one side of a curtain behind which are two tables, one with a computer to respond to questions, the other with a man to do the same. If the respondent is unable to distinguish the human response from that of the computer this suggests the fact that a human subject can be dispensed with since the computer has shown that it can "think", i.e., answer questions just as well. The second presents the case in philosophical terms in the title of Karl Popper's study of "Epistemology Without a Knowing Subject". Popper goes Descartes one better. Instead of Cartesian dualism of a world of mind and one of matter, Popper postulates three worlds, the third of which is the world of culture, of books, musical scores, etc., which contain knowledge in and of themselves without the intervention of any human subject. The third was James Jarrett's study of *The Educational Theories of the Sophists* which quotes Xenophon as saying "When Socrates argued out a question he advanced by steps that gained general assent holding this to be the only sure method. Accordingly whenever he argued he gained a greater measure of assent from his hearer than any man I have known." "This by the way," comments Professor Jarrett, "may be taken as an anticipation of programmed learning."[11] The transformation is complete. Two further effects can be noted for the record. In his debate with E.H. Carr, the Oxford philosopher Isaiah Berlin does not reject determinism on the ground that he does not know that it is false. The most that he can say is that if determinism were true then most or all of our language of praise and blame would require drastic revision. He does not make the point that if determinism were true he would not be a creative subject but an object, a programmable object like a computer and that his vast learning would in fact be programmed learning. He would in fact be something very much like a robot living (if that is the word) in a universe of robots. A second example *is* the article "Political Theory as a Vocation" by the political theorist Sheldon S. Wolin. In this erudite article Wolin argues against the idea of method itself as the backbone of political theory and political theory scholarship. The search for a right method he derides as "methodism," and he will have none of it. If he is right the case for method in the professional education of teachers collapses since there *is* no such thing. But a close look reveals the fact that Wolin conceives of method in purely mechanical terms, something like the folding of a shirt only more complicated. This is odd in the extreme since many of the great theorists he discusses from Marx and Macpherson to Strauss and Kendall have all been wedded to method in one or another sense. Indeed, as soon as the focus is shifted from the objective pole to that of the subject the various methods of discovery or Socratic teaching open up for us precisely as they did for Dewey and Bruner, Moore and Halmos, etc. The question is: do we think in the special way of the subject and understand as in the concept called *Verstehen*? Russell's answer is a flat "No" and he makes this answer in his critique of Descartes and his celebrated "*Cogito ergo sum*."

On the face of it Descartes' *Cogito* would appear to be simple enough, uncontroversial, and designed to guard against the acids of skepticism represented by the evil demon who would deceive him. In English it translates into two simple words "I think." Now who could possibly object to that? Well, one who can and does most forcefully is Bertrand Russell in his *History of Western Philosophy*[12] and the most Descartes is entitled to say, Russell contends, is that "There are thoughts." This move is critical and makes for three or four significant results. A close look reveals at least the following:

1. Russell has changed the formulation from the first person to the third. In place of "I think" we have the depersonalized "There are thoughts." And with this the notion of Descartes as a thinking subject has vanished. We are in the domain of "epistemology without a subject." Descartes' *Cogito* is followed by a logical result: "therefore I am."
2. If his *Cogito* is rendered impersonal then his "therefore" is misplaced and his "I am" does not in fact follow. The "I" or ego in "I am" has disappeared and the self has been erased from philosophy precisely as James advocated. But this is precisely the Hume theory in modern dress with Russell's development of the "propositional function" in which the subject has vanished completely. When Hume looked into himself, when he performed the act of introspection he failed to see any object which could properly be called a self. I contend that the reason for this is simple, fundamental, and obvious. In consciousness as perception (as in Christopher Isherwood's *I Am a Camera*) there is no subject and no experience of a self. The universal experience of a self with its thoughts, beliefs, opinions, personal understanding, and judgment is rejected in favor of the camera, machine, or computer model of

the mind in which computers "think" and thermostats have "beliefs![13] To frame the debate more fairly it is important to state precisely what the self is and what it is not. This was done in a concise paper called "What the Self Is Not" read before the Pacific Philosophical Society by Alburey Castell.

In the spectator theory of consciousness we are dealing, broadly speaking, with three types of objects, material objects such as chairs and tables, dogs and cats, mountains and trees, etc., etc., secondly with shapes and colors such as red patches and blue squares, and thirdly with mathematical objects of the kind familiar to Russell, Newman, cognitive scientists, and ordinary folk. Now, the self is emphatically not an object in this sense.

The point can be simply made. The three classes of entities mentioned are classed as objects in the strict sense of the word. In this sense an object is an entity that does not reason and cannot be reasoned with. But Descartes did reason and Russell is reasoning with us about him. Accordingly, we need a word for those entities from Descartes and Russell, philosophers and mathematicians, to you and me, who do reason and can in fact be reasoned with. And the name for this is subject in contradistinction to pure objects. In contradistinction the self is a subject which can reason and be reasoned with. But we can also theorize or think about the self, and in this sense it is also an object. In brief, then, the self is a subject which we, each of us, experiences as such and can think about as object. In short, the self is a subject which can subsequently be classified as object for purposes of analysis. Hume's inward look, his introspection, is pure mythology and Russell has made a category mistake mistaking a subject which is also an object for a pure object which cannot be reasoned with or reason.

The concept of method has emerged as central and decisive in our understanding of the rival positions of the two sides in the contemporary culture war in education. On the traditional side marked by the names of Patricia A. Graham and Diane Ravitch three forms of argument are employed in making the case against method. The first is that there are in fact many methods available and in light of this the writer will not take a stand for one over the other. In the second the writer, a historian like Diane Ravitch says "I don't know. I'm not a teacher." In the third the task is simply left to the teacher who is generally acknowledged to be untrained or poorly trained. In the absence of any rigorous program the pendulum has swung from traditional education to progressive education and back again, from *laissez faire*, which is no method at all, to the lecture and the textbook, homework, hard work, and tests. The arguments advanced by the two sides are on the level of theories of the middle level: Perhaps they are better than the clichés of pop culture but they never rise to the level of theories of first rank by mathematicians and scientists, philosophers and historians of rank in their professional fields. Outstanding among these is 1) the flat denial of *Verstehen* or a mode of understanding qualitatively different from simple and direct comprehension as in the comprehension of an object. 2) The consequent rejection of the student (or man in general) as a subject. 3) the willingness to embrace any result no matter how far-fetched such as the denial of the self, the attribution of beliefs to thermostats, and the assertion that water flowing down a hill has "information" because everything does. Information is everywhere. The roots of these beliefs can be found in theorists of the first rank whose work has created this climate of opinion and blurred the great divide between the Socratic and the anti-Socratic side in the debate on method. And to this we now turn.

The anti-Plato literature of our times can be dated precisely by a remarkable book called *Plato Today* by the Oxford scholar R.H.S. Crossman. *Plato Today* is remarkable on at least two counts. First, it has an excellent chapter titled "Plato Looks at British Education"[14] which presents a Platonic critique of modern mass education worth reading even today. Second, it makes a sharp distinction between Socrates, the symbol of free inquiry, and Plato, the authoritarian if not totalitarian. This is broadly the line of thought from Crossman to Russell and Karl Popper and calls for a comment, namely that the Socrates whom Crossman likes is entirely the creation of the Plato whom he hates. "It is Socrates, not Plato whom we need", he says in conclusion.

Socrates is synonymous with dialogue, with conversation, with question and answer advancing step by step toward the truth. In this, said Xenophon, there was no man superior to him. But this, says Bertrand Russell, is precisely the limitation of the dialectical method, which may be admirably suited to discovering truths of a certain kind such as in ethics (or metaphysics, or philosophy) but is incapable of discovering truths in science. Truths in the empirical domain lie outside its province. If correct this is certainly a drastic limitation. But is it correct? How true is it? Socrates himself restricted his inquiries primarily to questions of morals and politics, to moral and political philosophy, to the quest for justice and the best or right sort of life for man and citizen. But if his strictness is relaxed the picture changes dramatically and before our very eyes. At roughly the same time a scientist of rank, Professor

W.I.B. Beverage, Professor of Animal Husbandry at Cambridge, published a small book called *The Art of Scientific Investigation* showing precisely how this could be done in scientific research and teaching. In the sixties something was in the air in Britain and the United States and its similarity to the work of Stebbins and Hawkins can hardly be missed. But the case against method has a second and very able critic writing from right here in Berkeley.

"Political Theory as a Vocation" is Wolin's compact statement against method or the case for "the method of no method" as I call it. For the extended case, however, we must turn to his extremely well-written work called *Politics and Vision*.[15] In a way this is a curiously titled book for it contains little about politics itself and next to nothing about vision. In fact, all outward appearance to the contrary, is it not really a book at all but rather a collection of loosely connected chapters which could stand as independent articles. It has no single and sustained theme or argument, no discernible structure and no *locus standi* on which the argument is based. Indeed, it is not a work in political theory at all but a work in the history of ideas, erudite and well presented, but for all that it is a work of history in the Sabine tradition and not of theory or political philosophy. It tells its story with an air of neutrality, almost of studious neutrality one might say. But it has its heroes and villains nonetheless. Among the few scholars receiving favorable mention the names of Karl Popper, J.W.N. Watkins, and Dorothea Crook stand out in the study of Plato and Hobbes. While on the other side Strauss is dismissed as "fatuous," Kendall as "extreme," and Selznick as "manipulative."

The great adversary with whom the work opens is Plato. It closes with a sharp, somewhat condescending, critique of Marx. The book is, then, in the liberal tradition of Oxford philosophy from Wittgenstein to Isaiah Berlin, and closes with a warning against totalitarianism. Few today would have a good word to say about totalitarianism. But what precisely is the case against method?

The concepts of a political theory, writes Wolin, may be likened to a net. And what a political theorist will come up with depends on the structure of the net and where he casts it. Clearly some nets are better than others and some waters better to fish in. But there is no fixed standard, no best regime. The Socratic search was predicated on an illusion. There is only the cave of opinion lit by the shadows on the wall. Plato's graphic picture of the right and good state, the perfect state as one might say, is dismissed as "a frozen *Rechtsstaat*" in the phrase by Karl Popper and by this, I believe, Wolin means that it pays no attention to the brokerage of interests so vital to all politics.

Wolin is, of course, quite correct. But no picture of a final end, a snapshot of the ultimate stage, is designed to do this. The critique of Marx is still more curious. History itself had played a cruel trick on the creator of historical materialism. Instead of Adonis (in the form of the historical proletariat) it gave us *Quasimodo*. But Marx, of course, never pictured the proletariat as anything like Adonis. Quite the contrary, the hundreds of pages of the *Grundrisse* and the *Economic and Philosophical Manuscripts* are among the most graphic and moving picture of alienated labor and the disfigurement of the worker. And this analysis continues to move us to this day in reports on agriculture, undocumented Mexican and Central American labor, NAFTA and the deteriorating conditions of labor in Mexico.

Wolin's treatment of vision, of the nature of consciousness, is still more curious. He bases his view on Coleridge and the *Biographia Literaria* and the esemplastic nature of consciousness.

But the *Biographia Literaria* is exactly the wrong place to look for Coleridge on consciousness and method. Coleridge himself had devoted a full book to the subject and called it *A Treatise on Method*. The Treatise was one of his most brilliant and much discussed works on both sides of the Atlantic. In the United States, for example, Justus Buehler dedicated a long chapter to the Treatise in a study called *The Concept of Method* and ranges Coleridge on our side of the debate. While in Britain Rosamund Harding had only recently published an excellent and very thorough analysis of the creative process.

To sum up the investigation to date:

1. We began with a brief account of the Frontier Thinkers, an interesting group of progressive educators with special mention of two on the far left, Harold Rugg and George S. Counts, in an initial framing of the culture wars in America. In this brief Introduction we were involved with educators and historians of middle rank such as Diane Ravitch on the traditional side and her targets including Rugg and Counts himself. On this level the arguments made were superficial though widely accepted in the shaping of political culture then and now.

2. Accordingly, we set out to investigate the roots of the two main positions on the more fundamental level by theorists of rank in Britain and the United States. On the level of fundamental theory the two main positions could be bracketed by the work of R.S. Peters on "Education as Initiation" and the contrary view, the view that this is precisely the problem, by Bowles and Gintis in a three-year study funded by the Ford Foundation.

3. Peters' position, the position of Oxford philosophy, was ably seconded by John R. Searle and John Passmore with whom we come to the first direct confrontation with Bruner and discovery teaching the position defended in these pages.
4. The contrary position has several main roots, four of which are examined here. The first is the contention that "The Operation Called *Verstehen*" (or "understanding" or "sympathetic understanding") has never been described and does not exist. This argument is advanced with decisiveness, force, and clarity and strikes hard at our position. The pivotal role of insight (in our special sense, i.e., as distinct from comprehension) is flatly rejected and with it the investigator or student as subject. Scientific knowledge is "objective knowledge" as in normal scientific research and the case for method in developing a theory of instruction and craft of teaching is stopped before it can start.
5. The case against method is pressed to an extreme by Sheldon S. Wolin compactly in his article "Political Theory as a Vocation" and in expanded form in his widely read study *Politics and Vision*. Consciousness is understood as consciousness of an object, material, or sensible, or mathematical, and the notion of the self is discarded from Hume to Russell and Wittgenstein in Britain and from James and radical empiricism in this country. "The Vanishing Subject in the Psychology of James," as Dewey noted, had vanished completely till it was rediscovered by Bruner and associates, Moore and Halmos. To this strange story there is one interesting exception in the sharp debate between Harry V. Jaffa and Felix Oppenheim which calls for notice before presenting an outline of the case for the defense.

In March 1957 Felix Oppenheim published a revealing article titled "The Natural Law Thesis: Affirmation or Denial?"[16] swiftly answered in the next issue by Harry V. Jaffa with a brief rejoinder by Oppenheim. The debate pinpoints the central issue dividing the two sides in compact and clearly accessible form. But it is also interesting for a second reason: It represents a complete misfire. Two polished duelists take careful aim, fire at point blank range, and miss completely. This misfire points to a phenomenon here labeled "the flight from understanding." A careful reading of the structure of the arguments will show exactly how this works. Oppenheim makes the decisive point, and he makes it decisively: "Intrinsic value judgments can be neither valid nor invalid in a cognitive sense" because they are not objects of cognition in a scientific sense. Since they are not such objects they are intrinsically meaningless in the strictly cognitive sense required by modern science. And this creates an unbridgeable gap between the IS, the domain of science, and the Ought, the domain of moral philosophy. This is a crisp restatement of the Hume–Weber thesis which has dominated modern philosophy from Ayer and Russell to the Vienna Circle and the Wittgenstein of the *Tractatus* and later Oxford philosophy. Politically speaking it has led to relativism and pluralism in the celebrated work of Sir Isaiah Berlin in Britain and Robert Dahl, or Dahl and Lindblom, in the United States. This is merely to situate it. But our concern here is to illustrate the flight from understanding exemplified in the debate between the two sides. Here is how it proceeds.

First, natural right (and therefore moral cognition) does not lie in the domain of empirical or natural science. To say that all men have certain unalienable rights (let's call this X) is not like saying that all men have two eyes (let's call this Y). Between X and Y, moral judgment and factual or empirical judgment there is an "unbridgeable gap." And this gap cannot be bridged by the natural law thinker (of whom the theologian Brunner is an example) by a profession of unshakeable faith. Second, two poles are now sharply distinguished: natural law based on revelation versus the "intersubjectivity" of scientific discourse. This use of the term "intersubjectivity" is misleading. Scientific discourse is not merely intersubjective but impersonal and in that sense objective. It is characteristically third-person discourse rather than first-person discourse. Oppenheim's move made in the name of science is to rule out all personal knowledge in Michael Polanyi's sense of the term. The truths which Jefferson *et al.* took to be "self-evident" are ruled out by definition though they were intersubjective as marked by the "We" in the phrase "We hold these truths …." And with this "paradigmatic truth" in Kuhn's sense of the term is likewise ruled out. Truth in this sense is intersubjective and defines the relations between the truths in question and the community holding them (the Founders, Catholics, Marxists, etc.). But it is not the impersonal or objective or third-person truth of empirical science. No community could live by such truths because a community is a morally united group of people and distinguished from other communities precisely by this moral unity.

From Oppenheim's perspective, however, none of this makes any sense. And he now moves very fast to the rejection of natural right and a denial of moral cognitivism. "Intrinsic value judgments have no cognitive validity because they have no cognitive meaning." There it is in its stark simplicity from Hume to Ayer and Russell and now down to Oppenheim in the pages of

The American Political Science Review. The real-life implications are astounding coming as this does after the moral horrors of the Nazi regime and "the crimes of the Stalin era" to be confessed by Khrushchev himself. From Hume to Oppenheim there is an iron consistency in moral skepticism as a flight from understanding. Consider, for example, the American debate on slavery. If A says that "some men are by nature slaves" and B says that "all men have certain unalienable rights...," this according to Oppenheim is a meaningless debate. Why so? Because there is no intersubjective, i.e., impersonal, way of resolving the dispute as there is in science. Response: Of course not. Concisely stated, natural science is the study of the natural world, i.e., the universe of objects. Accordingly, normal science is for the most part a highly impersonal or objective study. And this in turn gives rise to an observational or spectator theory of consciousness. When viewed in this manner Hume is led to reject the idea of the self, James to deny the existence of consciousness, and Oppenheim following Ayer and Russell to deny the cognitive status of fundamental or "intrinsic" moral judgments. Modern philosophy denies the existence of what we all know to be the facts of psychic life and the meaningfulness and reality of fundamental moral discussion and debate. These have become "party questions" and we turn instead to studies of "the language of morals."

Oppenheim's challenging article received an immediate reply from Harry V. Jaffa in the next issue of the *APSR*.[17] Jaffa's response is a fine display of literary and dialectical forensics from the Straussian perspective. No brief summary can convey its quality in the literary and dramatic sense. A reader who enjoys fine writing should read it in the original.

Jaffa cuts right away to the heart of the issue between himself and Oppenheim or, more broadly, between Strauss and the scientific study of politics. To accept moral skeptics, he writes, "is to remove Justice itself from the court of reason." Our most fundamental moral principles would become ultimately arbitrary. They would in Russell's phrase be nothing more than "party questions." Against this Jaffa presents a number of arguments, minor and major, of varying force and quality (the argument from infinite regress, self-contradiction, and the case of the consistent Nazi, etc.). But these will persuade no one, least of all the consistent Nazi, or Communist, or even Marxist. Jaffa himself has failed to persuade Felix Oppenheim, a liberal democrat, let alone a consistent Marxist, or Communist, or Nazi.

To understand the misfire we cut to the chase and scrutinize his central proposition. The word "sweet," he argues reasonably, "presupposes a world of objects" to which the word by common consent applies. Were this not so the world of intersubjective experience to which all such words (sweet, sour, hot-cold, etc.) apply would lose its meaning because it would lose its objectivity. We would be plunged into the night in which all cows are black. And here is precisely where the flight from understanding begins.

Jaffa now engages in a smooth transition from the world of sensible and material objects which are (or can be) sweet or sour, hot or cold, red or green, hard or soft, to the self (which is not a material or sensible object). "Self-consciousness," he says, "is consciousness of oneself as an object." But this is precisely not the case as a moment's reflection will show. Let me call the world of material and sensible objects "the world of pure objects" or "objects in the primary sense." The self, however, is not an object in this pure or primary sense. The unity of internal experience which we call the self, which reasons and can be reasoned with, is a subject which, since it can then be studied, can secondly be classified as prime substance, or an object. All Jaffa's demonstrations fail because they all overlook this distinction. His star example is Mark Anthony invoking nature herself to say "This was a man." But this is a political or philosophical judgment, and these can vary with the cognizing subject. Consider Lukács on Lenin, or any number of acolytes on Stalin immediately after his death, or various and sundry Nazis on Reinhardt Heydrich on his assassination. Moral argument on the fundamental level is always argument made on a subjective dimension because it is argument made by a moral subject. If the nature of the cognizing subject is deformed (as were those of the Nazis, Stalinists, etc.) they will judge wrongly. And to the extent that they were not so deformed but on the contrary well formed, they will judge rightly as with Plato on the death of Socrates: "And so died our dear friend Socrates who was of all men the wisest, the justest, and the best." Moral cognition can be right or wrong. But not demonstrably so with a QED for all men as in Euclid because a Euclidean proof is (morally) impersonal. It merely requires intellectual competence. So, too, when Strauss imputes the inconclusive character of philosophy to its "comprehensive" quality, he is mistaken or, at least, ambiguous. Philosophy or the quest for knowledge of the whole is forever inconclusive because it includes knowledge of man. And knowledge of man is based on a subjective dimension which is the source of man's freedom not from error but from sin, if I may put it so. In his "Reply" Oppenheim wins every time or seems to because he has equated moral cognition which is subjective with scientific demonstration which is objective and impersonal. The sensible facts about Brutus (read Lenin, Stalin, Heydrich) are one thing. The moral facts are another.

Notes

1. David Tyack and Larry Cuban *Tinkering Toward Utopia*, Harvard University Press, Cambridge, Mass, 1995.
2. Richard Elmore, "Getting to Scale with Good Educational Practice." *Harvard Educational Review*: April 1996, Vol. 66, No. 1, pp. 1–27.
3. Bowles, S. & Gintis, H. *Education in Capitalist America: Education Reform and the Contradictions of Economic Life*. New York, NY: Basic Books, Inc. Publishers, 1976.
4. As Marx famously portrayed it in the *Critique of the Gotha Program*.
5. John Passmore, *The Philosophy of Teaching*, Cambridge, Mass: Harvard University Press, 1980.
6. William James, *The Principles of Psychology*, New York: Henry Holt & Company, 1890.
7. John Searle, "Can Information Theory Explain Consciousness?" *The New York Review of Books*, January 10, 2013 Issue.
8. R. G. Collingwood, *The Idea of History*, London: Oxford University Press, 1975; first published 1946.
9. John Passmore, *The Philosophy of Teaching*, op. cit., p. 69.
10. Theodore Abel, "*The Operation Called Verstehen*," American Journal of Sociology 54, no. 3 (Nov., 1948): 211–218.
11. James L. Jarrett, *The Educational Theories of The Sophists*, Teachers College Press, Columbia University, 1969, p. 48.
12. Bertrand Russell, *A History of Western Philosophy*, New York: Simon & Schuster, 1945, pp. 564–565. The book is available online: http://www.ntslibrary.com/PDF%20Books/History%20of%20Western%20Philosophy.pdf
13. Professor Searle reports a conversation with John Newman, an expert in artificial intelligence, in which Newman maintains that his thermostat has three beliefs: it's hot. It's cold. And it's fine.
14. R.H.S. Crossman, *Plato Today*, George Allen & Unwin Ltd., London, 1937, second revised edition, 1959, the sixth chapter, pp. 108–124.
15. Sheldon S. Wolin, *Politics and Vision*, Boston, Mass: Little, Brown and Company, 1960.
16. Felix Oppenheim, *American Political Science Review*, Volume 51, issue 1, March 1957, pp. 41–53.
17. Ibid.; Harry V. Jaffa, "Comment on Oppenheim: In Defense of the "Natural Law Thesis," pp. 54–64.

· 7 ·

BERTRAND RUSSELL AND THE EUREKA SYNDROME

Kekule's Dream

1

The philosophy of Bertrand Russell marks the spot where ends collide in the culture war in education. His philosophy of education was carefully criticized by Boyd H. Bode in the *Library of Living Philosophers*.[1] Russell replied by saying "Mr. Bode is the one contributor to this series whom I regard (in an impersonal sense) as an enemy." And with this the war was on. But what was the fighting really about? Russell says that the society desired by Bode is so different from what he desires that no constructive conversation on the topic is possible. The line of criticism developed here is very different and comes from a friend who desires a similar sort of society. But first a word about Bode's critique merely to set the stage.

Bode's critique is dialectical in structure and unfolds dialectically step by step from the first light touch to the final cut. A few lines will convey the style of the encounter. To the American public Russell has the attraction of a Mephisto. To read Russell is to enjoy the thrill of a *risqué* play or novel of meeting a man who smells of danger, of ideas subversive of your world and culture. The decisive issue is the split, the cleavage between the individual and the community of freedom versus organization and the pressures making for conformity. This, Bode contends, is the basic issue in American education. On the one side is the claim of the individual *psyche* for knowledge and culture, on the other is the claim of the state and the demands of citizenship and social cohesion. Russell needs a principle to bring them into harmony, and this is precisely what he does not have. In a democratic community the issue of conflicting wills is settled by majority decisions made continuously over time. The point is that these are conflicts always taking place *within* a culture itself developing over time. By contrast, the individual in Russell's educational philosophy is a pure abstraction standing over and against the community in a conflict that has no resolution within the tradition as it is actually lived. And this is all the more "reprehensible" in this time of crisis: "The simple fact of the matter is that our culture or tradition is cracking under the strain which is being put upon it" (636). Bode's conclusion is that "the only way is to reconstruct these (wills) so that they will coalesce in a common program" (637–638). And with these words he turns at last to the philosophy of pragmatism in James and Dewey where the tensions between the concrete individual and the evolving tradition are harmonized in the interplay between school and community, education and tradition and the search for balance and the good life.

By now, however, we are even more remote from school and the curriculum, the mathematics and science teacher, and the teacher in history, drama, and literature. But Dewey himself had a second and very different side to his teaching, curiously overlooked by both Bode and Russell. This was his cognitional theory developed in a substantial volume entitled *How We Think* and given sharper point in a brief article called *The Vanishing Subject in the Psychology of James*. Why this oversight? In the literature this is known as a *scotoma* or blind spot, and the condition is known as "the *scotosis* of the dramatic subject." And analysis of the line of argument in Russell, the paradigmatic figure in scientific philosophy, will illuminate the blind spots at the center of the problem of education and the culture clash.

For it is evident that once the vanishing subject is reintroduced into the equation and the student is treated as the knower, the problem of conflicting values has itself vanished. In the paradigm shift to Socratic teaching the Learner as the knowing subject is free to develop his ideas and values subject only to critical questioning by the teacher and his fellow students.

In this shift the teacher restricts himself to questioning and occasionally to a counterargument to see how it is met. He is as the midwife, herself barren who brings out what is there in others. The student as the knowing subject is free to develop his values and position subject only to critical questioning and analysis. There is then no need to harmonize the different wills in the class and the Russell–Bode dispute has itself gone with the wind.

Of the many figures who feature in our drama of moral conflict Russell is certainly the most many sided. He has something to say about nearly everything of any importance in philosophy, politics, and education. And he is always worth listening to with respect and the closest attention. To keep the account clear and clean I will begin by situating him in the main lines of the story.

1. Where does he fit in British empiricism and scientific philosophy?
2. How does this shape his judgment of the cardinal figures in his History from the Greeks and Aquinas to Hume and the present?
3. What can we learn from the conflict with Bode and American pragmatism?
4. What precisely is the cognitional theory dividing him from us?
5. What is the nature of the *eureka* phenomenon so missing from his conception of the functions of the teacher and so key to our view?

Russell's critique of classical political philosophy can be situated in the center of the rising stream of anti-Plato analysis originated by R.H.S. Crossman in the imaginative *Plato Today* (1937) written under the dark clouds of fascism and treating Plato as a precursor of totalitarianism.[2] This was followed by Karl Popper's widely read *The Open Society and Its Enemies* which broadened the attack to include Hegel and Marx and switched the focus to Marxism and socialism.[3] And Plato as an antidemocrat was the focus of a finely written article by Renford Bambrough titled "Plato's Political Analogies" in *Philosophy, Politics, and Society* (First Edition).[4] Russell falls squarely in the center of this influential line of thought. He recognizes the cast iron character of Socrates. But he does not share the view of the Delphic Oracle that "there was no man wiser than Socrates." Socrates, says Russell, refutes Thrasymachus with little more than a quibble. There was, he goes on to say, something smug and unctuous about the Platonic Socrates that reminds one of a bad type of cleric.

Russell's analysis of the Greeks highlights the mode of understanding flowing from the tradition of Hume and British empiricism. He begins at the beginning with Thales, universally credited as "the first philosopher." In these early days when the scientific and strictly philosophical were not clearly differentiated the scholar faces a choice: Are the words of Thales to be understood in an empirical and scientific sense or in a philosophical and even metaphysical sense? Russell unhesitatingly opts for the first. Of the two choices. Thales famously described water as the *arché* or principle underlying all things in the cosmos. Taken as protoscience, Russell tells us, this was not a bad conjecture. Water, we know, is composed of hydrogen and oxygen in two parts to one. And hydrogen, we now know, is the element composing the greatest part of the universe. Any reader interested in the dramatically contrasting flow of arguments should turn to the thoughtful study by Stanley Rosen titled "Thales: The Beginning of Philosophy" first published in the *Review of Metaphysics*.[5] Rosen's article is too tightly packed to permit ready comprehension. "Water" is here taken not as a simple material object but as the symbolic form of the underlying unity of the cosmos. A few sentences will convey the style of the new philosophical conception of Thales and the origin of philosophy. It is sad but true that we can never know that Thales was a philosopher unless we ourselves are philosophers. Thales is for us philosophy making its appearance in human history.

Water becomes the underlying principle of world order by submitting the immanent *nous psyche* which is the form of order. And water is then the water in the ordinary physical sense of the word. Water is the middle term between *nous psyche* and *anthropopsyche*, and regarded in this sense, it is a metaphorical expression of the superstructure of the whole within which cosmic order is extant structurally.

It has been traditional, Russell tells us, to praise Plato, to respect him rather than to understand him. Russell's position is the reverse: It is to understand Plato and to treat him with as little reverence as he would any English or American advocate of totalitarianism. So the lines are drawn between classical political philosophy and the new or modern philosophy issuing from Hume and British empiricism. Russell means to reverse the tradition and the bill of particulars runs as follows. The main influence on Plato were Pythagoras, Parmenides, Heraclitus, and Socrates from whom he derived his ethics and mystical vision of the Good. But it was Sparta, myth and reality, which shaped his political philosophy. The philosopher is defined as the lover of wisdom. But is there something clearly definable as "wisdom"? And if so what is the nature of the education required to develop it? The pursuit of wisdom demands leisure and much learning. Would we in modern society entrust government to plutocrats who have the one and Doctors of Divinity who are said to have the other? More: politics in any state is the arena where divergent interests come into play. Their reconciliation is the supreme art of politics and good government. And with this the purity of the philosopher's wisdom and the monopoly of the guardians are fatally compromised.

But Plato's utopia is altogether different from the ideals which inspire the modern democratic state. It has nothing to do with the compromise characteristic of democratic government and society. Rule by aristocracy is rule unchecked. Knowledge is power, and it has no concessions to make to the *demos*, the unphilosophical and ignorant. When we ask what this autocracy will achieve, the answer is rather "humdrum." Success in wars against cities of equal size, and enough to eat for the population as a whole, etc. But it will develop no science and with the banishment of the poets and dramatists, it will develop no art. The vision of the good which inspired Plato's celebrated parable, is a mystical vision, and not one of rational science. The problem is philosophical, and constitutes the fundamental problem in moral philosophy. Russell explains it like this: When we say of snow that it is white, this quality is available. But there is no similar quality which can be attributed to the good or to ethics generally. Later in his *History of Western Philosophy*, Russell imagines an argument between Nietzsche and Buddha,[6] the will to power versus the apostle of compassion, and comes to no conclusion as between them. On the fundamental level ethical dispute is rationally inconclusive and can, therefore, only be settled by force or emotional appeal. And this is the case for democracy, relativism, and pluralism. Ethical questions are in the final analysis "party questions" and call for compromise if society is to work. And with this we reach the root of the conflict between Russell, the paradigmatic liberal, and Strauss (or Voegelin, or Kendall) the paradigmatic conservative. Russell himself closes his study of *Human Society in Ethics and Politics* (Routledge, 1954) with the despairing cry that above and beyond all reason he hopes there is (a solution). But within the philosophy of Hume and British empiricism there is none. (How this came about will become more evident by visiting the fine study by A.J. Ayer called *Language, Truth, and Logic* which swept the field on publication.[7]

Plato and Aristotle are by common consent the two greatest and most influential philosophers of all time. But of the two, Russell tells us, it is Plato who was the more influential. And this for two reasons. First off it was Plato who influenced Aristotle. And secondly it was Plato who remained the more influential right through till St. Thomas and the thirteenth century. Russell's inclusive critique takes on a corresponding significance in the play of contrasting arguments evolving in culture war in the politics and education rising up in the interwar years, as revealed by our next three witnesses (Ayer, Crossman, Bambrough).

2

The critical significance of Ayer's treatise was caught right away by Leo Strauss who was to single it out for special mention in his critique of positivism in introduction to the *Essays on the Scientific Study of Politics*.[8] And rightly so for Ayer's study is the clearest, most coherent, and most ruthlessly consistent statement of the position to be found to date.

The prime source of Ayer's opinions was the burst of ideas in philosophy and mathematics in the previous twenty-five years. Most prominently these were marked by the Russell of the *Principia Mathematica* and the Wittgenstein of the *Tractatus*, G.E. Moore and F.P. Ramsey, and the cascade of articles brightening the pages of the *Proceedings of the Aristotelian Society*. Moore led the way with the refutation of idealism and Russell with the critique of monism and the theory of internal relations. By the time they were done traditional idealist philosophy in Britain was almost as dead as old Queen Anne. But there was also a second source of almost equal importance. This was the Vienna Circle and their pioneering in developing the philosophy of science in the model of physics. Here the most prominent names are those of Moritz Schlick and Phillip Frank, Carnap and Hahn and their contributions to *Erkenntnis*.

If the roots of Ayer's philosophy reach back to Locke, Berkeley, and Hume the presentation itself is as modern as tomorrow. The chapter headings of *Language, Truth, and Logic* tell the story. A stimulating Introduction is soon followed by "The Elimination of Metaphysics" followed in turn by "The Function of Philosophy" and "The Nature of Philosophical Analysis." The next to go is "The A *Priori*," followed by a chapter on "Truth and Probability" as applying to all empirical propositions which can be verified and assigned a degree of probability. And this in turn leads to a "Critique of Ethics" and the consequent formulation of emotive theory of ethics, later reformulated as the expressive theory of ethics. And finally we come to the notion of self as an entity, the elimination of the Ego as in Descartes celebrated "*Cogito ergo Sum*," and the resulting problem of a common world. So, we ask ourselves, what's left? The answer is given in the final chapter titled "Philosophy as the Logic of Science." So there we have it in its stark simplicity and unassailable logic.

Some sample quotations will convey the sweep of Ayer's argument from its possible beginnings to its breathtaking conclusions. The baseline is formed by the philosophy of empiricism deriving from Locke and Berkeley, and especially Hume, and developed by Russell and Wittgenstein in Britain, and by the Vienna Circle in Austria. In modern empiricism three features stand out as the points of critical importance. The three features are these: (1) the role of sense contents, (2) the analytic/synthetic distinction, and (3) the criterion of verifiability as the test of meaning. From these all else follows.

Ayer's text on each of these points is clear and decisive. "A putative proposition is significant only if it is verifiable" (p. 38).[9] The rejection of metaphysics follows quite logically, and Ayer does not hesitate for a moment. "The utterances of the metaphysicians are nonsensical" (p. 41). Or again, as if for emphasis: "All metaphysical propositions are nonsensical." What then is the function of philosophy? "The function of philosophy is wholly critical." It is the critical clarification of the logic of science (p. 48). In his role as a critical analyst the philosopher should "confine himself to works of clarification and analysis" (p. 51). "If," he cites Hume as saying, "we take in our hands any volume of divinity; of school metaphysics, for instance, let us ask; Does it contain any abstract reasoning concerning quantity or number? No. Does it contain any experimental reasoning concerning matters of fact or existence? No. Commit it then to the flames. It can contain nothing but sophistry and illusion" (p. 54).

The second key distinction is the distinction between synthetic and analytic propositions. An analytic proposition is that of an unmarried man. All such propositions are, therefore, tautologies and devoid of content. It is only the synthetic proposition that has any content, and this content is an empirical content. "A sentence," Ayer tells us, "says nothing unless it is empirically verifiable" (p. 73). Or again, "... all propositions are either empirical or *a priori*" (p. 87). And the *a priori* is by definition not empirically verifiable and devoid of meaning. This is the basis of the refutation of rationalism ancient and modern. And this analysis culminates in the controversial critique of ethics well known as the emotive theory of ethics.

Once again a few quotations will deliver the punch of the argument: "... in so far as statements of value are significant they are ordinary scientific statements, and where they are not scientific they are not in the literal sense significant but are simply expressions of emotion which can be neither true nor false" (p. 103). They are expressions of feeling, verbal ejaculations, or commands. But they have no cognitive status or value.

It follows that "A strictly philosophical treatise on ethics should therefore make no ethical pronouncements." (p. 103) Fundamental ethical concepts, Ayer tells us, are unanalyzable. "They are mere pseudo concepts." (p. 112) To say that "you acted wrongly in stealing that money." The term "wrongly" merely expresses your feeling of moral disapproval. And this has no cognitive status because as a feeling it is unverifiable. They may be of interest to the psychologist, but they have no interest to the philosopher because they enjoy no cognitive status. Ayer is explicit: "We have seen that as ethical judgements are mere expressions of feeling, there can be no way of determining [their] validity..." (p. 112). As a pronouncement made in the mid-thirties and the rise of Stalin and Hitler, this is breathtaking. The reason or rather the explanation is equally astonishing if not more so. According to Ayer "one really never disputes about questions of value" but only of fact (p. 110). Accordingly, "there can be no such thing as an ethical science" (p. 112). Philosophical inquiry is limited to an analysis of the language of ethics.

In this treatise, the most significant of the day, Ayer began with the elimination of metaphysics only to end with the elimination of ethics, aesthetics, and philosophical theology. If Ockham's razor shaved Plato's beard then Ayer's blade has taken off the whole head. And this with refinements came to dominate academic study till the revolt by Polanyi *et al.* in Britain and Strauss *et al.* in the United States. The issue at stake between Ayer and the critics is the validity and relevance of the scientific outlook to the study of man and not simply the material world in the model of physics. What is the place of value in a world of facts? The core of the problem is this: Values are subjective and can be verified. Values in their objectivity and externality can be verified. Values in their subjectivity and internality, cannot. This difference forms the heart of the problem in the conflict between the two sides. The sharpest, most stark response was that of Leo Strauss in his critique of Max Weber and the fact/value distinction. "This, I contend," said Strauss, "leads to nihilism, nay it is identical with nihilism." If sound, the critique is dispositive. But modern thought has generally not accepted it.

More convincing is the theory of the subject developed by a score of thinkers from Hegel to Kierkegaard and Buber to Dewey. Most prominent among them is the work of Bernard Lonergan, S.J. in a number of writings. The subject–act–object view is ruled out by Ayer (p. 122) and by Russell in his chapter on Marx in his book *A History of Western Philosophy*.[10] The rationale is the more fundamental quality of "sense contents" - the accent falls naturally on "contents." "Sense contents" is a unified term unifying sense and contents.

The five senses are simply the tributaries along which the contents flow. Two radically different features of experience are here fused into a whole with the accent falling on the empirical contents, and not the sense of the human subject. Lonergan phrases it like this. We all perform certain operations such as seeing, hearing, feeling, tasting, and smelling. In these operations there is the thing seen, the sound heard, etc., and the act of seeing, hearing, feeling, etc. The former, the first of these is the object and lies on the experiencing side of the equation and can be termed the subject. And surely we all experience ourselves as subjects with a sense of personal identity, a sense of self without which a man would be a clinical case. Castell's article mentioned earlier (See chapter six.) tells us precisely what a self is not, and what it is. This is the case for the "substantive ego" which we all experience as in Descartes "I think." This is our universal sense or experience of human consciousness. And it is a mistake to rule it out saying only "there are thoughts." Consistently applied, the scientific outlook provoked the *Brave New World* of Huxley's satire, the consumer society of Postman, Strauss's "joyless quest for joy," and Voegelin's charting of progressive deculturation. But a more balanced view is presented by our next witness, R.H.S. Crossman whose *Plato Today* takes us straight to the problem of education and culture, or the moral quality of society.

3

The culture of the community, that is to say the moral quality of society, is the specific province of education and its supreme responsibility. This is the issue confronted by R.H.S. Crossman in a remarkable study called *Plato Today* first published in the interwar years (1937), and then republished a decade later.[11] Crossman comes to the table after teaching Plato at Oxford for a dozen years or more. After the war he became a practicing politician, an intellectual light of the British Labor Party, and the celebrated editor of *The God That Failed*.[12] *Plato Today* is the earliest work in the series of anti-Plato literature marked by the names of Bertrand Russell, Karl Popper, and Renford Bambrough in the case of liberal democracy versus autocracy, the totalitarian mind, and fascism for which the figure of Plato serves as a compact symbol in the war of ideas.

In a remarkable exercise in imagination Crossman presents Plato as the critic liberal society and particularly of British education. The chapter is called "Plato Looks at British Education"[13] and presents the Platonic critique and the response to it by an Educationalist in an unfolding dialectic of ever harsher severity. The lines are drawn with the first exchange. "We," says the

Educationalist, "are democrats." As democrats we believe in the principle of freedom, the right of each man to choose his way of life, and universal suffrage going back to 1870. And with the extension of the vote we have developed a system of universal education to create an informed electorate. Crossman's Plato replies by contrasting the principle of freedom (which is devoid of content) with the principle of virtue and the knowledge required by it. This poses the problem of the distinction between the rulers and the demos. To proceed as you do, Plato says, is to muddle along with no criterion to distinguish truth from falsehood. Farming and building, carpentry and shoe making all require a special skill and education a *techné* to be developed by the study of mathematics and philosophy to attain virtue. This is beyond the reach of the *demos* who cannot become philosophers and must therefore be included in a popular mythology with noble lies.

But virtue requires freedom as its condition. Replies the Educationalist, rightly and "Englishmen are free to choose." "I believe." He says, "you are no better than a fascist." Crossman's Plato does not side step the charge. On the contrary, he advises the democratic educator not to be frightened by "the bogey of fascism." You must, he says, be ready to look to the practices of other lands, presumably Italy and Germany.

Plato's critique, then, is a compound of two lines of thought. The first is a critique, always discerning, often incisive of liberal democracy now evolving into a mass democracy. The second is the prescription for reform which earned him a newfound reputation as an advocate of totalitarianism and a fascist. Liberal democracy, Plato contends, is flawed in principle. It is in principle incurable. Its principle is itself the bad seed from which we have the bad fruit to be seen wherever we look. The fundamental principle of liberalism is the principle of freedom, followed by equality, democracy, and the open society. To this Plato counterposes the principle of virtue and knowledge, followed swiftly by hierarchy, aristocracy, and autocracy in the ruling group. The two sets of principles are mutually exclusive and Crossman writes with the rising power of Germany and Italy in background and Franco's rising success in the foreground.

The Educationalist takes his stand on democracy, pointing to the extension of the suffrage in 1870 and the institution of general education to create an informed public at the polls. Virtue, he argues rightly, is meaningless in the absence of choice. In the absence of freedom as a condition the practice of virtue is a hollow formality functioning lifelessly in an authoritarian political machine. Plato replies with an incisive critique, now known as the aristocratic critique of mass society. For Plato the key problem is the problem of Truth, and the imperative to understand it, to make it one's own, in an ever more comprehensive sense. Without a criterion of truth opinion remains crude and confused: There is no ascent from the lower to the higher, from the *doxa* to the *logos*. And this is the role of philosophy in the education of the rulers. Plato's critique of mass democracy is unanswerable, and the Educationalist fails to meet it fairly and squarely on its merits. Of the several facets of this critique two or three stand out in bold relief. First off, the entire system is dominated by a plutocracy bent on profit and devoid of culture. You are ruled, says Plato, by men no better than yourselves. In the logic of domination your educators become the slaves of vested interests and not inquirers after philosophic truth in a spirit of disinterested search and scientific research. The lip service they pay to the idea of academic freedom is merely part of the folklore of capitalism and the façade of liberal democracy. Self-rule or rule by the *demos* is a contradiction in terms, if the terms include virtue and knowledge or culture and moral quality in the highest degree. The present-day American reader will appreciate the point in the age of Trump and his choice of Secretary of Education.

Made in the course of conversation, Plato's observations were soon to be confirmed in the most widely read study of the time. In his study of *The Twenty Years Crisis*[14] E.H. Carr drives the point home in passage after passage. "the oldest and still perhaps the most powerful instrument," writes Mr. Carr, "is universal popular education."[15] The state which provides the education necessarily determines its content. No state will allow its citizens to imbibe in its school's teachings subversive of the principles on which it is based. In democracies the child is taught to prize the liberties of democracy. In totalitarian states to imbibe the strengths and discipline of totalitarianism. In both he is taught to respect his own country (p. 134). Or again, "The mass production of opinion is a corollary of the mass production of goods." (p. 134) Or yet again, "The nationalization of opinion has proceeded everywhere *pari passu* with the nationalization of industry." (p. 135) The problem is inherent in the ever-growing size of the nation state, the power conferred by science and technology, and the seductions of elite control and mass indoctrination in the folklore of the tradition. To this Plato and Carr, conservative and liberal, have two widely differing prescriptions for reform. What, then, does Crossman's Plato prescribe?

Crossman's Plato is as remarkable for what he does *not* say as for what he does. He does not begin, as we might expect, by saying: You must first cut down the size of your state. England is too large, and even London too populous. The right size is one which makes for community, for friendship between men and citizens, and for genuine dialogue or face to face conversation which alone makes for philosophy. More: since the debasement of culture and mass indoctrination is made possible by technology, you must set limits on all further technological development and the science on which it is based. I do not approve of book burning as they do in other lands so I recommend that you place them in your newly formed archives named, perhaps, after my teacher Socrates who also was not overly fond of books. When he questioned them, he said, they did not answer back. So begin with a polis and the reinstatement of the dialogue as the central feature of a philosophy that goes beyond language, important as that is, to morals and metaphysics.

Plato's proposals are made with clarity and flow consistently from his idea of the perfect state. At root this means the subordination of the principle of freedom to the principle of virtue and the rejection of democracy in favor of aristocracy and autocracy. His specific recommendations, laid down in steps of mounting severity, earn him the reputation of the complete fascist by the close of the exchange. The masses are to receive a vocational education suitable for the craftsmen they are fitted to be in a rigid class structure. The old ways, Plato avers, were the better ways. The rulers were men of substance and supported by the Church of England. In those days England produced the men of letters of whom she is still justly proud. The function of the educational system is to create true gentlemen with a sense of civic obligation, and not the elegant and pampered ladies and gentlemen of present day. Aristocratic rule is rule by the gentlemen. The new Universities will give them the requisite knowledge and training for statesmanship in the new society.

However, Plato continues, truth and wisdom by themselves cannot prevail against the forces of greed and self-interest of acquisitiveness and cunning. Against these forces mere talk and goodwill are unavailing. So you must tell yourself not simply to go as far as your adversaries but even further if the rule of reason is to prevail as the leitmotif of the state. You must acquire absolute control of the press, radio, and the film industry. And no opinion contrary to yours is to be permitted. On the contrary, the publication of any such opinion is to commit a crime punishable by death. And finally you must not be frightened away by the bogey of fascism for any of my ideas. Understand that even bad governments have good ideas. And to this the Educationalist can only reply that Sir Oswald Mosley would certainly appreciate Plato's recommendations and endorsement in the days ahead.

The signal achievement of *Plato Today* is to place the modern principle, the principle of freedom and democracy, against the classical principle, the principle of virtue and autocracy, against one another and resolve the issue in favor of the modern. The problem posed has two dimensions, and not just one. The first is the dimension of truth or validity. The second is the dimension of relevance to the world as it is and will be. The ideas developed by Plato are on a highly abstract level in the course of an inquiry into the true nature of justice and the best or perfect state in pure theory. It is hazardous to read them as a straightforward policy proposal made without radical amendment. The context is not the modern state but the polis with its small size and the face to face community of which it is composed. And the bonds of this community are laid in friendship and the good in Plato's dialogue and Aristotle's well-known treatise on ethics. In this context the unbridled development of technology would be a fatal flaw. Technology unbridled promotes the extension of the state and makes community impossible. The lonely crowd is the other side of technology.

The society projected by Plato was a small, essentially landed society ruled by gentlemen. But the gentleman has had his innings as Russell once observed, and it has been a short one. The day of the gentleman has given way to the day of the *demos*, and now the mass. What precisely does this mean for education and the political culture of the nation state? To this the Educationalist has no good answer, and nor does Crossman himself and it is here that his construction of Plato as a proto fascist breaks down. The breakdown occurs in two ways, the second of which is more significant than the first. Bad governments, says Plato, referring to Nazi Germany and Italy, can have "good ideas." Well what precisely were they? Beyond the idea of race Hitler's Germany had no ideas at all. In fact, the fascist movement in Germany and Italy was notoriously devoid of ideas. The revolution in Germany was famously called The Revolution of Nihilism. Fascism in Germany was imperialist from the start, dedicated to the development of the *Grossraum* and the unbridled development of technology and science. German culture was destroyed. The Jews were forced to flee, and the universities and schools became centers of party indoctrination. Simply said, a fascist is not merely one who has a certain definite set of ideas. He is at one and the same time a person with a certain definite sort of personality. The critical interconnection here is the relation of ideas or political constitution to personality. Fascism was primarily a lower middle class phenomenon. And its underlying dimension, the dimension that fueled the fire, was that blend of envy, anger, resentment, and spite which

Nietzsche called *ressentiment*, and which in this country we saw in Nixon and his popular support. Fascism without *ressentiment* is all but a contradiction in terms. But of all this there is not a trace in Plato's many dialogues. In fact, *Socratic Humanism*, as portrayed in Versenyi's fine work by that name,[16] is precisely the opposite. It is the antidote to the poisons of resentment welling up in mass society and the lower middle class.

In fact it is the contrast between Plato and the fascist that emerges most forcefully from Crossman's own text. In his fair-minded presentation Crossman stresses the dominance of truth and the presiding role of "the rule of reason" in Plato's doctrine. The search for truth is to be conducted in a spirit of impartiality and intellectual disinterestedness. But these are the very qualities most notoriously missing in Rosenberg, Hitler, Mussolini, and the fascists. If anything they are suggestive of Marx and the early Lenin of the *Philosophical Notebooks*, not to mention Marcus's *Reason and Revolution* and *The Critique of Pure Tolerance*. Strictly speaking, totalitarianism is a product, an outgrowth of the modern state. And there is something a little forced and anachronistic in the attempt to fit it to the classical and premodern mind, though this is an important line of thought. One example is Thorsen in his study of Rousseau, though Rousseau wrote as a critic and even an adversary of the modern state. A second example, in the citation by E.H. Carr, is the historian G.D. Coulton who presents the Catholic Church as the first totalitarian state or organization in history. Much depends on how you look at it and how you frame your question. Frame it in terms of the open society versus the closed (or partly closed) society then Rousseau, the Catholic Church, and Plato will certainly come down on the wrong side of the equation. Frame it in terms of the open society and the principle of freedom versus the consensual society and the principle of virtue, and the issue becomes more debatable. Rousseau, the Church, and Plato are the missing actors in Hannah Arendt's drama of the origins of totalitarianism as they are in Carl Friedrich's collection of studies on the topic of totalitarianism.

Crossman closes his book with a contrast between a Socrates whom he loves and a Plato whom he has come to hate. But let us remind ourselves that the Socrates he loves, the iconic free inquiring mind, is entirely the creation of the Plato he hates. Crossman bridges the span between the philosopher and the fascist with the conception of knowledge acquired as a *techné* drawn from the famous examples of Socrates himself. If knowledge is *techné* and only *techné*, Crossman has half made his case. He himself does not explore the theme which became the problem studied by Renford Bambrough in the finest article devoted to our problem and to which we now turn.

4

The decisive stroke in the anti-Plato critique was made by Renford Bambrough in his fine study of Plato's political analogies.[17] Trained in Oxford philosophy, and the author of a work on Plato and another on Aristotle, Bambrough writes with authority on his subject. The tone is cool, the argument measured, and the statement of the problem precise and accurate. Within the limitations of its methodology it is as clear and dispositive a critique as any from the side of modern British empiricism in the tradition of Russell and Wittgenstein. If right it should close the debate, for we can now see precisely where Plato went wrong in his many and celebrated political analogies.

Recent work in analytic philosophy, Bambrough tells us, has developed well beyond the early days of focus on epistemology and ethics, the philosophy of mathematics and science. It now studies *The Vocabulary of Politics* as in T.D. Weldon's recent book and to a critique of the great figures of the past as in Stuart Hampshire's critique of Spinoza. It centers its interest on the logic of the doctrine itself, and it does so with "sympathy and penetration." And Bambrough's critique is presented in this spirit of sympathy and penetration. It aims to present Plato's reasoning as accurately and fairly as possible, to do justice to its power and plausibility and to reveal the precise point where it becomes "radically misleading." Plato has presented us with "the characteristically Socratic mode of argument," and Bambrough is here to show why it fails. And with this we come to a high point in the play of contrasting arguments.

The way he sets up his argument is fascinating. He formulates it in terms of the sharpest, most clear-cut distinctions, and the analogies do lend themselves to precisely that. They are well known as the shoe maker, the builder, the craftsmen of various sorts, and most famously the navigator. Each of these calls for a special skill, and the skill developed makes one a specialist in the art or craft, an expert in the trade. And what the expert commands, what makes him an expert, is mastery of a *techné* suitable to the trade in question. Craftsman, specialist, expert, *techné*, this is the core of the litany Bambrough holds up against the analogies with a fateful question: Is there a similar *techné* by which ethical questions can be resolved and which can form the basis of a veritable, true, and correct political science? If there is not then the analogies fail and the case of the Platonic Socrates is lost. This is the key to what Bambrough calls "the Platonic error," and he has exposed its nerve.

The precise nerve of the argument is Plato's confusion of ends and means, of applying the logic of means to the logic of ends. The logic of means is a *techné* and results in a science as in the science of architecture or of navigation. But there is no such science of ends and no *techné* by which we can ever begin to develop any such science even in the broadest sense of the term. Even in the broadest sense of the term there is no such body of knowledge to be learned and passed on. Between means and ends there is an impassable gulf, so Bambrough proceeds to correct Plato and the analogy of the navigator. The skill of navigation is a technical skill enabling the navigator to steer the course with safety and reach the other shore. But the choice of the right shore or island to be reached is properly that of the owner or set of passengers. Correctly interpreted Plato's analogy leads to democracy and democratic choice and precisely not to aristocracy, let alone rule by the philosopher king if such could ever be found. Scientific controversy can (in principle) be settled as indeed we have settled it from the days of Galileo and Newton to the present. Where it remains unsettled we know the procedures by which it can (in principle) be settled and the experts who will agree on the outcome. But in matters of morals and politics there are no such experts and procedures, and no such body of knowledge. So "the characteristically Socratic argument" is "radically misleading." This is the sum and substance of Bambrough's contribution in his breathtaking "correction" of Plato.

Bambrough has made the case for democracy, and rested it on moral skepticism. But this was precisely not Plato's intention in designing the analogies and in the celebrated parable of the cave. Plato's intention was to recommend aristocracy and the rule of the wisest and the best in the vision of the good. And the analogies are designed to serve this intention if they are read quite differently. And in so doing we will, I contend, be more faithful to Plato's intention and to the true meaning of the analogies. Plato's intention is precisely to bridge the gap between means and ends, *techné* and philosophy, the ends for which shoes and ships are made and the ends for which life is led or, at least, should be led. The place to begin with was with all ordinary folk, i.e., with nonphilosophers, with their experience and daily life and with the wisdom or at least common sense that can be learned from it. Socrates, I venture to say, likes to begin not with an abstract propositional content but with a performance from which the right or most appropriate ethical and political ends and means can be derived. From these, the humblest, he presses on upward to the highest. The Socratic dialectic is an *ascent* and not a flat propositional content. Socratic dialectic is a transformative dialectic and not an exercise in logical or conceptual or linguistic analysis. Socrates, said a critic, must have been a strange reformer indeed if he hoped to make men good by logic. There's the error in a nutshell.

The precision and penetration of Bambrough's statement make it the most convenient point of inflection in the turn to the contrasting arguments. The flow of contrasting arguments develops in the following way (see Table 7.1) in model or concise form.

Table 7.1. Contrasting Arguments.

A) The tone of the logician is cool and detached, almost clinical in its dissection.	B) The tone of the moral reformer is warm, critical but also sympathetic, and always engaged.
A) The logician focuses on the logic of the argument.	B) The moral reformer focuses on the *psycho*-logic of the argumentation.
A) The logician focuses on the doctrine, its structure and vocabulary.	B) The reformer focuses quite as much on the mind or moral character of the subject.
A) The critic centers attention on the critical means–end distinction and the gulf between the Is and the Ought, the indicative and the imperative.	B) The reformer is well aware of the problem of transition and searches for ways to bridge the gulf in the light of common experience and common sense and some shared vision of the good.
A) The critic as technician sees knowledge as reducible to a *teché*.	B) To the moral reformer knowledge in the larger sense begins where *techné* leaves off, and this is why we call it wisdom and not expertise.
A) The upper reaches of the critic's world is populated by specialists, experts of one kind or another.	B) The reformer's search is for the knowledgeable and virtuous among the citizens, the statesmen and not merely the politicians, the wise among men and not merely the prudent or canny.
So the Oracle famously said that there was no man wiser than Socrates.	
A) To the critic the litmus test is the test of verification understood as resting on the data of sense and nothing else.	B) To the moral reformer this is simply the first step. He reaches beyond the data of sense to the data of consciousness without which there can be no conversion, no ascent toward the true, the beautiful and the good.

A) To the critic, James famous question: Does consciousness exist (as an entity)? The answer from Russell to James is "No."	B) To the moral reformer consciousness is not reducible to a bodily function like digestion in animals and photosynthesis in plants. It is there in our awareness.
A) It follows that the idea of the self is radically undermined because the experience of the self in consciousness is disallowed.	B) Philosophy famously began in the moral sense with the centrality of dialogue, the "*cor ad cor loquitur*" essential to moral understanding and "the improvement of the soul." All such philosophical conversation represents a moral ascent beginning with the familiar examples of ordinary life and striving toward the fuller vision of the good contained in them in rudimentary form. In this ascent words subtly change their meaning and significance from the "navigator" with a small "n" to the "Navigator" with a capital "N." The appeal in them is to the moral consciousness and *techné per se* can make no such transformative appeal. In its frozen impersonality it leaves the passengers right where they were at the beginning of the voyage. *Techné per se* is morally tone deaf.

Source: Author.

A few examples will illustrate the point where Bambrough stops short and Socrates presses on to the next inevitable step. This occurs whenever the interlocutor is called upon to consult his experience as a thinking subject and not merely the abstract logic of a doctrine viewed as an object of knowledge and analysis. Socratic teaching is always an ascent. But the question is: an ascent from what to what? The answer is "an ascent from opinion to knowledge, that is the transition to be made in the consciousness and character of the interlocutor." The examples from daily life are familiar in the roles of teacher, lawyer, judge, and statesman. In each case we try to raise the student or citizen to a new and high level of consciousness with a better, more comprehensive grasp of the ends to be served in his education as man and citizen. The quality this requires at each step is judgment, and judgment stretches beyond the reach of *techné* as a pure skill. In the political domain this takes us from the politician to the statesman and from the expert to the wise man. Between the knowledge possessed by the two parties there is an interesting asymmetry of which Bambrough takes no cognizance. The good or wise man can see and understand evil. But the man of evil, a Hitler or Stalin, cannot understand the good. The higher can perceive the lower, as Strauss liked to say, but the lower cannot perceive the higher. And this is precisely the union of knowledge and virtue.

Ends and Means: The abstract quality of Bambrough's analysis is itself part of the problem in the school he represents so ably and well. As a philosopher of language he distinguishes sharply between ends and means. But in politics as in life there is an interplay between them all the way to the end. The ends pursued by Hitler were the wrong ends in the moral sense, ends that were intrinsically evil. The Nazi's could not see this because they were morally corrupt. Our failure to do so is the failure of liberal theory and marks the night in which all cows are black. Less clear is the distinction between ends and means at any particular point in time or stage in history. So, for example, in his excellent study *Hitler and Stalin: Parallel Lives* Alan Bullock sees the corruption of ends in Nazism with perfect clarity.[18] But in the case of Marxism and communism the corruption lay solely in the means. Bullock noted that the corruption at the heart of communist ideology lay in the means. Greater social justice, freedom and equality, an end to exploitation and alienation are noble humane ends. What compromised them fatally were the methods employed to achieve them. But in the minds of Lenin and Trotsky, Stalin and his followers the methods were inseparable from the ends to be achieved, hence Lenin's *What Is To Be Done?*, Trotsky's *In Defense of Terror*, and Stalin's later writings. But did these abstractions which sound more like a liberal credo constitute the ends of communism? The end was surely the stateless, lawless, classless, familyless realization of reason which marked "the end of history." And this was a myth forever unattainable and way off in the future but constituting the mythic power of the movement and the sacrifices endured by millions from Lenin and Trotsky to Mao and Chou and the epic of "The Long March." But it is as an end that it is false, and we can know it to be.[19]

The line of thought sketched above leads to a paradoxical conclusion. We cannot be certain that Nazism or Communism is wrong until the last Nazi or Communist agrees that it is. But then of course he would have ceased to be a Nazi or a Communist. He would be converted to another point of view, say the point of view of liberal democracy. The line of argument represented by Bambrough overlooks the central role of conversion in the parable of the Navigator or the doctor of the soul. The aim of the Socratic teacher or Navigator is to produce the insight that leads to conversion and the discovery of a new solution and a higher, more noble way of life. Passengers and Navigator, patient and physician now agree and can proceed to the next step in moral education. But there is no conclusive test for moral knowledge. Moral knowledge requires an act of will in a moment of decision made in fear and trembling. The requirement of objective and impersonal verification rules out the critical variable, namely the person or moral agent, the subject in his subjectivity who is always part of the moral equation.

Another way to see the problem is this. The moral education suggested by the analogies is in essence a problem posing education. The analogies are designed to make the other party experience a problem in his moral life where before all was still. Question and answer are intended to lead not to the indefinite refinement of a doctrine but to "the improvement of the soul." They are intended to lead from the *doxa* to the *logos*, and not merely to the indefinite refinement of the *doxa* as *techné*. The modern stumbling block is the word "soul" understood in a metaphysical if not religious sense. In a secularized world the phrase "the improvement of the soul" has no resonance. We need the idea but have no word to express it. The term proposed (by Michael Novak I believe) is "intelligent subjectivity." This catches the vital point which is the union of thought and feeling, or mind and character or personality which is evident in us all.

It is to this, the seat of moral intelligence, that Plato is appealing in the various analogies such as the analogy of the physician. This is what Oscar Wilde had in mind in talking about "The Soul of Man Under Socialism." And this is surely what Tawney referred to in "The Sickness of an Acquisitive Society." By severing the two Bambrough has given us the analysis and dissection of a soulless doctrine incapable of informing a way of life.

5

The transition to the contrasting view is most readily made by consideration of the *eureka* experience, its nature and structure, for it is here that the subject can be seen in full display.

The story is told by Isaac Asimov with the skill of a born raconteur and spins out in three parts. The first introduces the reader to the dynamics of insight in Asimov's own case. The second recounts the classic case of Archimedes. And the third sketches out the way insight actually occurred in a dream state in the problem of the structure of the benzene molecule. Here's how the story goes. When, in the course of his writing, Asimov tells us, he felt stymied by a problem, he learned not to continue on the same track. Instead, he discovered it was critical to do something quite different. In his case it was to go to a movie, preferably an action movie of some kind. And soon after, the solution would suddenly come to his mind. For others it might be some different sort of activity. But the principle is the same and points to the dual nature of thought. Creative thinking is both involuntary and voluntary, unconscious and conscious. It is often this relaxed, involuntary or unconscious turn that produces the flash of intuition which breaks the deadlock and solves the problem. The case of Archimedes is the most celebrated example of this phenomenon.

Back around the year 250 BC when Syracuse was a thriving city, the king Hieron ordered and was duly presented with a crown of gold. The craftsmanship was excellent and the King was pleased. But Hieron was a king and wise to the ways of the world, and in due time he came to wonder whether the crown had been alloyed and he had been cheated. He knew no way to solve the problem and put his doubts to rest. But he had a friend or relative named Archimedes, the greatest scientific mind of the ancient world, and put the problem to him. There were ways of solving the problem. But they all involved flattening or otherwise damaging the crown. And this the King could not permit. Archimedes was stymied, and stymied for days on end. Then one afternoon he decided to forget his troubles and relax in one of those Roman baths. As he immersed himself he noticed the level of the water rising and, perhaps, even spilling over the top of the tub.

Suddenly two seemingly unrelated facts clicked together in his mind and he had it. The solution was clear and Archimedes rushed out still naked shouting "*Eureka!*" I've got it! The density of gold is just over nineteen grams per cc, that of copper is less than half that at 8.92 grams per cc. The two densities and volumes are quite different, and it follows that the quantity of water displaced will be very different between a crown of pure gold and one alloyed with copper. All one has to do is to measure the amount of water displaced and running through a tap on the side. This was the blinding flash which made for the ecstasy of the eureka experience.[20]

But the most fascinating story in this always engaging narrative is the story of Kekule's dream, and I shall recount it as before in the words of the story teller himself. For some years in the mid eighteen hundreds the chemist Friedrich August Kekule had been working on the structure of the benzene molecule. This was a difficult and often frustrating task because the structure of organic molecules such as benzene and hexene is more complex than that of inorganic molecules such as those of water and salt, H_2O and NaCl are familiar to every school boy. But the structures of alcohol and cane sugar are immediately more complex. When sketched in the form of a picture the structure of these molecules can be laid out as a chain or something resembling a snake. And each of them has an extension called a valence for bonding with the other atoms. But somehow benzene did not fit the general picture. You could call it an exception and go on with life. But this is not the way of science: Science does not fudge the edges to make the exception fit the rule. Kekule had focused on the problem for months and even years of concentrated work. It had been at the forefront of his attention. Then one day in the year eighteen sixty-five he took a break from it and journeyed to a nearby place in a public carriage. Perhaps it was the motion of the carriage or the sound of the horses hoofs on the cobblestones and he fell asleep and had his famous dream. In the dream he saw the structure forming not a chain or long snake but a ring or snake with its tail curved around toward its mouth. *Eureka!* He had it. The benzene molecule was an exception: it formed a ring. Organic molecules, it seems, come in two sets, one forming rings and the other chains. Asimov's point is simply this: First-rate scientific discovery and the insight from which it flows is not always the result of the conscious organized research that is written up in textbooks and journal articles. It is often the result of the psycho-logic of involuntary and unconscious experience, typically overlooked in the formal writeup of the discovery. This is frequently the core of creative thought of the highest order and of much fundamental scientific discovery. Any other such examples? Asimov gives us three, James Watt and the steam engine, William Rowan Hamilton and the discovery of quaternions, and Otto Loewi in the physiology of the nerve and nerve endings. But of course there are many more, and the pages of science and art are replete with them. But the case of Poincaré, a mathematician, is particularly significant for our story of insight and its role in education and the craft of teaching.[21]

6

Poincaré's study is significant on two main grounds. First, it is an authoritative account of mathematical creation by a most distinguished mathematician writing in Russell's own field at the time of the *Principia Mathematica* (1910). And second, it is the most perceptive exploration to date of the relationship between conscious and unconscious thought in the creative process. He devotes his first four pages to the graphic account of a day in the working life of the professional mathematician.[22] These few pages are all but a must for the layman interested in the process of conscious activity in the mathematical fields. Every word and phrase is carefully chosen, and every word carries exactly the right weight. Poincaré's introduction is a masterpiece in the economy of effective presentation with no frills added. This picture of the kind of activity involved in conscious thought is vital as background for the radically different kind of activity involved in the complementary process of unconscious thought in the creative process and the sudden illumination of insight. In a brief passage which is not without its charm he contrasts the mind of the mathematician with that of the expert card player or better yet the chess master. But all this is purely preliminary, serving only to contrast conscious working activity with the altogether different flow in the involuntary activity working under the surface in the creative act.

The act of creation occurred, Poincaré tells us, sometime after he had a cup of black coffee. He had been working at his desk for some time on a set of functions he called Fuchsian functions. He had been working on them, focusing on them for days and days with no real result. Like Kekule before him and Asimov after, he felt stymied. Then one evening he decided to take a little break and enjoy a cup of good, strong black coffee. This was not his usual custom and the coffee kept him up in something like a half sleep. Then suddenly hey presto! the solution came to him in a flash and all that remained was to write it down and the problem was solved. Poincaré relates this little story to go beyond the geometer's scrutiny of the theorems in the world of objects and "penetrate deeper and see what goes on in the very soul of the mathematician." This is precisely the Copernican shift from object to subject, marking the development of modern thought possibly since Kant and certainly since Hegel. Poincaré continues his story like this.

The question before us is simple, and fundamental. The question is: What is the essential nature of the act of creation in mathematics? The answer he proposes is likewise simple and fundamental. In its innermost essence, the act of creation comes about as a blending of two aspects of thought, the conscious and voluntary and the unconscious and involuntary producing the sudden flash of insight. In the course of his conscious work, the mathematician might well run into an impasse. He faces an infinity of possibilities and needs to make a choice. But which? The wrong choice can easily lead to work whose results are unproductive and uninteresting to the profession. Continued work along these lines just gets nowhere. This is where the unconscious comes into play. So here's how the story continues. Poincaré was, as he has mentioned, working on a set of functions he called Fuchsian functions. And he asks the reader not to be frightened off by these formidable technical terms. The geometer, he tells us is interested in the theorems, the psychologist in the attendant psychological factors which come into play precisely when the attention is relaxed.

In his case the big moment came about like this. His work was not really getting anywhere. Little progress was in sight. So he decided to forget mathematics for the while and take a trip. He left Cannes where he had been residing, to take a trip with the school of mines. As he stepped onto the omnibus the solution hit him like a flash with a feeling of unrivaled certainty; he had only to write it out.

We have, then, the classic story of Archimedes, the scientist's story of Kekule, the mathematician's story of Poincaré, and the story teller's story of Isaac Asimov. And interestingly enough, they all tell the same story. Knowledge, the theory goes, consists of two parts: there is tacit knowledge and explicit knowledge, focal knowledge and subsidiary knowledge (Polanyi), voluntary knowledge and involuntary knowledge, conscious knowledge and unconscious knowledge, and it is the interplay between them that makes for insight in creative thinking of the highest order, and to a lesser extent in us all.

The point to notice in our four very different examples is simply this:

1. The external features which make for a graphic story are in fact the accidentals of the case and vary from person to person, time and circumstance. Many a person has taken a Roman bath, gone to see an action movie, stepped onto an omnibus, or had a dream. But they did not experience that intoxicating flash of insight.
2. In each case a period, often a long period of prior focal work, was the necessary and indispensable condition for the resulting insight.
3. This antecedent activity had not produced the solution of the puzzle in the problem at hand. On the contrary, further work along these lines appeared to be getting exactly nowhere. Thought was moving along the familiar grooves of the brain and getting nowhere in what seemed to be a repetitive pattern.
4. The critical move was to get away from it, to forget it, the crown, the structure of a particular molecule, or a special type of mathematical function.

5. Only with this, with the complete relaxation of focal attention and the conscious mind does the unconscious come into play to make for the release of tension which solves the problem and produce the cry of *Eureka!* in French or German. Of course it goes without saying that the insight has to be verified and the proof written down for colleagues to check. But the process of creation and the process of verification are two very different processes, though related to one another in the act of supreme creation. And this is the domain of the subject to which Bernard Lonergan has given such rich and regarding attention.

7

In the literature on our topic, the idea of the subject presents itself in two forms, the implicit and the explicit. The implicit is generally overlooked but it is there, present to the *eye* of the theorist in the work of Michael Polanyi and the scientists he cites, prominently including W.I.B. Beveridge. And it is likewise present in the work of the culture critic Theodore Roszak in the second to last chapter of *The Making of a Counter Culture*.[23] After a brief, almost cameo appearance in Kant, the idea of the subject moved to center stage in the philosophy of Hegel. Soon after, it appeared in explicit form in such varied thinkers as Kierkegaard and Buber to become the informing principle in E.F. Schumacher's widely read *Small is Beautiful*.[24] Then in the two central chapters of another book by Schumacher, *A Guide for the Perplexed*, called "Adaequatio One" and "Adaequatio Two."[25] But these were singular achievements. However, as a central dimension of theory, the idea of the subject manifested itself in four major schools of thought. The first of these was the Hegelian left, where the two most prominent names were those of the early Lukács and the later Bloch, the titles of whose works makes this amply clear.[26] The second to follow in this trail was, quite naturally, the Marxist school of thought deriving from Labriola to Gramsci in Italy, and Freire in Brazil, and the school of thought following Lukács in Europe with Baran, and Marcuse in the United States.

The third is Dewey explicitly in the book and article mentioned earlier and in the early Postman of *Subversive Activity* fame and implicitly in the work of Bruner and his colleagues in science and mathematics. And, finally, the fourth is associated with the name of Bernard Lonergan and the transcendental movement in Catholic theology of which he was certainly the most prominent member to have written explicitly on our topic.

"The notion of the subject," Lonergan tells us, "is difficult, recent, and primitive." It is as recent as modern philosophy, and not to be found in the writings of the classical and medieval philosophers from Plato on down. As mentioned, it made its first brief almost cameo appearance in the philosophy of Kant. This first appearance in Kant is significant since it forms the underlying dimension in Lukács' evocative essays in *Soul and Form* in his Kantian phase. In his next and Hegelian phase he devoted a long article to the subject–object relationship in the Aesthetic and to Bloch's later book on the topic.[27] The notion is also difficult, as it cannot be formed by combining other and simpler notions. Phrased differently, it is not a complex idea which is the result of some purely ideational activity. Quite the contrary, it is itself a "primitive" idea in the precise sense that one cannot reach it by combining other simpler, i.e., more primitive ideas. The subject is a fundamental idea and in the opening pages of his study of method, Lonergan explains it like this:[28] we all perform certain operations such as seeing, hearing, etc. The thing seen, the sound heard, etc., is named the object, and the operator doing the seeing, hearing, etc., is named the subject. The subject, then, is the operator engaged in the operation of seeing, hearing, feeling, tasting, etc., and the entity seen, heard, felt, etc., is the corresponding object. So far so good. It all seems like plain sailing. But there may be some rocks ahead on which a word or two is due. Lonergan's earlier and more compendious study, a book of notes for theological students titled *De Constitutione Christi: Ontologica et Psychologica*,[29] caught the eye of one Rev. Angelo Perrego who criticized it sharply in the pages of a prominent Catholic journal.[30] At issue was the nature of Christ as dual nature or as a duality (God and man at one and the same time) or as having two natures, one as God and the other as man with only an abstract unity. Lonergan felt that the latter position imputed to him was a misrepresentation amounting to heresy, and drafted a response titled "Christ As Subject: A Reply" to settle the matter. The reply is made in three parts: (1) A Misrepresentation, (2) The Notion of the Subject, and (3) Concluding Remarks for Theological Students and the Literate Jesuit Public. Here we focus exclusively on the second for obvious reasons. Lonergan presents the rival theories and directs attention to the clear and cleancut conflict between them. The two opposed theories are labeled "*conscientia* experimental" and "*conscientia* perception," and the difference between them is simply this: when consciousness is understood as an experience, we have a psychological subject having the experience. When consciousness is understood as fundamentally the perception of an object, there is no psychological subject. The first view can be traced back to Aristotle. The second was the achievement of David Hume and his eminent followers from Russell, Ayer, *et al.* to the Vienna Circle. This is the fundamental difference between Gramsci and Freire, Polanyi and Beveridge, Dewey and his successors in discovery teaching, on the one hand, and the traditional conception from Entwistle on to the present day with its emphasis on knowledge as a compendium of contents derived from the lecture, the textbook, and the encyclopedia. Whitehead said he found reading the encyclopedia a bore. Peters replies that he enjoys reading it. And there we have the difference and the conflict in a nutshell. Still, what more precisely is the difference between the two conceptions and how does the conception of consciousness as perception arise in the minds of its distinguished adherents? In this, the fourth of six differences outlined in the original study, Lonergan offers a simple and homely example. Consider the proposition "John knows his dog," or any other material or sensible object. We call this "direct knowing" in which John is the grammatical subject and dog the object. Nothing could be clearer. Now consider the proposition "John knows himself." We call this "reflexive knowing" in which John, the grammatical subject, knows not his dog but reflexively himself. In this reflexive form of knowing, the subject, John himself, is now known as an object of knowledge, for all that can be known by the act of perception is an object in a universe of objects. In the theory of consciousness as perception there is no room for the psychological subject: The notion of the subject has been radically eliminated from the outset. As in physics, and science generally, "all that is known is known as an object." And once this is grasped, the appeal of the emotive theory of ethics to Ayer and their followers is readily understood. The theory is exceedingly plausible and dominates the higher learning in America. Still it is wise to attend to a singular difficulty. The difficulty lies in the one-dimensional character of the view and is clearly this: when one sees or knows a chair or table, dog or cat, or indeed any material or sensible object, the cognitive act does not in itself transform or in any way change the object perceived. It simply reveals it for what it *is* as this chair or table, this dog or cat, or this material or sensible object in the common world outside the niceties of atomic physics. But in man (as distinct from the lower animals), consciousness has a second and equally important quality. And this is its constitutive quality or character. In each and every one of us, consciousness is constitutive of ourselves as subjects, each with a self without which he would not be whom he is as one machine of a certain kind is indistinguishable from another of the same kind. Consciousness as perception cannot account for this second function. With Hume it is easy to deny the existence of the self. With James it is prompted to question the existence of consciousness itself (as an entity) as in his well-known article "Does Consciousness Exist?" published in his essays on radical empiricism. But if consciousness is conceived as experience the difficulty mentioned above is immediately transcended. For here we have both the experiencing subject and the thoughts experienced "thought thinking" and "thought thought," *pensée pensante* and *pensée pensée*. The first is the subject in dialogue, conversation, or argument. The second is the progressive, ever-changing contents argued about in the dialogue or conversation. One mode though stresses the priority of thinking over things thought, of the student or theorist as subject. The other stresses the value of things thought and as presented in the lecture, textbook, article, monograph, or encyclopedia for it has no room for the student as subject. When viewed from this perspective, Socrates' criticism of books for not answering back, and his criticism of Protagoras for lecturing him all around take on a new and significant meaning.

A final point will cast light on the breakthrough in ethics by one side and the nature of its rejection by the other. Lonergan distinguishes between the major levels into which the concept of the subject can be divided. There is first the empirical subject who acquires knowledge via the five senses. There is, secondly, the intelligent subject using his mind to organize and understand his knowledge. So, too, there is the rational subject, and the free subject making his choices and decisions in his everyday life, and the moral subject making his acts of decision in the moral domain. The first two or three are readily translatable into Polanyi's theory of tacit knowledge, and the last three the tacit dimension. And this is why Polanyi subtitles his book "Toward a Post-Critical Philosophy." The contrast with Ayer is striking. Ayer's basic constituent is "sense content," a compactly unified concept in which the emphasis falls on the content (which is objective) with the senses acting as the tributaries along which the content flows. The result is to make any progress along the lines developed by the transcendental movement quite impossible. This line of progress is briefly sketched by Lonergan in a densely packed review of a study called *Metaphysics* by Emerich Coreth, Ordinary Professor of Metaphysics at the University of Innsbruck in Austria.[31]

Coreth begins with the fundamental distinction between performance and concept or *Vollzug* and *Begriff* as he puts it. Instead of a purely conceptual analysis of the right or the good, he suggests that we begin with a performance, namely the performance of our daily acts in the course of our normal lives as men and citizens. Is there not an ethic (and indeed a metaphysics) involved in these acts? Of course there is, and it is the task of philosophy to articulate them and subject them to rational analysis now in the clear light of day. The reply by Ayer, Russell, and scientific philosophy is predictable. The radical division here is between science, which is objective, and the personal which is subjective. The objective is interpersonally verifiable and leads to an international science. The subjective varies from faith to faith and blows with the winds of doctrine. One is knowledge. The other is belief, opinion, emotion, and radically noncognitive. All such beliefs fail to survive the criterion of empirical verifiability. They are pseudo-concepts, and the Ordinary Professor of Metaphysics was studying a field that does not exist. Begin with the operator as one who has the experience of his five senses and build upon it, and you have the subject from the act of seeing, etc., to the act of understanding and the thing seen, etc., and understood as the object, and you have a theory of consciousness as experience and the possibility of a rational ethics. Begin with the compact concept of "sense contents," and Ayer will take you down the road from "the elimination of metaphysics" to the emotive theory of ethics which is unable to pronounce judgment on the eve of the Moscow Trials and *Kristallnacht*. Coreth's dialectic of subject and object, of *Vollzug* and *Begriff* will not work in the framework built on the foundations supplied by the theory of sense contents as objective fact. The notion of "intelligent subjectivity" distinguishing Churchill, Roosevelt, and Cardenas from Mussolini, Hitler, and Stalin does not arise to explain the seat of moral consciousness which, in an earlier day, Socrates called the soul. Instead, the person in his performance is divided into two parts, an empirical or scientific part which makes empirical judgments about the victims in the Moscow Trials, the Jews in Nazi Germany, and a purely emotive or expressive part being denuded of morals in anything more than a purely relative sense. In brief, the flow of British philosophy from Hume to Ayer has culminated in a radically nonmoral philosophy of politics and culture which the historian of the counter culture has called "The Myth of Objective Consciousness"[32] with thoughts but no thinker (as in Descartes), dreams but no dreamer (as in Kekule), and insights but no subject and cognitional theory (as in Archimedes, Kekule, Poincaré, Asimov, and countless others). What, then, is the myth in "the myth of objective consciousness?" And why did the young react so desperately against the void they felt?

8

Roszak's critique of the objective consciousness is the culmination of his more general critique of technocratic society, and appreciation of its youthful adversaries in the sixties. The book is written in a fluent, easy to read style and marked by a number of sharp antitheses. So we have the technocracy, on the one hand, and "its children," the youth of the Haight-Ashbury, on the other. We have the objective consciousness cultivated by science and technology, and the subjective consciousness celebrated by the young. So, too, we have the humanities being transformed into the behavioral sciences, artificial intelligence, and Herman Kahn. And we have their more humanistic critics in the form of Michael Polanyi and Thomas Kuhn, Abraham Maslow on *The Psychology of Science* and Max Eliade on *The Technocratic Society*. We also find some strange couplings in the body of the book. Except as a critic of capitalist society in decay, what has Herbert Marcuse to do with the counterculture? What has Norman O. Brown, a classicist and author of *Hermes the Thief*, to do with the children in the Haight-Ashbury of San Francisco or the Village in New York? The title *Love's Body*, Brown's next book, caught the attention of many but was read by few. Technocracy children had turned their backs on Western culture and neither the classics nor Hegel, nor Marx had any appeal for them. What is it that did appeal to them in their search for something to live by?

In their search they turned to the Orient, particularly India and Japan, to Indian music and the trappings of Hindu culture, and to Buddhism and Zen. Some took on Indian names like Ram Das, formerly Richard Alpert of Harvard University, and Archana, the name assumed by a very personable young lady, an artist in Berkeley, who took to visiting one Bahaji, a holy man of sorts who had taken a vow of silence and now wrote only on a slate. One whom I came to know rather well was Angela Atwood, later of SLA fame, whom I visited for the better part of an hour in her small San Francisco apartment. I was treated to Indian music, Morning Ragas and Evening Ragas, and the immediate burning of incense with us both sitting on the floor on carpets, legs crossed, since there were no chairs. Technocracy children took to the arts and crafts, to folk dancing and folk music, to communes and something like a back-to-the-land movement.

The apostles of the youth culture were Allen Ginsberg, whose *Howl* voiced the evangel of despair, Lawrence Ferlinghetti whose City Lights bookstore became a San Francisco beacon, and Kenneth Rexroth, the talented translator from the Japanese, and occasional voice over our local radio station. There was also Alan Watts, with the most articulate lectures on Buddhism, Zen, and the subjective consciousness, and a variety of lesser lights now forgotten. While on the other hand, there is the psychedelic movement and Timothy Leary of whom Roszak is critical, and Marcuse whose Marxism and rationalism he rejects. Such, then, is the context for the critique of objective consciousness with which Roszak concludes his book. "It is," Roszak tells us, "The psychology not the epistemology of science that urgently requires our critical attention."[33] The critique is developed in three major theses of which the first is the most fruitful. He calls this "the alienative dichotomy"[34] characteristic of consciousness as perception with its radical division of subject and object from Hume to Russell and Ayer and the Vienna Circle. In this view, the subject–object identity, famous since Aristotle, is rejected, and with it the interplay between subject and object in the study of man and society. The foundation was laid by the work of Kuhn and Polanyi; Roszak supplements it with the contribution made by Maslow in *The Psychology of Science*. But he does not attend to the major point suggested by Kuhn's title, namely that it is the structure of scientific revolution that Kuhn is investigating so brilliantly in this provocative study.[35] It is here that the subjective factor comes so prominently into play in the creation of a new scientific paradigm. It is far less in evidence in normal science, which constitutes much of the greater part of the activity of the body of working scientists for most of their scientific careers. The personal factor highlighted by Polanyi comes into play in the examples of Poincaré and Kekule as outstanding examples of creative thinking of a very high order. But it is relatively small in the workday life of the working scientist. And this leads to the problem with his second thesis titled "The Invidious Hierarchy."[36]

"The Invidious Hierarchy" fixes attention on the predominance of "out there" over "in here."[37] "Out there" is the universe of objects, words, and things in their facticity, while "in here" is the domain and world of subjectivity. In the objective consciousness, the first is an imperial world whose empire is forever expanding. And this expansion is at the cost of the subject, the self, the person whose dimensions are simultaneously shrinking, becoming concentrated into a point. We see this every day in all normal scientific research. And in a way how could it be otherwise? The truths of science and mathematics are by their very nature universal. We do not have as many sciences, Catholic, Republican, and feminine, as we have varieties of belief. The imperial "out there" is the universal empire of modern science. Still it is wise to attend to a difficulty or two in the conventional wisdom. In *The Art of Scientific Investigation*, W.I.B. Beveridge draws attention to the role of chance in scientific discovery (as with the discovery of X-rays) and has a full chapter on the cultivation of taste in the scientific investigator. And Freire has an excellent couple of pages on the critique of the "banking theory"[38] reducing the earner to a cypher. And in "The Act of Study" the student has become an equal partner.

Roszak's third thesis, "The Mechanist Imperative,"[39] caps his argument by contrasting the culture of technocratic society with the spirit of the counter-culture, which is "to greet every object with a song."[40] The strain toward mechanism, more evident than ever today, is to measure and quantify all knowledge breaking up all holes into their atomic units, tabulating, pigeon holing, measuring, quantifying everything from voting behavior to the risks and consequences of thermonuclear war. McNamara and Herman Kahn came into their own and we could estimate the number of probable dead depending on which way the wind blew. Observing, measuring, classifying, an army of specialists all well versed in technique now populate the Departments of Political Science and Sociology and think tanks in an invasion of centaurs as from another world. "Out there" is everywhere and "In here" has shrunk to little more than a point. To what remains of "in here," Roszak puts a critical question: "Who are you when you are being objective?" And the answer is "I am no one in particular, a nobody fabricated by the technocracy as in a dream."[41]

And once more we need to interrupt Roszak's song with a question, or rather a reservation. Observing, measuring, and classifying, tabulating, and pigeon holing are not noble as ends but necessary as means. Without such instrumentation we would not have any social science worthy of the name, no Durkheim, Michaels, or Pareto, no Marshall or Keynes, no studies like the Lynds of Muncie, Indiana or of Dahl's New Haven study of the party system like *Democracy and the American Party System* by Austin Ranney and Willmoore Kendall, a liberal and a conservative in productive partnership.[42] We all want to understand society and history and not merely to greet every object with a song. Here we have "the drive to understand" which Roszak overlooks and which Lonergan identifies with a simple example. When a box is empty, Lonergan tells us, it does not want to be filled. But when the mind is empty of the knowledge in question, it does often with an urgency which is quite compelling. Roszak's "non intellective consciousness" overlooks the drive to understand from Thales to Russell and beyond. The sixties were an episode in American culture, a dead end with Roszak's book as its swan song and technocracy children have passed from the scene.

9

"The myth of objective consciousness" marks the dividing line between Roszak and Russell, the children of light and the children of darkness, technology, programmed learning, and culture. It marks the divide between classical and modern philosophy: Socrates, Plato, and Aristotle, on the one side, and Hume and empiricism on the other. To see this more clearly, Roszak's term "objective consciousness" needs to be clarified and stated more precisely. What exactly is "objective" consciousness? What does it lead to, and wherein does the power of the myth reside? The objectivity of the objective consciousness lies in the fact that here (as in Hume's classic exposition), consciousness is understood as perception pure and simple. The mental universe formed by this view is radically a universe of objects. The opposite view clearly is the reality of subjective consciousness. For if consciousness is not objective it must be subjective. And the subjectivity of consciousness lies in the fact that consciousness is now understood not as the perception of an object but as the experience of a subject. Once this is seen, all else follows, including the irreconcilable conflict between the two views. For neither is capable of final and conclusive demonstration to the satisfaction of all competent observers.

There is no neutral point from which a final decision can be made. The choice between them can only be made by an act of judgment, which is in its nature a subjective act. If we take sense contents as fundamental, as in the Hume–Russell–Ayer view, we arrive at one theory. And if we divide this into its two constituent parts, such as seeing and the thing seen, hearing and the sound waves heard, we arrive at another and very different view of the universe and moral man. The case of Bertrand Russell from his initial conception of Socrates to his final view of the functions of the teacher is a striking example of this. Either Russell has framed the functions of the teacher correctly and with precision, or the whole enterprise has failed and resulted in the sterility of a dead end street at the end of a long journey.

Russell's view of "The Functions of the Teacher," first published in *The Atlantic Monthly* in 1937 and reprinted in *Unpopular Essays* (1950),[43] is his most on-point contribution to our problem. We would do well, therefore, to follow its precise line of argument from beginning to end.

The profession of the teacher has, Russell tells us, been transformed over the past hundred years. In former days the teacher was valued as the tutor of a small group of select students. Today he is little more than a minor civil servant, a low-level employee of the state. The change since ancient times is even more dramatic. In ancient times the teacher was a free agent, free to teach useful skills and the truth as he saw it. Today he is obliged to indoctrinate the youth in the prejudices useful to the state. What was once a vocation has been degraded into a profession in the service industry. And it is not easy to see how this process can be reversed.

The teacher must of course perform the necessary function of developing the skills required in an industrial society and critical for the defense of the state. But these are merely the *minima moralia* of teaching as a profession. If teaching is to regain something of its status as a vocation, it must once again be conceived in broader and more elevated terms. Right teaching, good teaching is the antidote to the rival dogmatisms prevailing in much of the world as in Russia, Germany, and Japan. (This was first written in 1937.) He can only do this by cultivating an attitude of reasonableness and the habit of impartial inquiry in his students. He must go beyond the narrow limits of nationalism and introduce them to the idea of civilization. But to do this he must himself know what civilization is. Civilization is not merely a matter of machinery and machines, of motor cars, steam engines, and bathrooms, important as these are. More importantly, it is a matter of mind and emotion, of knowing the best that has been created in the arts and sciences and making them one's own, of steeping oneself in them to mold one's personality and character. And the teacher can only do this if he relates to his students with love and affection, with a quality that goes well beyond the rapport required in a purely professional encounter. But, the critic will ask, "How is this to be done?" The production of teachers of quality can only be the creation of a nation or community that sets a high premium, if not the highest, on culture and moral excellence. And this is precisely what we don't have on Russell's own showing. Teachers today are overworked and underpaid, some working a second job. Where will they find the leisure and energy to become the gatekeepers to civilization, to Pindar, Aeschylus, and Sophocles, Plato, Aristotle, and a new Enlightenment, introducing their students to *Faust, Part Two* and Hölderlin. No one expects a clergyman to give five sermons a day. But we do expect that of teachers. The teacher should not simply transmit the orthodoxy, the "correct opinions" of the community, but should subject them to impartial inquiry. But who is to tell a "correct opinion" from an "incorrect" one? One man's "nationalism" is another man's "patriotism," with the value judgment changed. Which, then, is the right value judgment?

To this question, the iconic Russell, the Russell standing for the stream of thought from Ayer to Bambrough, has no answer. The criterion of interpersonal verifiability and the resulting emotivist theory of ethics have seen to that. In the debate between Buddha and Nietzsche, namely in the domain where ends collide, Russell cannot venture a decision. But education as culture, as the formative moral experience of the student, is predicated on a moral decision which will inform the culture as a whole. To appeal to "impartial inquiry" is not enough. Impartial inquiry alone does not result in a decision between Nietzsche and Buddha or the ideals of Greek and Indian civilizations. Only such a decision can produce a concrete result. Without such a decision, Russell's analysis remains on a purely abstract level adorned by such copybook maxims as the appeal to love and affection, to caring in the teacher, ill trained, overworked, and underpaid, as the messenger of a new world, indeed of civilization itself.

The abstract quality of Russell's reasoning reveals itself in two ways. First published in the *Atlantic Monthly*, it was clearly addressed to an American audience. But it is precisely in America that education is reserved to the states and funded by taxes raised in the local community. The Tenth Amendment stands as a bar against any supervening national system. And it is the states and local communities, especially in the South, that would oppose Russell's demand. Without their support and generous funding, his proposals were fated to fall on deaf ears. The essay itself was the subject of an excellent article by Professor William Hare of Halifax University. But this was only to speak to the converted. The only occasion in which the limitation of states' rights has been overcome was in the late fifties, when under the pressure occasioned by Sputnik, President Kennedy persuaded the Congress to allocate billions to fund the National Science Foundation and the work by Jerome S. Bruner and his colleagues in mathematics and science. The key feature of this new method, well-known as "discovery teaching," was the development of insight on the part of the student. The student was transformed into "the discoverer of new truths" in mathematics and science. On the level of the schools this was the work of Robert Davis in mathematics and of David Hawkins and Robert Stebbins in physics and biology. On the graduate level it was developed by R.L. Moore and written up by Paul Halmos, another mathematician and teacher of distinction. And the process of insight itself was studied in detail by Jacques Hadamard in *An Essay on the Process of Invention in the Mathematical Fields* (Princeton University Press).[44] But no one was more familiar with mathematics and the *eureka* syndrome than Lord Russell, a friend of the mathematician Henri Poincaré, who had written on the topic. Why did Russell not put two and two together in a unique act of insight? We can only conjecture, and my conjecture is this.

In Hume and the stream of thought flowing from Hume, consciousness is regarded purely as the perception of an object. The universe of Hume is a universe of objects there to be perceived, analyzed, and understood as objects. This is the "myth" of objective consciousness in which the experience of the subject is radically denied and rejected as the basis of a cognitional theory and philosophy. In fact, philosophy is recontoured into the philosophy of science which is itself broken up into its various parts, of which psychology now understood as an objective study, is one. Russell has accepted this from the start, and the result is his picture of Thales and Plato, and animadversions against Socrates for introducing an ethical bias into philosophy. For Russell, accordingly, insight and the *eureka* syndrome are an interesting part of psychology. But this has no part to play in philosophy or education in any important and technical sense. He is well aware of the subject–act–object as revealed by a passage in his brief Marx chapter. But he dismisses it as not fundamental, and proceeds with a sense content theory and the neutral monism of James who denies the very conception of consciousness (as an entity). So, without a conception of consciousness as subjective, as the experience of a subject, Russell disregards the experience of insight and its promotion as the central aim of the teacher with the student transformed into "the discoverer of new truths." In the absence of a valid cognitional theory Russell's treatment can only be historical and moral. But his *History* is tendentious, and his ethics are without a foundation. As a practical proposal, "The Functions of the Teacher" is a policy statement without a constituency in the community to which it is addressed. And with this we come to the end of the road and the sterility of a movement marked by the most distinguished names, of whom Russell will be remembered as the most brilliant.

Notes

1. Bertrand Russell, *The Philosophy of Bertrand Russell*, The Library of Living Philosophers, Inc., Vol. V, 1944. Boyd H. Bode's critical essay, "Russell's Educational Philosophy," is also included in this volume, pp. 619–642. For the text online see: https://archive.org/stream/in.ernet.dli.2015.11868/2015.11868.The-Philosophy-Of-Bertrand-Russell_djvu.txt Then Bertrand Russell, "Reply to Criticisms," in the *Philosophy of Bertrand Russell*, ed., Paul A. Schilpp, New York: Harper Torchbooks, 1963. For this Russell excerpt see P.L. Smith, Socialization and Personal Freedom: the Debate between Boyd H. Bode and Bertrand Russell, University of Illinois, 1980: https://onlinelibrary.wiley.com/doi/full/10.1111/j.1741-5446.1979.tb00852.x Pagination for volume V is given in parentheses following the quotations.
2. R.H.S. Crossman. *Plato Today*, George Allen & Unwin Ltd., London, 1937, second revised edition, 1959.
3. Karl Popper, *The Open Society and Its Enemies*, Abingdon, U.K., Routledge, 1945.

4. Renford Bambrough, "Plato's Political Analogies," in *Philosophy, Politics, and Society*, ed. Peter Laslett (Oxford: Blackwell, 1956). The essay is also in *Plato, Popper, and Politics* edited by Renford Bambrough (Cambridge: Heffer, 1967).
5. Stanley H. Rosen, "Thales: the Beginning of Philosophy", in Essays in Philosophy. University Park: Pennsylvania State University Press, 1962.
6. Bertrand Russell, *A History of Western Philosophy*, New York: Simon & Schuster, 1945, pp. 771–772. The book is available online: http://www.ntslibrary.com/PDF%20Books/History%20of%20Western%20Philosophy.pdf
7. A. J. Ayer, *Language, Truth, and Logic*, New York: Dover Publications, Inc., 1952.
8. Leo Strauss, *Essays on the Scientific Study of Politics*, New York: Holt, Rinehart and Winston, 1962.
9. A. J. Ayer, *Language, Truth, and Logic*, op. cit., p. 38. Pagination is given in parentheses for the following quotations from this book.
10. Bertrand Russell, *A History of Western Philosophy*, op. cit., p. 782–790.
11. R.H.S. Crossman. *Plato Today*, George Allen & Unwin Ltd., London, 1937, second revised edition, 1959.
12. R.H.S. Crossman, ed., *The God that Failed*, New York: Columbia University Press, 1949 and reprinted by Harper Collins Publishers, Inc., 2001.
13. R.H.S. Crossman. *Plato Today*, op. cit., the sixth chapter, pp. 108–124.
14. E.H. Carr, *The Twenty Years' Crisis (1919–1939)*. London: The Macmillan & Company, Ltd., 1961. (E. H. Carr's first edition of this book came out in 1939.)
15. Ibid., p. 134. Pagination for E. H. Carr is given in parentheses following the quotations.
16. Laszlo Versenyi, *Socratic Humanism*, foreword by Robert S. Brumbaugh. (New Haven and London: Yale University Press, 1963.
17. Renford Bambrough, "Plato's Political Analogies," in *Philosophy, Politics, and Society*, op.cit.
18. Alan Bullock, *Hitler and Stalin: Parallel Lives*, Vintage Books, Alfred A. Knopf, New York, NY, 1991, p. 413.
19. See, for example, the convincing argument in the closing pages of Nicholas Berdyaev, *The Origins of Russian Communism*, University of Michigan Press, Ann Arbor, 1960.
20. Isaac Asimov, "The Eureka Phenomenon," *Fantasy and Science Fiction*, June 1971, pp. 107–116.
21. For the case of literature see Rosamund Harding, *An Anatomy of Inspiration*, W. Heffer & Sons Ltd., Cambridge, 1942.
22. Isaac Asimov, "The Eureka Phenomenon," op. cit.
23. Theodore Roszak, *The Making of a Counter Culture*, Berkeley: The University of California Press, 1969, pp. 205ff. chapter VII, "The Myth of Objective Consciousness."
24. E.F. Schumacher, *Small Is Beautiful: Economics as if People Mattered*, New York: Harper & Row Publishers, Inc., Perennial Library edition, 1973.
25. E.F. Schumacher, *A Guide for the Perplexed*, London: Jonathan Cape, Ltd., 1977.
26. Georg Lukács, "Die Subjekt-Objekt Beziehung in der Aesthetik," *Logos*, Vol. 7, No. 1, 1917/1918, pp. 1–40. Ernst Bloch, *Subjekt-Objekt Erläuterungen zu Hegel*, Suhrkamp Verlag, Frankfurt-Am-Man, 1951.
27. Ibid.

28. Bernard Lonergan, *Method in Theology*. Herder and Herder, New York and Darton, Longman, & Todd, London, 1972.
29. Bernard J.F. Lonergan, (Latin and English), The ontological and psychological constitution of Christ, translated by Michael G. Shields from the 4th edition. In the Collected Works of Bernard Lonergan, vol. 7.
30. Angelo Perrego, "Una nuovo opinione sule'unità psicologica de Cristo," *Divinitas* 2 (1958) 409–424.
31. Emerich Coreth, *Metaphysics*, New York: Herder and Herder, 1968.
32. Theodore Roszak, *The Making of a Counter Culture*, Berkeley: *op. cit.*, p. 205–238.
33. Ibid., p. 217.
34. Ibid.
35. Thomas S. Kuhn, *The Structure of Scientific Revolutions*, Chicago: The University of Chicago Press, 1962.
36. Theodore Roszak, *The Making of a Counter Culture*, Berkeley: *op. cit.*, p. 217. Pagination in parentheses are from Roszak's book.
37. Ibid., p. 220ff.
38. Paulo Freire, *Pedagogy of the Oppressed*, translated by Myra Bergman Ramos, New York: Seabury Press, 1968. The first page of the second chapter.
39. Theodore Roszak, *The Making of a Counter Culture*, Berkeley: *op. cit.*, p. 217 and 227ff.
40. Ibid., p. 268. The final line of the book.
41. Ibid., second to last chapter, VII, the "Myth of Objective Consciousness."
42. Austin Ranney and Willmoore Kendall, *Democracy and the American Party System*, New York: Harcourt, Brace and Company. 1956.
43. Bertrand *Russell*, The *Atlantic Monthly* Press, London: Williams and Norgate; New York: Holt. And Company, *1937.* And *Unpopular Essays* (1950), New York: Simon and Schuster.
44. Jacques Hadamard in *An Essay on the Process of Invention in the Mathematical Fields*, Princeton University Press, 1945 and New York: Dover Publications, 1954.

· 8 ·

WHERE ENDS COLLIDE

The Liberal-Conservative Debate in Philosophy

1

At the very time Russell was writing "The Functions of the Teacher", R.G. Collingwood, Waynflete Professor of Metaphysics at Oxford, was drafting a major work which was to culminate in precisely the opposite point of view. The *Idea of History*[1] is a panoramic survey extending from the Greeks and Romans to the present time in the work of Bury and Oakeshott. It is a learned and sweeping presentation of the philosophy of history as seen from an Idealist point of view. The book closes with a fable, little noticed by most critics, which gives point to the entire argument.[2] The story runs like this: One day the body of a gentleman, perhaps the owner of a property, was found stabbed to death at his writing table. The local constabulary, called to investigate the crime, proved to be at a loss. To resolve the impasse, Inspector Jenkins of Scotland Yard is called in to investigate the murder. Jenkins proceeds to question the suspects, testing their alibis against a series of clues and false clues. Did the murderer escape by the window? Why then were there no foot marks on the grass outside? What was the motive for the crime? Was the victim changing his will? Etc. Jenkins' procedure in radically questioning everything is in marked contrast to that of the local constabulary which consists in compiling the relevant information in search of a solution there. This is the procedure of the ordinary historian writing the ordinary books of history which

Collingwood dismisses as scissors and paste history. By contrast, Jenkins begins with the centrality of the question in all genuine historical investigation. The question, writes Collingwood, is the gas which fires the pistons and drives the car forward.

The salient features of the Collingwood view now stand out in clear relief. History in the significant sense is not the mere narration of events seen from the outside. Genuine history is not composed by the method of "scissors and paste" of the ordinary historian and the ordinary books following from his pen. History is not narration but begins with a problem, here the problem of a murder, what prompted it at this date and who stood to benefit by it. Jenkins' questions and the answers he receives constitute the dialectic of interrogation with right and wrong answers, clues and false clues for the historian as detective. The right stance for the historian is that of the detective. And the interplay between Jenkins, questions and the facts of the case (How big was the knife? How did the murderer learn to use it so well? Etc.) emerge as the interplay between subject and object in dialectical investigation. When Jenkins' procedure is seen in model form it can be likened to two or three seemingly different models of inquiry. One of these is the Lonergan model framed as insight–understanding–judgment, which flows from it and fits it exactly. Another is Freire's model of problem-posing education based on student cognitive models contrasted with the lecture and textbook or a narration of contents based on a teacher cognitive model. And a third is, of course, Gramsci's sketch of the creative school based on the same subject–object dimension in Hegel and contrary to the positivism of Bukharin in Russia and the flow of British empiricism and positivism.

The second feature to notice is the fact that this is a purely cognitional theory, a neutral analysis of how the mind works when it is working at its best in the development of insight and the discovery of new truths. As a technical or value-neutral analysis, it can be fitted into any one of a number of philosophies or meta-theories. It can, for example, be made to fit the Jesuit philosophy or the liberal philosophy of Dewey, Bruner, and associates. It follows that to reject the Marxist philosophy of Freire and Gramsci is not to reject the cognitional theory advanced in Freire's "The Act of Study." In his hands the two are closely related. But they are not the same. And precisely the same can be said for Collingwood, a fairly conservative writer at a distance from Marxism, Freire, and Gramsci. For example, in terms of political philosophy Collingwood was led to a belief in the doctrine of progress in the context of a pronounced historicism. Classical political philosophy, he tells us, should not be criticized for the well-known limitations pointed out by a score of writers. Far from being limitations they can be regarded as its merits, for this was the highest view possible in this historical situation. But we have in the modern age progressed well beyond that. And this in a nutshell is "the quarrel between the ancients and the moderns" and it provoked a sharp reply by Leo Strauss. But that is a different part of the story. Here we restrict ourselves to the cognitional theory and Collingwood on history and the historian, which was the theme of E.H. Carr's first lecture in *What Is History?*

2

The cognitional theory implicit in Inspector Jenkins' interrogation of his witnesses surfaces and becomes explicit in E.H. Carr's study *What Is History?*[3] Collingwood's theory came to be known as the "in here" / "out there" theory, where "in here" represents the mind of the historian and "out there" stands for history. Before you study history, Carr advises to study the historian. And with this the turn from "out there" to "in here" is deftly executed. The fundamental distinction is the distinction between history as reportage or a chronicle of events and critical history or history as a reenactment of the past in the mind of the historian. History, Carr tells us, is the result of a constant dialogue between the past and the present. "All history," said Croce, is contemporary history."[4] So when you study the historian pay close attention to the date when his history was written. The date is the clue to the perspective or contemporary scene out of which his history produced. Carr illustrates this with the striking case of Meinecke and his three or four works, each different in tone and character from the preceding work down to *Die Deutsche Katastrophe*.

Conventional history is history in which the historian first organizes the facts in his notebooks, then writes the connecting narrative. This is the notion of history advocated by Chester Finn and practiced by Diane Ravitch and Entwistle in their well-known works. Collingwood calls this "scissors and paste" as a form of history writing in the production of the ordinary books dominating the market then and now. In the "ordinary" history books we have a sharp distinction between facts and values, and the facts always come first: First get your facts right, organize and arrange, and then draw your conclusions. Facts are the bricks in the wall, and thought is the mortar that binds them together and shapes the narrative. In his opening chapter, titled "The Historian and His Facts," Carr exposes the shallowness of this view flowing from positivist historiography. Of the infinity of facts confronting the historian what is it that makes this an historical fact? We know that in 48 BC Caesar crossed the Rubicon. But so did many others before and after. What is it that elevates this to the rank of a historical fact? Carr offers us an intriguing example. In the year 1850 an unknown vendor of ginger bread was kicked to death by an angry mob.[5] This was noted in some papers but was not yet a historical fact. Later it was mentioned in a book on history and entered the antechamber of historical facts, there to await a second. If it is picked up and enters the footnotes and finally the textbooks, it will have been transformed into a historical fact. If not, it will lapse into the myriad of facts from which it was briefly rescued. It is the critical judgment of the historian, the thought behind the facts, that determines the relevant facts of history and their significance. The critical point in the Collingwood view is the intimate and reciprocal relation between the subject and the object, the historian and his facts.

The idea of the subject (and the correlative idea of the object) are categories of thought. In this sense neither subject nor object are to be understood in any material or sensible sense. The subject is not there like a rock on the beach waiting to be discovered. So when Wittgenstein says "there is no such thing as the subject," he is not to be understood as merely saying that there is no such thing as a rock on the beach. And when Russell says that the idea of subject–act–object is not fundamental, he is nearer the mark, for in the Hume tradition it cannot be. What is always more fundamental in this tradition is the fused notion of a sense content in which the emphasis falls naturally on the content. These, then, are two rival ways of seeing things, two different modes of understanding giving rise to two contrasting forms of argument neither of which can ever be conclusive. Carr presents a striking illustration of the priority of mind over matter, of "in here" over "out there."

When Gustav Stresemann died his papers were packed into boxes and filled some three hundred of them.[6] In time, he entrusted the task of editing to Bernhardt, his secretary of many years. Stresemann's Eastern policies which led nowhere were cut to the bone. His Western policies, which led to the triumph of Locarno and success with the League of Nations, were given prime billing in a volume titled *Stresemann's Vermächtnis* or *The Legacy of Stresemann*. In time an English publisher decided on an English version and entrusted the task of translating and editing the Bernhardt collection. This resulted in a single volume some one-third the size of Bernhardt's original in which policies and conversations leading nowhere were trimmed still further to the benefit of his Western policies and the success with which they crowned his career. And it is the crucial move. The conventional mind can still object saying that if the scholar wished to consult the original papers they were there and available to him in the copies made by the British and American authorities after the war. The bedrock reality remains in the documents "out there" in external reality. The answer to this is insightful and fascinating. In the Stresemann papers you will find that Stresemann's case is well and persuasively presented, while Chicherin's responses are more fragmentary and not as well considered. The original act of editing occurred not by Bernhardt or Sutton but in the mind of Gustav Stresemann himself. And no doubt the same would be true of Chicherin if we had access to his papers. And "in here" always trumps "out there."

Look at Thales from the viewpoint of scientific philosophy and we have Russell's interpretation of "water" as H_2O. Look at the same fragments from the perspective of classical philosophy and we have Rosen's rich and subtle presentation in hermeneutics. And more to the point: look at Russell, Crossman, and Bambrough writing on Plato in the interwar years and we have Plato the fascist and totalitarian. Look at the same dialogues as did Jaeger, Friedländer, and Versenyi and we have a very different picture of Socratic humanism. There is no point in asking who is right, Plato or his modern critics, Collingwood advises us. Each is presenting the only picture he can in the circumstances in an infinity of interpretations which make the problem of historical knowledge and the teaching of history. Where is the objectivity of history to be found?

Carr's most daring *démarche* lies in his solution to the problem of historical objectivity. The dilemma into which his acute criticism has cast him is obvious. He has begun by rejecting fidelity to fact and the crude positivism of history as scissors and paste and a chronicle of things past. And to this one can say "so far so good." This is the essence of the Collingwood critique of "out there." But he has also rejected the Collingwood contribution of history as a reenactment of the past in the mind of the historian, or the celebration of "in here." So the question is what remains? How is the historian to escape from nihilism and the sea of an infinity of meanings? The answer is to shift the stress from fact to relation. So the question becomes "relation to what?" And here is where Carr's daring and originality become most evident. History was defined as a dialogue between the past and the present. But this was clearly provisional and short hand, for the present is but an instant in time, a moving point into the future. A more comprehensive view is the view of history as a dialogue between the past and the future.[7] The historian par excellence is the one who has the future in his bones.[8] It is this relationship with the future which alone can create real history by resolving the problem of historical objectivity to escape the crisis of historical nihilism and the chaos of an infinity of purely subjective interpretations. History is of necessity written from the point of view of the winners! And this is what Trevor Roper called "E.H. Carr's Success Story."

To be sure, Carr has a ready answer at hand. It would be odd, he tells us, to write a history of the United States except from the point of the winners in the War of Independence. Or of the Civil War, we might add, except from the perspective of the North, the cause of the Union and antislavery. But surely this is because we have a moral consensus against slavery and, therefore, in favor of Lincoln and the preservation of the Union. More generally stated, do we not require a moral theory of politics to control the discussion and our history of the debate? Carr's earlier work was criticized, rightly or wrongly, for advocating a policy of appeasement toward the new regime in Germany between the mid-thirties and Munich. In an article on "The Political Science of E H Carr," Hans Morgenthau called his work, particularly *The Twenty Years Crisis*, "a monumental failure." And this failure he diagnosed as philosophical. He meant the absence of a controlling moral point of view forming the horizon from which the analysis would be based. In its absence the winners tend to emerge as right and their policies the ones to be followed by the losers and the weaker. "The economic impact of the Soviet Union on the Western world," Carr wrote, "can be summed up in one word: planning." But with the implosion of the Soviet Union, it was abandoned in Russia and has had no impact on the Western world. He writes appreciatively of the contribution collectivization made to Soviet industrialization. But surely this "contribution" could have been better made without the slaughter of millions of farm animals by the *kulaks* and of millions of *kulaks* by the regime. Success and failure are not so easy to gauge when the costs are added in. The problem here was totalitarian autocracy, tyranny, and an indifference to human lives and moral costs resulting in the murders of Ignace Reiss, Julia Points, and Leon Trotsky, to the Moscow Trials, the shooting of the Red Marshals, the Nazi-Soviet Pact, and Stalin's trust in Hitler, another loser.

Carr picks up the distinction proposed by C.P. Snow between literary intellectuals and the scientific elite. Literary intellectuals look back to the past with nostalgia: the historian is urged to love the past. The scientific elite "have the future in their bones."[9] Carr sides with the latter. He too has the future in his bones and concludes his book with a chapter on "The Widening Universe." But the future's a plastic and wide-open term. And tomorrow's future may be very different from that of the day after tomorrow. Two who had the future in their bones were Marx and Lenin. But on the day after tomorrow their future lay interred with their bones. Lenin's future was the more grotesque as War Communism had to be rescued by the New Economic Policy, his body paralyzed by stroke after stroke till death brought release and he was mummified and placed on display by his pupil and follower, "the wonderful Georgian." His brief reign was revealed as the preface to tyranny in the framing and murder of his closest colleagues from Zinoviev to Trotsky, and finally the implosion of the whole structure and the disappearance of Leninism in the Western world. Two others who felt the future in their bones were the philosopher Georg Lukács and Carr himself. "Only he who is called," wrote Lukács, "and is willing to usher in the future can understand the concrete truth of the present, can understand the present as history." This was in his legendary work of 1923, and follows suit without the Marxism and metaphysics. And the flaws in his analysis flow directly from this source. He has not solved the problem of historical objectivity, but spirited it off from a formless past to an equally formless future. The future can be *almost* anything. To be sure, anyone who talked about the reunion of the United States with the British Crown would be talking utopian nonsense. The future is not open to anything. But it is plastic and wide open to any one of a set of possibilities no single one of which stands out as anchor for a healthy relation to the present. If it is to be of any value the historian's relation to the future must be a healthy relation. And this makes it a moral consideration. But this is precisely what is swept aside in Carr's analysis, which decides the choice between morals and power as between utopia and reality. Power is steady and always real. The structure of moral philosophy, like philosophy itself, is transient, vulnerable to realist analysis, and destined to fade into the past. It is the recurrent chronicle of the losers facing the ferity and corruption of power. And to this meaningless progression of utopia and reality Carr has no solution for the future in the abstract can offer no solution.

In the widening horizon to which Carr directed our attention two of the main actors were soon to walk off the stage. With Khrushchev's revelation of "the crimes of the Stalin era" the myths which had served to sustain the regime were dissipated and Stalinism rapidly became a thing of the past. Gorbachev's attempt to save the relics of Marxism–Leninism were brushed aside and the rest is history though not in Carr's sense. In China the red star only flies at half mast with a Communist Party presiding over a capitalist economy with billionaires and all. And in the US we have not progressed from the legacy of the New Deal but turned instead to Reagan, Bush One and Two, and finally to Trump and the untutored mass feared by Plato in Crossman's fable. In retrospect "The Widening Horizon" has proved to be a realist fantasy, a long journey into the night and leading nowhere. Tomorrow is as problematic as today and the historian can have no determinate and safe relation to it without the exercise of moral judgment between the emerging forces of right and wrong, good and evil—the Churchill of tomorrow and the Hitler in us all.

In place of the causeless universe of Kafka's novel we have a predetermined universe of winners and losers from which the dimension of choice and decision, that is to say of moral decision, has all but disappeared. The subject–object distinction is also known as the subject–act–object distinction, where the act refers to the act of understanding, judgment, of decision when faced with a choice. The element of choice is vital in all human affairs and acts of understanding. Without it human affairs and statesmanship become unintelligible. The world we live in is composed not only of causes but also of choices and decisions. We do certain things, choose this and not that, not only because there are causes pressing upon us but also because we have reasons flowing from choice. Lenin, who suffered a premature death, could have chosen to preserve intraparty democracy to the fullest by allowing a multiparty system to flourish as the political context for a genuine democratic centralism within the party. Surely this was a choice made by him with Trotsky to follow. Perhaps the "cause" was Lenin's fundamentally autocratic personality. But he could be flexible as in the Iskra period and the tensions with Plekhanov, or again in inaugurating the New Economic Policy (NEP). Here he made a good decision, and there a bad decision leading to a monolithic party soon to be controlled by the General Secretary. Lenin was always a man of decision(s), and this always implied a choice. In brief: there are not only causes of what we do (as in mechanical fields) but also reasons for the choices we make. Carr underplays the element of choice and with it the dimension of reason and judgment, of reason and unreason in, say, Lenin and Hitler. In place of moral responsibility as the test of statesmanship he pins his flag to the future as the test of objectivity in historical writing. But even his eye, the keenest of the keen, could not see the future unfolding before him. *The Twenty Years Crisis* was criticized, rightly or wrongly, for advocating a policy of appeasement.

History as progress, history as the record and charter of man's progress toward liberty and equality in an ever-widening horizon, this is the answer of Britain's foremost historian to the question *What Is History?* His argument is compounded of five major elements. First off, Carr begins with a very fine analysis of the historian and his facts based on the subject–object distinction introduced by Collingwood and rejected by the traditional historian. This vivid richly illustrated account is entirely successful. More problematic are the next few elements of which the role of accident in history is the first and led to a sharp debate with Sir Isaiah Berlin in the pages of *The Listener*.[10] Carr calls this the case of Cleopatra's nose.[11] If Cleopatra's nose had been much larger (or smaller) Anthony would not have been lost, and the course of Roman history would have been very different. Carr dismissed this argument from the trivial to the momentous as made in its various forms: What if Trotsky had not fallen sick on an afternoon spent duck hunting in the midst of his struggle for power with Stalin, what if Lenin had not died prematurely after his final stroke, what if the Emperor Alexander had not died from the bite of a pet monkey, etc., etc.? But Cleopatra's beauty was what it was, a fact of history and her nose was precisely the right size and shape. And much the same can be said about all the many trivial accidents advanced by speculative historians and historiographers. But how if the accident were not trivial, as Trevor Roper suggests in his *Encounter* critique "E.H. Carr's Success Story?" What if Churchill had died in nineteen thirty-nine? Speculation of this kind, Carr replies, leads inevitably to a history of what might have been an alternative history that does not exist and has no real significance. So much for the accidental view of history propounded by Bernard Berenson and defended by Sir Isaiah in his study of *Historical Inevitability*.

History has a certain inevitability because things are what they are and not something else. And they are what they are because all things have their cause or causes. To suppose otherwise, to presuppose a caseless freedom of action, is to live in a Kafkaesque nightmare, a world of which no history can be written. Carr illustrates his point with a little story.[12] Jones has had one last drink too many before picking up his car from the garage where the mechanic has not done a good job with the brakes. Driving home that night Jones comes to a blind, poorly lighted intersection and sees a man in the shadows. But too late, and the man is killed. The victim is Robinson, who stepped out late that night to pick up a fresh pack of cigarettes. What was the cause of the accident? Was it that Jones had one drink too many? Or was it the mechanic's bad job with the brakes? Or perhaps it was the blind intersection, or Robinson's need for more cigarettes? In his writeup of the report the historian must look for a cause or set of causes which have social significance. To impute the cause to smoking is to isolate a cause which has no social significance in reducing future traffic fatalities. It is a cause without general significance and therefore unworthy of the attention of the historian.

The issue on which the Carr–Berlin debate turns is a fundamental and dividing issue in philosophy. It can be framed in a simple question: Is the social universe one of radical contingency or is it one in which events and human actions are strictly determined? If you accept the fact that all events have causes, says Carr, then I am a determinist. With this the gauntlet is cast, and Sir Isaiah has picked it up in his response. Carr phrases it thus: Was the Bolshevik Revolution (read Second World War, First World War) inevitable? He regards this as a parlor game and says if you saw the question "Was the war of the Roses inevitable?" you would regard this as a joke! A student asked to name the cause of the Bolshevik revolution might name a half dozen. A superior student might go a step further and list them in order of importance. But it is not till we have searched out their interrelations and presented a coherent, unified, and synoptic picture can we be said to have done the job. The question is now answered and the Bolshevik revolution would emerge as inevitable. And with this we come to "E.H. Carr's Success Story" and the wide-ranging critique by the critics.

If Lenin's victory, and that of Stalin after him, was predetermined then the story of the losers, their advocacy and their arguments, loses much, if not all, of its significance and history emerges as the story of the winners. If the historian Carr were citizen Carr in mid-nineteen seventeen which way would he, should he, have thrown his weight? We know how critics from Rosa Luxemburg to the Plekhanov of *Our Differences* from the early Berdyaev to the later Trotsky warned of the danger as they made their case. Were they not right from the perspective of the future which is Carr's touchstone of historical objectivity? The historian, Carr writes, must have the future in his bones. But which future is that?

Even at the time of writing (1961) the future had begun to unravel with the publication of Khrushchev's "Secret Speech" on "The Crimes of the Stalin Era." Carr minimizes the horrors of collectivization by reminding us of the dreadful extremes in the conditions of the worker, including child labor, in the course of British industrialization. This, he says, is now written off as the costs of industrialization. But surely the slaughter of farm animals in the millions and the resulting slaughter of the kulaks also in the millions cannot lightly be written off as "the costs of progress" in industry. In fact, they produced a famine which the regime covered up, and the forced industrialization was poorly managed with waste and a scarcity of consumer products in the stores as reported by numerous visitors at the time. Trotsky's exposé in *The Revolution Betrayed* would appear to be nearer the truth as an objective analysis. But then Trotsky was a loser, and losers hardly count. And what of the other losers in the party hierarchy, tried, found guilty, and shot after the Moscow Trials, and the shooting of Tukhachevsky and the red Marshals? They, too, were losers so what do we chalk this up to?

The Soviet Union was left vulnerable to the Nazi attack. Stalin distrusted everyone, everyone that is except Hitler who violated the pact and came near to destroying him. But the Soviet regime survived thanks to the bravery of its soldiers and the genius of Zhukov *et al.* only to enter into a Cold War with the United States which it lost in a big way disintegrating progressively to Gorbachev and the final implosion with Yeltsin. Its future, if Mr. Carr could have seen that far, is the story of the biggest loser in the century.

All this is familiar to the most casual reader of history and in no sense intended as a lesson from the pupil to the master of a many volume history of the Soviet Union. I mention it here only to indicate that the future as the touchstone of objectivity is a broken reed for the historian to lean on. Is there a better one to which we can point, for if there is not we are back to Collingwood's problem of variety of meanings in a sea of subjectivity. I think, there is, and I hesitantly make a small commonsensical suggestion intended for further thought.

Past and future: If the future is a broken reed for the historian to lean on, then he has only the past. The Injunction to love the past is dubious injunction for the twentieth-century historian writing on fascist Italy, Nazi Germany, or the Soviet Union. How should the historian relate to the past even in these extreme cases? I think this involves a two-step process with the second in some tension with the first. The first is to analyze and present the events and actions of the past exactly as the main actors understood them. This includes the losers as well as the winners, for the losers might have had a real point. Indeed they might have been right! Broadly speaking, this is to reason from within the horizon from which the actors, losers as well as winners, saw things and made decisions. The second step is to write from a second horizon, which is the historian's own horizon, to supply a critical perspective. Objectivity in history is the successful blending of the two horizons. And this is what we see in Trotsky's *History of the Russian Revolution* and Deutscher's biography of Trotsky and history of his life and work. We can illustrate this from the work of Carr himself. Mr. Carr was the notable biographer of three most notable figures, Bakunin, Marx, and Dostoevsky. But he never relates them one to another and so misses the most salient feature in the controversies surrounding their names. His study of Marx is subtitled "A Study in

Fanaticism," which misses the real point in the conservative–liberal debate. In the conservative view, if we fast forward to the US after the war, as the House Committee members repeat time and again, concern is not with "free speech" as understood by *The Nation* then and now, but by the very different issue of espionage in the service of the Soviet Union. This was the real issue in the Hiss case and the investigation of the Perlo group and the Silvermaster group as related by Chambers, Elizabeth T. Bentley, and Hede Massing. And this is the issue as defended by Buckley and Bozell, Kendall and Burnham, and the editors of *National Review*. And the investigation of some fine novelists and script writers from Dashiell Hammett to the Hollywood Ten was an investigation into the work of those whose message was paving the way with such fine novels and films as *The Maltese Falcon, High Noon, Bad Day at Black Rock, Lonely Are The Brave,* and *Johnny Guitar*. The view of the conservative elite was more subtle and more explosive. Allow me a personal recollection.

At the Lincoln Conference, which I organized for Governor Bob Kerrey, I gave the first panel to Henry Giroux, Stanley Aronwicz, and Donaldo Macedo with Siegfried Grosser, a mathematician, Gerhart Niemeyer, a political philosopher, and myself from education, acting as the three discussants. In his critique Niemeyer characterized Giroux *et al.* as ideologues and not philosophers, and as con men seducing an innocent audience. But his real charge which he then came to was that they were demons and that this represented an eruption of the demonic in our midst! To many this charge was incredible, idiosyncratic and fantastic, a voice from another world. And in a way it was, but not in the way understood. The theory of demonism, of the demonic erupting in our midst, has a long and distinguished history going back to Dostoyevsky who wrote a long novel on this theme and called it *The Demons or The Devils*, and Mr. Carr has a chapter on it precisely under that title. At the time of its writing, Dostoyevsky's novel was dismissed as extreme, idiosyncratic, and fantastic, a voice from another world. But soon after the murder of the student Ivanov gave it flesh as a starting prediction. And as the events in the Soviet Union began to unfold, the novel and its hero, Stavrogin, were no longer seen as creations from a world of fantasy and its author was no longer regarded as "The Shakespeare of the Lunatic Asylum." This is the view championed by Chambers in *Witness*, by Voegelin in the Munich lectures now published as *Science, Politics, and Gnosticism*, by Vyacheslav Ivanov, the Symbolist poet and critic, in a long chapter on Dostoevsky's theory of demonism, and by his foremost Russian biographer Konstantin Mochulsky. The problem as seen by the conservative elite is not the psychological problem of fanaticism, but the metaphysical and theological problem of the Devil... and God. "The problem of socialism," wrote Dostoyevsky, "is not an economic problem. The problem of socialism is the problem of atheism." In confronting the conservative case in the culture war, each of us must make their own decision in morals and metaphysics or philosophy. And the doctrine of contrasting arguments is designed to enable them to make it on a progressively more fundamental level step by step. It prompts the student not to solve a puzzle but to make a choice, or rather a continuous series of choices and decisions on a moral level.

3

Isaiah talks nonsense, says E.H. Carr. But, he adds more graciously, "even when he talks nonsense he earns our indulgence by talking it in an engaging and attractive way."[13]

The criticism turns on the theory of determinism and the role of accident in history presented by Berlin in *Historical Inevitability*. But the roots of the conflict run deeper still. The fundamental conflict is between the Oxford philosophy of Austin and Berlin, notably in *Concepts and Categories*, and the pronounced historicism of Carr with its origins in Collingwood. Carr carries the argument to its ultimate conclusion, and by making it consistent he makes it incredible and a scandal to his critics like Trevor Roper and Hans Morgenthau. Trevor Roper's brisk polemic was published in *Encounter*, under the title "E.H. Carr's Success Story." And Hans Morgenthau called his earlier work *The Twenty Years Crisis* "a monumental failure." Sir Isaiah is more moderate, and more puzzling. "I do not assert that determinism is false," he says, "because I do not know that it is false." "My reason for not asserting that determinism must be false is simple. I did not and do not know that it is false...." What Sir Isaiah does know, and therefore, can assert, is that if determinism were true then our language of praise and blame, i.e., of moral responsibility, would have to be completely overhauled. There we have the problem in a nutshell. Oxford philosophy has nothing to say about the world. It prides itself on leaving things exactly as they are. Its concern is solely with words and not things. But the words in our language of praise and blame all flow from our universal experience of ourselves as subjects. And this is precisely what will not be overturned by a purified language compatible only with a universe of objects. Carr's solution is brilliant and problematic. Berlin's solution is equally problematic if no less brilliant. The dilemma is there for all to see, and neither solution will satisfy the critics.

The immediate cause of the dispute with Sir Isaiah is the issue of determinism in history provoked by Berlin's article on "Historical Inevitability." The article is based on Bernard Berenson's study titled *The Accidental View of History* and begins with a suggestive quote "...vast impersonal forces." But all effects have a cause or perhaps more than one. Consider this simple example. One night before driving home Jones has a last drink and it is one too many.

Notes

1. R. G. Collingwood, *The Idea of History*, London: Oxford University Press, 1956. First published by the Clarendon Press in 1946.
2. Ibid., pp. 270ff.
3. E.H. Carr, *What Is History?* London: Penguin Books, 1961; second edition, 1987. The debate is recorded in the *Listener*; see the discussion on "objectivity in history," pp. 159–165 and the brief passages on Carr in Ved Mehta, *Fly and the Fly Bottle: Encounters with British Intellectuals*, Columbia University Press, New York, 1983, pp. 107ff.
4. E.H. Carr, *What Is History?* op. cit., p. 22.
5. Ibid., p. 10.
6. Ibid., p. 16–19.
7. Ibid., p. 164.
8. Ibid., p. 143.
9. Ibid.
10. Isaiah Berlin. "What Is History? (Letters to the Editor)." *The Listener*, May 18, 1961, p. 877; June 15 1961, pp., 1048-49. Ending publication in 1991, the archives of *The* Listener, a BBC weekly magazine have all been digitalized by the Immediate Media Company of London.
11. E.H. Carr, *What Is History?* op. cit., p. 128.
12. Ibid., p. 137.
13. Ibid., p. 121.

· 9 ·

THE CONSERVATIVE CRITIQUE

In the conservative critique of liberal democracy, the most outstanding name is that of Leo Strauss and the vast body of his writing constitutes the most fundamental, intransigent, and extreme indictment of liberal democracy in all its many facets and features. Most notable among these are his books, *Natural Right and History*[1] and *What Is Political Philosophy? and Other Studies*,[2] and a later work called *The City and Man*.[3] But he also published substantial studies on Xenophon and Aristophanes in their relation to Socrates, a set of essays collected under the title *The Rebirth of Classical Political Rationalism*,[4] and edited a *History of Political Philosophy* with Joseph Cropsey.[5]

After his education at Marburg, Strauss began his professional life as a research scholar specializing in Talmudic and classical studies at a Jewish Institute in Germany. In the mid-thirties he left for Britain and Oxford where he published his first major work, a study of *The Political Philosophy of Hobbes: Its Basis and Its Genesis*,[6] which Isaiah Berlin considered his best book. Strauss then emigrated to the United States and a position on the faculty of The New School for Social Research and soon assumed the position of Editor of its journal *Social Research* where he published a number of important essays and reviews. Some of the essays of this first period were published under the title *Persecution and the Art of Writing*[7] and began to bring him to the attention of the scholarly world, prominently including Robert M. Hutchins, then President of the University of Chicago. Strauss was invited to become the Robert M. Hutchins Distinguished Service Professor at the University of Chicago where he delivered the Walgreen Lectures published under the title *Natural Right and History* which was to be his most significant impact on the world of liberal scholarship. He also began attracting an increasing number of talented students, such as Bloom and Jaffa, and Anastaplo and Berns all making their contributions to the culture war now getting stronger after the break of the war years.

The Strauss critique is the most comprehensive in American letters. It presents a synoptic perspective as the alternative of choice as against the joyless and empty world of liberalism and the decaying orthodoxy of Marxism. Though its appeal to the young was non-existent, it attracted a score of professors teaching at one University or another from coast to coast and they are now known as Straussians. The magic that created this sect is obscure. But perhaps this much can be said. The Strauss investigation unfolds over time like a detective story complete with Sherlock Holmes and a Professor Moriarty.

Behind the more robust figure of Thomas Hobbes, the original villain of the story, we see emerging "the fine hand of the Italian," and thus in *Thoughts on Machiavelli*,[8] Strauss reveals the master mind, the prophet unarmed but with a gift for propaganda, working silently and successfully behind the scene to create a criminal syndicate and spread "the evil teaching." In Strauss the master question is: Who killed political philosophy? And the answer developed with the suspense of a detective story is the syndicate of modern philosophers from Hobbes and Locke to Rousseau and Burke, Montesquieu and the Federalist Papers. The original teaching was too bold to go down, as the "justly decried names of Spinoza and Hobbes" attest. So, it was softened by Locke, then by Rousseau and Burke in the critique of modern natural right and made more charming and corrupting by Montesquieu before crossing the ocean to emerge in the Federalist Papers. To understand the evil teaching is to break the spell by going beyond it. Strauss reaches back to classical political philosophy with its origins in Socrates, its dramatization in the dialogues of Plato and its completion in the treatise form in Aristotle. Classical political philosophy makes the claim to have solved the riddle of justice. It presents itself as the final solution in principle and the city as the complete political good, again in principle. Strauss' achievement is to have made classical political philosophy, the philosophy of Plato and Aristotle come alive as worthy of fresh and direct consideration as fundamentally right and not as mere subjects of historical investigation in what has now become the history of ideas and marks his rank as one of the most significant political philosophers of the century. Strauss himself admits, in the *City and Man*, I believe, that some of Plato's theories like the theory of forms are fantastic. And to this one might surely add the theory of knowledge as recollection. Plato has formulated the problem of knowledge with a brilliance that was unsurpassed. But his solution to the problem was fantastic and the problem remains to this day. So too Strauss formulated certain problems in liberal philosophy as seen from a Platonic perspective. But his solutions are extreme and little short of fantastic in the modern world of letters. A few examples from his lecture on political philosophy will convey the point. 1. Philosophy, says Strauss in the opening pages, is search for knowledge of the whole. The whole is the totality of the parts. We know the parts but the whole alludes us. All political actions, says Strauss, again in the opening pages, aim either at stability or change. In preserving things as they are, we wish to avoid change for the worse and in aiming for change we aim at change for the better. And all thought of better and worse implies thought of the good. This thought of the good is the measure of the centrality of the moral in politics and political philosophy. But, of course, change for the better or worse might be change in a purely economic or political sense as in the century of colonization. 1. Strauss' argument is pure verbalism, for the better and the worse need not contain a moral dimension at their core. 2. Strauss commends classical political philosophy for its freshness and directness. The classics did not employ any term that was not already employed in the marketplace of popular political controversy. The right and appropriate line of development in the articulation of political philosophy is from natural public debate to the level of philosophy, from the *doxa* to the *logos*. In all such public debates the umpire was naturally the philosopher. As an example, he cites the public use of the term "cold war" in his introduction to *The Essays on the Scientific Study of Politics*.[9] But as his critics pointed out, the public did not create the term, Walter Lippmann did, and Walter Lippmann was a political scientist. More generally speaking, the model Strauss holds up could develop quite naturally in a small city. It is out of place dealing with a vast country like the United States, where the issue presently before congress is the debate about a trillion dollar budget and its allocations as between the military and the improvement of the infrastructure. At the time of Strauss' writing, the issues involved in the cold war led to the Marshall Plan, NATO, and the Truman Doctrine. The public might have had to be sold on the Marshall Plan, but it had no role in conceiving it. Nor can one see how the philosopher, whoever he be, could be the umpire in the resulting controversy. Strauss gives us four names as the greatest philosophers of the century. Husserl, Heidegger, Bergson, and Whitehead. All Europeans with little knowledge and no authority to umpire political decisions in this country. On a more general level, in the opening pages of "What is Political Philosophy,"[10] as mentioned above, Strauss, you will recall, defines philosophy as search for knowledge of the whole. The whole he tells us is the totality of the parts. We know the parts but the whole alludes us. The allusive quality of the whole is due to its comprehensive character and this comprehensive character has three main elements: God, nature and man. Precisely what the parts are he does not say. Presumable they are the economy and the economic, society and sociology and the political system or political science and we are said to know them. But if the whole includes knowledge of God or nature in the Straussian or philosophical sense and man, in more than an anthropological sense, then it is destined to allude us forever in this blend of God and man. Strauss evades the problem by shifting from one position to another. Some say that the various positions composing the register of philosophy show that they refute one another and that there is, therefore, no final fixed and determinate truth to be had. Actually, Strauss' answer merely shows that they contradict one another and continue to pose the question of the truth and the imperative to search for knowledge of the best. At other times, however, he insists that we take seriously the claim of the classics to have solved the problem of justice and the best regime definitely once and for all. He himself proceeds as if this latter claim were true in his critique of Max Weber and the great philosophers from Hobbes and Locke to Rousseau and Burke in *Natural Right and History*. His critique is clear, detailed and explicit. His running attack on relativism and historicism is the most fundamental to come from the conservative side. But it assumes the complete validity of the classical position. The modern political scientist is much interested in questions of method. But the classics showed no interest in the question of methodology as it is now called. Modern writers have been preoccupied with the philosophy of history and the problem of historical knowledge. But the classics had no philosophy of history and developed no historiography in the Carr, Collingwood, or any other sense. All this is to presuppose the validity of what it is intended to prove as in the case of Max Weber and Hume. Strauss' procedure is to furnish a purely negative critique without any attempt to prove his positive position. This emerges most clearly in his critique of Hume. In developing his arguments, Strauss tells us, he would like to make use of the convenient terminology of David Hume. According to Hume all our ideas are formed by combining impressions made on the mind by the external world. One can see this readily with objects such as chairs and tables, dogs and cats. But how, Strauss asks, can this theory of perception work in giving us the idea of the state, which is precisely not a material or sensible object. This is a good question and I do not have the answer. But I have little doubt that a scholar in the tradition of Hume could provide us with an ingenious reply. My point here is that in rejecting all of modern philosophy, Strauss has misguided us with a superficial response intended as decisive. In rejecting Hegel *tout court* he fails to recognize the critical significance of the theory of the subject, which informs much of modern philosophy from Dewey to Lonergan and the development of the *conscientia experiential* as the fundamental alternative to Hume's consciousness as perception with its consequent denial of the subject and personal identity. Strauss' critique of Max Weber is more extreme and certainly much more fantastic than the brief remarks on Hume. It is developed in the second chapter of *Natural Right and History* under the title, "The Distinction between Fact and Value" and marks his complete break with modern philosophy and social science. It is here from the second chapter on that we can see the working of "the fine Italian hand" in turning philosophy from the study of republics that never existed to regimes that actually exist, from the study of natural right to the empirical study of politics, their justification and dynamics. Strauss' critique presents itself as a master-piece of textual analysis. Weber's writings are searched for one and another of his various statements on methodology and these are condensed into some half dozen fundamental contentions. Strauss' procedure is to raise a question in the form of a general, "But why?" at each critical point. Some of Strauss' rhetorical questions will strike a reader as decidedly strange. An example is the instrumental value of social science. If you wish to succeed by achieving X, you must do Y and Z, if you are not to fail in a useless or irrelevant waste of time and money. To question this and the instrumental value of social science generally is decidedly strange. Reflection on Strauss' purpose, however, dispels this original sense of strangeness. But this fundamental purpose makes his position even more remote from contemporary or modern reality. Strauss' purpose is the reinstatement of nature as opposed to convention as the *ens realissimum*. The ontological rock of reality and with it the study of natural right as the grand theme of political philosophy. Once this is grasped in its full implication his indictment makes more sense in the intensity of his language and particular charges. The two outstanding charges are the charge of nihilism and the charge of an ensuing chaos. Natural right provides the ultimate criterion of truth and agreement can produce peace, but it cannot produce truth. Once the ontological rock is destroyed there is nothing left to fill the void. Of Weber's methodology Strauss says, this leads necessarily to nihilism. Nay, it is identical with nihilism. The removal of an objective standard can only lead to the chaos of subjectivity and the night in which all cows are black. This theme is developed by Sammy Rosen in *Nihilism from Wittgenstein to Heidegger*. But the concrete arguments advanced are unconvincing. Typically these take the form of posing the most extreme cases. What would we think of a historian, who set out to write a history of art, but ended by writing a history of trash. In fact the distinction is not always so easy to make. In settled times we have a massive consensus not only in science but also in music and painting. But when confronted with a revolutionary new form as in Stravinsky's *Rite of Spring* the critic reviewed the performance in these words, "Who wrote this terrible *Rite of Spring*? What right had he to write this thing? And on our helpless ears to fling. It's bing bang, bing bang, bing bang bing." It is only when the ear has been musically educated that we can hear it as music and art. Where the fundamental framework, the horizon itself, is in question, it is no longer easy or perhaps even possible to tell sense from nonsense and the reasonable from the absurd. So in *Politics and Vision* in a passage on Locke, Sheldon Wolin dismissed Strauss' argument as fatuous[11] and in the conversations with Isaiah Berlin, Sir Isaiah dismisses the Strauss view on the Machiavellianization of modern philosophy as bordering on the absurd. The Strauss problem flows from the fact that he takes the classical philosophy to be the final fixed and complete truth and refuses to advance a step beyond it to address the problems of the modern world. To understand the nature of totalitarianism and tyranny is not to study the classic framework but to analyze the nature of Stalin's regime and "the abolition of facts" and the Moscow Trials mentioned by Polanyi as part of the elixir of making the magic of Marxism. Or to take a more striking example, Strauss notes that the classics paid little or no attention to foreign policy since treason is not a debatable subject in political philosophy. In the simpler world of the city-state this is readily understandable. But with the rise of world communism the persons to read were not Xenophon and the classics, but Rebecca West, Whittaker Chambers and Earl Latham. The distinction between the internal and external was steadily erased and in Britain, Canada and the United States, men turned to treason, subversion and espionage out of broad political and philosophical convictions. In Britain this was certainly the case with Kim Philby, his friends Burgess and Maclean,

Anthony Blunt, and, of course, Alan Nunn May and Klaus Fuchs, while in this country the witness of Alger Hiss is still debated, as is the naming of names from the Hollywood Ten to the Ware Group, the Perlo Group, and the Silvermaster Group. But neither Strauss nor his followers have addressed the problem and enlightened us on the new meaning of treason. Around the time these momentous events were unfolding, Strauss was lecturing on "*Euthyphro* on Piety" an essay published in the *Rebirth of Political Rationalism*.[12] Strauss' remoteness from the great events of the day flows from two causes: as a political philosopher he swiftly promotes all empirical questions to an investigation on the fundamental level of philosophy. We cannot know much of the state as it exists without first knowing the nature of the state and in particular, the best state or regime. And this requires an analysis of Plato's laws, the search for justice in *The Republic*, and the study of piety in the *Euthyphro*, etc., etc. and this search is never completed. Of political controversy in the *Agora* or marketplace of ideas, the best umpire is the philosopher. But of the great events and controversies of his day, Strauss, the philosopher has nothing to say. But he does have a question to ask. Contemplating the possible victory of world communism he feels forced to ask whether the destruction of the world might not be a preferable alternative. These were the two alternatives that Strauss could see in the late 40's and early 50's. But with Khrushchev's secret speech of 1956 on the crimes of the Stalin era, the criminal empire began its process of disintegration and the Marshall Plan, the Truman Doctrine and the policy of containment, were proved right after all. There is a striking discrepancy between the richness of Strauss' textual analysis of the dialogues (and other studies) and the poverty of concrete proposals implicit in them. For example, Strauss opens his Walgreen Lectures by quoting the opening lines of the Declaration of Independence, in a handsome tribute to Jefferson and the American founding. The power and the success of the United States in resisting Soviet imperialism, he says, undoubtedly flows from them. American power proved successful in meeting the Soviet challenge and won the cold war. But this power and these policies, all liberal to a fault, were based on science and technology. And Strauss has earlier told us that on the issue of slavery, for example, the difference between the classics and modern turns on the issue of technology. The unbridling of technology leads inevitably to the dehumanization of man. This is certainly the theme of Crossman's Plato and the sad state of British and American education as a testament to it. But the emancipation of science and technology is built into the modern principle of freedom and consent as the standard of right action by the state and this is precisely what

Strauss condemns from Locke to "the crisis of modern natural right" in Rousseau and Burke and finally to the Federalist Papers. More: he is critical of modern political theory for its concern with such an "empty" concept as the concept of power. But Kenan's concern in American diplomacy was precisely with "the challenge of Soviet power." Power has rightly been a central theme in modern thought from Russell and Kenan to Morgenthau and E.H. Carr and the essential instrument of foreign policy *vis a vis* the Soviet Union. What have Strauss and his students put in its place?

The second source is his rejection of moral judgment as subjective. This is framed most extensively in his critique of Max Weber and the distinction between facts and values. For Strauss there is no fundamental distinction between the world of facts and that of values. Values are, in his opinion, precisely as objective as the facts of the case in question. Strauss and his students like Bloom are critical of the term value because this implies an evaluating subject, whose judgement is subjective. This is the theme of the opening section of Bloom's critique in *The Closing of the American Mind* and to Jaffa's reply to Oppenheim, where he accuses Oppenheim of a naïve acceptance of the one (the world of sensible fact) and an extreme skepticism of the other (the world of moral judgement). For Jaffa as for Bloom and Strauss the objectivity of fact and the objectivity of values stand of fall together. A rejection of the objective validity of values leads necessarily to nihilism, because the standard of validity is denied any objective status. Strauss' major statement is made in his critique of Isaiah Berlin in an article titled "Relativism," now available in the *Rebirth of Classical Political Rationalism*.[13] In the preliminary skirmishing Strauss makes a good point when he criticizes the opinion that to realize the relative validity of one's ideals and yet stand for them unflinchingly is the mark of a truly civilized mind as against a barbarian. By this standard says Strauss, any liberal hack would be more civilized than Plato and, of course, this goes too far. But we should take it in context. Schumpeter, who is Isaiah Berlin's authority for the quotation, was writing in 1942 with the conflict between liberal democracy and the Fascist powers in mind and surely Berlin understood that. But the more fundamental argument Strauss makes is simply this. According to Berlin we make a circle around each man in which he is sovereign and master of his goods and possessions. As the British say, "An Englishman's home is his castle" and cannot be entered without due process of the law. Autocracy stops here. To this Strauss relies, that any laying down of a circle involves Berlin in a self-contradiction. For the laying down of any such line is to create an absolute and Berlin is a relativist. The liberal position in Weber and social science leads to nihilism and the position taken by Berlin, its second greatest advocate, leads to self-contradiction. In brief the liberal position cannot be maintained on the level of philosophy and the classical tradition. The source which Strauss sees as the heart of the problem is the consensus. In this case the 100 percent consensus of the people in a democratic government based on the consent of the people. All this is simple and obvious. The problem with the Strauss argument runs much deeper. It lies in his unwillingness to recognize the fact that moral judgement is at base subjective and not at all like facts. Finally, Strauss' second line of argument marks his remoteness from modern academic life and indeed from modern times itself. As against modern times he makes the case for the ancient city as representing "the complete political good." And classical political philosophy as furnishing the ultimate criterion of political right. He articulates the position with a variety of arguments similar in style and structure to those mentioned above. I shall call one the Twin Peaks argument: the fact that you cannot tell which of two peaks sitting in the clouds is the higher, does not mean that you cannot tell a mountain from a mole hill. But the real arguments like those presented in the Russell chapter are not about mole hills but about the question whether classical political philosophy as represented by Plato is a Fascist enterprise. The question is, why are these peaks forever hidden in the clouds? And Strauss has no answer to this question. Or rather the only answer that he can make is incredible and borders on the absurd. Much the same can be said of his defense of the laws of the city which condemned an innocent man to death as a "revolutionary agitator." I take the words from Willmoore Kendall in the case of "The People versus Socrates Revisited". In this case the most Strauss can say is that they let him live for 70 long years. This view of the rightness of the laws and the public orthodoxy is maintained not only by Kendall but also by Burnham. But would Burnham maintain that the laws were just if they had tried and put him to death in the early 30's, when he was a disciple of Trotsky and a flaming advocate of world revolution? The grand principle is the principle of virtue as against freedom, including freedom of speech and rule by an aristocracy or at the limit by a mixed regime. This line of argument was more fully developed by Walter Berns in *Freedom, Virtue and the First Amendment*.[14] Berns tells us that freedom is a "problem" because it is an "empty process" and does not distinguish good from evil as in the teaching of Earl Browder or Gus Hall and the communist leaders. Berns analysis proves that the history of the courts decisions is in shambles and we should return to first principles and in particular, the principle of virtue. But virtue too is a "problem" and who is to identify the twelve virtuous men or women to fill the courts? Court decisions have frequently split five to four. Would the principle of virtue change the margin or simply give us a radically conservative court? In any case court decisions are governed at times not only by precedent, law and high principle, but also by expediency, as I would hazard, the pressure for unanimity in cases like Brown versus Board of Education. The Straussian view overlooks the role of expediency in all democratic decision making. Democracy is compromise. And rule by an aristocratic elite is remote from the realities of democratic life. But in a way, all this is not to say too much. It reveals the intensity of feeling and the nigh total rejection of modernity and philosophical theory and political practice. But it does not come to grips with the central problem running through the entire Strauss enterprise and that of his foremost students such as Bloom and Jaffa. Let us circle in on this with a few small steps. The fundamental value is truth and Strauss has found it with the discovery of nature in classical political philosophy. The finished form of philosophy is the treatise. But preparatory form is dialectical. And we may ask, why so? The answer is that in the dialectical form we face one another more nearly as subjects, where the aims, character and context of the conversation is relevant to any deeper understanding. This is how the world looks to a Thrasymachus or Callicles, a Crito, but not to a Socrates. And this is how it looked to the court that judged and condemned him. Each of us is a subject and lives within an horizon that he has chosen. There is always an interplay between the subject and his ultimate framework or horizon. The one defines the other and is incomprehensible without it. When Jefferson says, "We hold these truths to be self-evident…," the "we" defines the collective subject and the truths enumerated constitute the structure of the framework or horizon defining the objective pole of the conversation. This raises two problems and not just one. The first is obviously the problem of truth, the truth of the liberty and equality with which their Creator is said to have endowed all men, a thesis which remains controversial to this day. And the second is the problem of communication. To whom can the declaration communicate? Certainly to the "we" the Americans who signed it as the charter of their liberties and of the foundation of self government. But also certainly not to George III and the British who could well regard it as a call to sedition and treason. In the dialectical form of conversation we speak with the other as subject to subject with each willing to alter or modify a position in the light of what the other has said. But in the second case we confront an adversary with a view to refuting a point and destroying a position. The first is a friendly engagement in the search for truth.

The second is confrontational and a rhetorical war of words. We are no longer conversing with the other, but talking at him with a presumed audience in mind. Strauss fixes all attention of the problem of truth understood as an objective reality. In exaggerating the objective value of truth he overlooks the role of the subject and his horizon in the pursuit of truth. In brief he has conflated our two problems into one in a declaration of independence from all things modern, except the right to live in peace and pursue his work. In a passage at the beginning of *Natural Right and History* Strauss identifies two sets of critics.[15] The first are liberals of various persuasions. The second are the neo-Thomists. But he adds "they are all modern men." He stands alone as the only one who is not a modern man, but an ancient with a set of adversaries on either side. But Lonergan and his followers were not adversaries. They were friends respectful of Strauss and naturally sympathetic to the critique of positivism and liberal relativism. An outstanding example of this is the fine article by Stanley Parry called "Reason and the Restoration of Tradition," published in *Modern Age*, a conservative journal founded by Russell Kirk.[16] Parry opens with a sketch of the crisis in culture and mentions Strauss as among the few contributions of note in addressing it. But while these, including Strauss might have significant effect in a healthy state they are ineffective when the tradition itself is in crisis. When the tradition itself is in crisis reason becomes impotent and the contending parties talk past one another. They no longer share enough in the way of common assumptions, method and rules of evidence to reach agreement on the formal or objective level. The reason is that moral judgment is subjective as his section heading proclaims. This does not mean that it is without foundation or untrue in a particular case and not cognitive as Oppenheim, *et al.* believe. It simply means that its truth cannot be demonstrated to those who do not share the basic framework within which moral truth is understood and within which it can be communicated. The subjective dimension creates a problem of communication rather than one of truth *per se* and Lonergan himself has treated the problem of relativism in his study of "Doctrinal Pluralism."[17] Concisely stated the problem is this: 1. It is certainly true that God exists. 2. What God has revealed is also certainly true. 3. Why then is it not possible to prove the truth of the Word? The answer is that the truth of God's existence is a truth in the mind of believers but not of unbelievers. And the same is true of revelation and the Word. These once more are truths in the minds of the faithful, but not of unbelievers. Believers in the faith share one horizon; unbelievers share another. And words change their meaning when they are transposed from one horizon to another. So it is that the moral judgments of the framers became "psychological axioms" in Dahl's analysis of Federalist Ten in a *Preface to Democratic Theory*.[18] After all Dahl might say, what else could they be? In conflating two problems into one, Strauss is left with a political philosophy without the cognitional theory which was the distinctive modern achievement in the work of particularly Lonergan and modern men. And his charges of nihilism in Weber and social science convinces no one. A modern state cannot govern itself without the social sciences, at least as an adjunct to political philosophy. So for all his vast learning and unrivaled skill as a textual analyst, Strauss remains an isolated figure, admired by the conservative elite, but without any substantial impact on American politics and culture.

The theme of inversion forms the underlying dimension of Eric Voegelin's contribution to the conservative critique on the most fundamental level. But this is not inversion in the more normal sense in which it is developed by Michael Polanyi. Quite the contrary, in Voegelin the idea of inversion is widened and deepened to form the grand theme which illustrates the mounting intensity and destructiveness of modern politics from the Enlightenment to the present day. This is the inversion of the transcendental and the immanent over the course of the century from Voltaire to Marx, Lenin, and the Soviet Union. The death of God, His murder if you will, lies at the heart of the problem. And it is one of the problems and no part of the solution. Voegelin's writings fall into three major groups. There are first his early writings which are now somewhat dated. Secondly, there are his last works, the multivolume *Order and History*, which lies beyond the scope of this writer. *Israel and Revelation* makes the introduction of revelation into the subject matter of philosophy and politics.[19] The next two volumes, *The World of the Polis*[20] and *Plato and Aristotle*,[21] are Voegelin's study of the classical world from the later Christian point of view and his closing the story with the analysis of modernity and *The Ecumenic Age*.[22] The sweep of Voegelin's thought is breathtaking. The language is clear and clean and at times even muscular. We have left the remote quality of Strauss's philosophic enterprise and arid prose for a turn to the experience of the thinker and the mind it has shaped from the polemics of Voltaire to the pathos of revolutionary existence in Bakunin. The three main works of this middle period to which we turn will be *From Enlightenment to Revolution*,[23] *The New Science of Politics*, and the Munich lectures on *Science, Politics, and Gnosticism* which takes us to the heart of the problem as understood by the conservative elite prominently including such diverse figures as Willmoore Kendall and Whittaker Chambers, and in part William F. Buckley,

Jr. With these we should mention the article titled "On Classical Studies," published in *Modern Age* and presenting Voegelin's theory in concise or model form.[24] The model ranging over a mere three pages gives us the quintessential Voegelin in a few simple sentences. One item runs as follows in the contrasting of the two positions: the life of reason (or classical political philosophy) is seen as a fascist enterprise. How did this perversion come about? And how can the life of reason be reconstituted? *From Enlightenment to Revolution* presents the most detailed account of the problem.

This book might never have been published except for the intervention of Professor John H. Hallowell. On completing it Voegelin put it aside in light of a new and fundamental insight. In all such studies ideas and concepts are treated as if they had a life and meaning of their own, and the debate between rival theories took place within a community of ideas which in fact does not exist. Voegelin's insight lay in the fact that it is the experience, the feelings and sentiments behind the ideas that give them their vitality as symbols in a social order with *society* as the true unit of comprehension. The most fundamental idea is the idea of reason itself. Is reason to be understood as logical or technical or scientific and restricted to the immanent field of forces which constitute the natural world? Or is it rather to be understood as the bridge between the immanent and the transcendental order of true being? The first is the modern and secular view from Hume and the Enlightenment to Russell and Ayer, Crossman, and Bambrough. The second is the view from Plato and Aristotle to Augustine and Thomas before the secularization of history and the growth of societies without spirit and men without souls. *From Enlightenment to Revolution* charts the course of progressive despiritualization from Bossuet and Voltaire to Helvetius and Bentham and, finally down to Bakunin and Marx, and the dark shadow of totalitarianism in Stalin and Hitler.

From Enlightenment to Revolution opens interestingly enough with a chapter of Bossuet and Voltaire signaling the emergence of secular history. This furnishes the theme which is developed in the next ten chapters on to its denouement in Bakunin and Marx. The perspective is not philosophy and natural right or the relation between the city and man but that of the Christian faith, of the word that became flesh and articulated from the New Testament to Augustine and Thomas. This chapter and the succeeding ones do not move exclusively on the level of high philosophical abstraction. On the contrary, Voegelin is intimately familiar with the body of primary and secondary literature and the analysis is developed with a wealth of historical detail. With Bossuet and his *Conférence avec Monsieur Claude*[25] we see the importance of a corporate body of truth interpreted by the hierarchy and the Church as against the right of individual conscience and a spreading flood of truths. For Bossuet, Voegelin tells us, it was not the content of heresy but the fact of schism that posed the danger. But it is with Voltaire and his friend, the *Marquise du Châtelet-Lorraine* that we come face to face with the danger immanent in the revolt against reason.

The danger emerges in the secularization of history and the concomitant despiritualization of Christianity. In time Christ would appear not as the Savior but as a moral reformer like Confucius or Buddha or other wise men. As the age progressed the classic symbols of the Christian faith would be robbed of their power to illuminate the truths of the transcendental realm and finally become incomprehensible. In fact, in a further stage they would be transformed into the principles and vocabulary of the new secular order created by Marx. And this signals the breakdown of dialogue, of critical conversation on the philosophical level. Anyone who has had a conversation with a Marxist, Voegelin tells us, can see that it is of no use to tell him that his governing ideas are not part of a critical theory but perversions of Christian ideas and symbols. The point to emerge from this story of the progressive decay of the symbols of the transcendental order of truth is nicely caught up in Voegelin's title *From Enlightenment to Revolution* as charting the course from the one to the other. It was the Enlightenment whose dynamics led to the revolution of thought which we witness in Hegel, the Left Hegelians, Bakunin, and Marx. To phrase the Voegelin thesis in its most startling form, it is the liberalism of the Enlightenment, which paved the way for the revolution of Marx and the Marxist movement. Voegelin makes the point, and more than once, that there is no fundamental conflict between the enlightened progressive such as Condorcet and the communism of Marx. Strange as it may sound to contemporary ears, this view is by no means idiosyncratic or unique to Voegelin. On the contrary, that it goes back to Dostoyevsky who originated it, is mentioned by his biographers and critics such as Konstantin Mochulsky and Vyacheslav Ivanov, and strongly supported by Whittaker Chambers who regarded the New Deal as making a revolution by "bookkeeping." Dostoyevsky himself was clear on his point and made the figure of Timofey Granovsky, a widely renowned liberal historian, into the initial character in the unfolding of events in *The Devils*. To the Catholic and conservative elite following in Voegelin's footsteps Marxism and socialism are only the final or terminal point. Till then, till that final battle, the main enemy is liberalism and the corrupting creed on which it is based. And no one has done more to clarify this than Eric Voegelin in the four studies which make up his middle period.

At stake is the idea of reason itself and its transformation in the new world of science marked by the figure of Isaac Newton. Voltaire had returned from his visit to England a convert to the philosophy of Newton on which he wrote a book by that name. Voegelin analyses the dynamics of this transformation in a few brief pages (*From Enlightenment to Revolution*, p. 30ff.)[2] which the interested reader will want to read and assess for himself. The analysis is critical in forming the first stage in "the wasteland of the Enlightenment" soon to be followed by the second and third steps taken by Helvetius and then by Comte and St. Simon. History has been secularized and Christianity historicized. The new standard is the standard of science and the philosophy to which it gives shape. All else is medieval and superstitious. As Voltaire phrases it "...for every *raisonneur* is born perverse." But Voltaire existed in a sort of in-between state of prerevolutionary suspense. His sallies, criticisms, and jibes at the old order were brilliant and colorful. But he was not yet capable of mapping out the shape of the new order to come. The evangel of immanent social transformation was initiated by Helvetius, and to be followed by the rise of positivism and utilitarianism in Comte and Bentham with "the new religion of humanity" in Comte and the "satanic vision of the Panopticon" in Bentham.

In the development of ideas from Voltaire to Marx the first notable figure is that of Helvetius, closely followed by those of Comte and St. Simon. Helvetius (1715–1771) was a minor figure compared with his illustrious contemporaries such as Locke and Rousseau. Yet his role in the insertion of ideas is critical to Voegelin's narrative. In his two works, *De l'Esprit et De l'Homme*, Helvetius functioned as a transmitter of Lockean ideas. But in the transmission Helvetius oversimplified Locke's theory. And with this oversimplification came the critical distortion that bent toward inversion. In Locke knowledge is gained from the senses. But in a passage down the line Locke clarifies this with the phrase "*sensu interno et externo.*"[26]

In Helvetius, however, the emphasis has shifted and the accent falls purely on the external. This shift is decisive and leads Helvetius to argue that a science of morals should be developed along the model of science in experimental physics.[27] And this inversion toward the immanent is followed by a Tonkinese myth which is a furious attack on Christianity. In place of the *logos* and the articulation of the transcendental basis of morals, Helvetius substitutes the pleasure-pain calculus as the basis of natural morality. The inversion could not be more complete: In the obliteration of the transcendental Helvetius is compelled to find the new basis of morality in the dynamics of somatic experience. From this to the later theories of conditioning was only a matter of a few steps. The road leads from Helvetius to Skinner in our times.

Next to come in this analysis is the progressive instrumentalization of knowledge, and with this the perversion of education. In concise form the inversion proceeds along the following steps: First, we have a clean break with the transcendental in the form of philosophical theology. Second, we have the elimination of metaphysics, as its close accompaniment. Third, and this is accompanied by reducing Locke's "*sensu interno et externo*" to the purely external. Gone are such aspects of the mind as reflection, believing, doubting, willing, etc., etc. Fourth, the new model is the model of experimental physics in the age of Newton and with this the turn to the scientism of the Enlightenment thinkers or at least some of them. And fifth, there is a turn toward conditioning as part of the education process, a turn later developed in the behaviorism of William James in *The Principles of Psychology* and B.F. Skinner in various works, most famously in *Walden Two*. A word more will clarify the structure of this development.

Man is subject to two sets of opposing forces. The first of these is a tendency toward rest or inertia which Helvetius calls *paresse*. The second is a tendency toward activity prompted by a certain inquietude which he calls *ennui*. With this fundamental insight Helvetius develops a *Genealogy of The Passions* which was to attract the interest of Nietzsche a century later. Among the passions is the desire for power (*désir du pouvoir*) which can be uncommonly strong in some men. This he calls a "*passion forte*." This passion, common to all men in its general form, is, of course, the "*amor sui*" of the Christian tradition, whereas in St. Augustine, it is contrasted by the "*amor Dei*." In the secularized theory of Helvetius, however, the absent "*amor Dei*" is transformed into the divinization of the educational process and popular culture as the new emerging force. "The respect paid to virtue is transitory," Helvetius tells us. "The respect paid to force is eternal" (p. 48). And this brief sketch is presented as much for the initial light it casts on the mind of one of the two leading conservative critics as on the figure of Helvetius himself in the genealogy of ideas from the *Encyclopédie* to the encyclopedic works of Marx. For further light on Voegelin and the conservative view we must visit his chapter on Comte and swell more extensively on his study of Marx.

But it is with Comte and the rise of positivism that we come to the real issue and the sharpest clash between Voegelin and the Enlightenment. Comte may be little read these days, but in the academic world he still stands as the father of the science of sociology. To Voegelin, however, he is primarily an "intramundane eschatologist." The turning of the tables could not be more complete. How, then, has the inversion occurred? It all began with D'Alembert, Condorcet, and Helvetius. But in Comte it has taken a monstrous step forward in the direction of a satanic vision to unfold in Bentham and the Panopticon, Lenin and the Soviet state. It begins with the replacement of the *bios theoretikos* with a science of phenomena and the truths of Christianity with those of the Religion of Humanity, with a new being, the *Grande Etre*, which Comte has conjured into existence. In this totally secularized world Jesus naturally appears as a sort of philosopher and Christianity as a sort of morally reforming movement. In fact, the name of Jesus does not even appear in the Calendar which Comte drew up for the New Age. The others are all there, Moses, Abraham, Mohammad, etc., but not Jesus. "The satanic apocalypse of Man," writes Voegelin, "begins with Comte."[28]

We now witness the emergence of the religious motivation underlying progressivism and the new science which J.L. Talmon has studied under the title of *Political Messianism* from its Enlightenment origins to Marx and Marxism.[29] In the newly secularized world we encounter a sinister phenomenon unknown to the ancient world: the Prohibition of Questioning.

To the philosopher who ventures to ask the fundamental questions of metaphysics, Comte has an answer read at hand: "Don't ask idle questions." All such questions are idle questions because they cannot be answered within the context of a science of phenomena modeled after the science of physics in the Age of Newton. (The reader will recall Ayer's chapter on "The Elimination of Metaphysics" written after his stay with the Vienna Circle two centuries later.) Comte is locked in within "the walls of the phenomenal world which deny the affective nature of man and the spiritual organization of man and human personality. The restoration of spiritual order lies beyond his compass. All that remains to him is the disorder of particulars in the world of pragmatic history. In this contest between spirit and power Voegelin is despairing of success: "The light of reason is a dubious guide in the night of the spirit."[30] To amplify his meaning he cites the work of De Bonald, Novalis, and De Maistre and later of Cardinal De Lubac on *The Drama of Atheist Humanism*.[31] Comte's solution is the creation of the *Grande Etre* or Humanity as the collective subject, an idea to assume sinister proportions in Turgot's conception of the *"masse totale"* celebrated by deadly effect by Marx and Lenin. And this is why "the satanic apocalypse of man begins with Comte."[32]

Sociology has indeed developed to become a science with the work of Durkheim, Pareto, and Michels. But Comte's contribution such as his Law of Three Phases is largely forgotten. Voegelin at any rate spends no time on Comte the social scientist. For Voegelin it is the process of inversion that is critical in the analysis of Comte as the key transitional figure from positivism to Marxism. In Comte the process of inversion takes three major forms. The first is the divinization of man in the creation of the *Grande Etre* or humanity seen as a concrete subject. The second is the Religion of Humanity or worship of the family of man. And the third is the complementary divinization of woman in the incarnation of Clotilde de Vaux, his friend and intimate. She had come to visit him on Wednesdays and the room in which she visited was made into a chapel. Everything was left the way it was when she last came. This event included the chair on which Clotilde de Vaux sat. The process was meticulous and extreme. So extreme was the process that some commentators have spoken of two periods on the life of Comte, with the second showing signs of divine madness or insanity. But in fact, Voegelin tells us, Comte was as sane as anyone though he may have suffered a nervous breakdown. For Voegelin it is the marked inversion from the transcendental to the immanent that is the real point revealed in the process of redivinization of which Comte is the supreme example till Marx and Russian communism. This story is featured in the chapter on "Inverted Dialectics"[33] and the final chapter on the genesis of Marx's ideas in the revolt against philosophy.[34]

Voegelin's two chapters on Bakunin are among the richest we have on the pathos of revolutionary existence. Though a man of powerful intellect, Bakunin was not primarily a man of ideas. His criticism of rivals, including Marx, often shows flashes of insight and brilliance. But he was not an organized and systematic thinker. He was a man of action who was rightly called "the poet of the revolution." He was consumed by an all-encompassing anger and hatred of the entire ruling system in Europe and in his own land. And he set himself out to destroy it with what began as a one-man crusade. The passion for destruction, he said, was also a creative passion, and he began to pick up allies from sheer force of personality. These ranged from Marx to Nechayev and seldom lasted very long. He became internationally famous, especially in Italy and Spain. But he spent part of his later life languishing in solitary confinement on the orders of Tsar Nicholas the First, his mortal adversary said to have had the soul of an inquisitor. Bakunin was an unscrupulous man and much given to fantasy. But he met his match and more in Sergei Nechayev, a student in his early twenties whose imaginary support system matches that of Bakunin phantom for phantom.

Though Bakunin was not primarily a man of ideas he did write one well-known work which he titled *God and The State*, placing the two in sharpest conjunction. God is the symbol of all that is wrong in the State in its concentrated essence. The supreme task is, therefore, to destroy the State and the God who sustains it. In the opening pages Bakunin describes his turning away from God and toward the Devil as a satanic inversion in the turning of the tables. He understood perfectly well what he was doing, and the rest is history. Voegelin sums up his critique in these few words: First off, Bakunin has no concept of order either in society or in history. The destruction of order is his "joyful passion" and the root of his anarchism. Second, the discovery of the masses, the emergence of the *masse totale*, becomes his agent of destruction on a world scale. Third, while he can be celebrated by his followers as "the poet of the revolution," it is in Bakunin that we can see most clearly the spiritually diseased form in which the inversion has erupted: Bakunin and Nechayev, Tkachev and Lenin, these figures mark the blending of German philosophy and Russian communism.[35] In this procession Bakunin alone stands out as advocating the *metanoia* of the human person as we have known him through the past several millennia. This is the underlying theme in Bakunin and Marx, and we do not understand them as thinkers until this is fully realized. This is the innermost meaning of the desire to create "a new heaven and a new earth."[36] And this is the source of the inspiration in the message and the power in the turning of the tables. It is what distinguishes the revolution of Marx (and that of the Marxist movement) from a Fabian-style movement for social reform and makes their war against liberal democracy a war between two faiths.

Voegelin's study of the process of inversion begins with the emergence of secular history marking the beginning of modern times. The modern mind knows no other kind of history. The Christian interpretation of history from St. Augustine to Joachim of Flora is by now a long forgotten secularized discipline. So E.H. Carr can with consistency criticize Berdyaev's profound and original study of *The Origins of Russian Communism* as extending beyond the bounds of history into that of the orthodox persuasion tinged with French personalism.[37] The fact that this is the single most acute analysis of the topic makes no difference to the historiographer in E.H. Carr, himself the noted historian of the Soviet Union. Voegelin's narrative concludes with an analysis of the "Inverted Dialectics" of Karl Marx, its genesis and meaning. This brace of chapters is the climax of the work and when placed beside *Order and History*, ranks Voegelin among the two or three commanding figures in the conservative critique of liberal democracy.

The theme of inversion forms the underlying dimension of Eric Voegelin's contribution to the conservative critique on the most fundamental level. But this is not inversion in the more normal sense in which it is developed by Michael Polanyi. Quite the contrary, in Voegelin the idea of inversion is widened and deepened to form the grand theme which illustrates the mounting intensity and destructiveness of modern politics from the Enlightenment to the present day. This is the inversion of the transcendental and the immanent over the course of the century from Voltaire to Marx, Lenin, and the Soviet Union. The death of God, His murder if you will, lies at the heart of the problem. And it is one of the problems and no part of the solution.

Notes

1. Leo Strauss, *Natural Right and History*, University of Chicago Press, first edition, 1959.
2. Leo Strauss, *What Is Political Philosophy? and Other Studies*, University of Chicago Press, 1988. First edition, New York: The Free Press, 1959.
3. Leo Strauss, *The City and Man*, Charlottesville, VA: The University of Virginia Press, 1964; University of Chicago Press, 1978.
4. Leo Strauss, *The Rebirth of Classical Political Rationalism: An Introduction to the Thought of Leo Strauss*. His Lectures and Essays selected and introduced by Thomas L. Pangle. University of Chicago Press, 1989.
5. Leo Strauss and Joseph Cropsey, *History of Political Philosophy* with University of Chicago Press, 1963.
6. Leo Strauss, *The Political Philosophy of Hobbes: Its Basis and Its Genesis*, University of Chicago Press, 1952 and 1963.
7. Leo Strauss, *Persecution and the Art of Writing*, New York: The Free Press, 1952 and 1980; University of Chicago Press, 1988.
8. Leo Strauss, *Thoughts on Machiavelli*, University of Chicago, 1958 and 1978.
9. Walter Berns, [et al.] and Herbert J. Storing, ed., *The Essays on the Scientific Study of Politics*, New York: Holt, Rinehart, and Winston, 1962.
10. The first article in his book *What is Political Philosophy? and Other Studies*, op. cit.
11. Sheldon Wolin, *Politics and Vision: Continuity and Innovation in Western Political Thought*, Boston: Little, Brown and Company, 1960, cf. p. 478–479, endnote 282.
12. Thomas Pangle, ed., *The Rebirth of Classical Political Rationalism: Essays and Lectures by Leo Strauss*, Chicago and London: University of Chicago Press, 1989.
13. Ibid.
14. Walter Berns, *Freedom, Virtue and the First Amendment*. Baton Rouge: Louisiana State University, 1957.
15. Leo Strauss, *Natural Right and History*, op. cit., p. 7.
16. Stanley Parry, "Reason and the Restoration of Tradition," *Modern Age* 5 (Spring 1961): 125–138.
17. Bernard Lonergan, *Doctrinal Pluralism*, The Père Marquette Lecture in Theology Series. Volume 3, 1971. Pages 1–74.
18. Robert A. Dahl, *A Preface to Democratic Theory*: University of Chicago Press, 1956.

19. Eric Voegelin, *the Collected Works*, vol. 14–17, Volume I–IV with the general title: *Order and History*, Columbia, Missouri: University of Missouri Press, 2000–2001. Eric Voegelin, *the Collected Works*, vol. 14, vol. I: *Israel and Revelation*.
20. Eric Voegelin, *the Collected Works*, vol. 15, Volume II: *The World of the Polis*.
21. Eric Voegelin, *the Collected Works*, vol. 16, Volume III: *Plato and Aristotle*.
22. Eric Voegelin, *the Collected Works*, vol. 17, Volume IV: *The Ecumenic Age*.
23. Eric Voegelin, *From Enlightenment to Revolution*. Durham, NC: Duke University Press, 1975.
24. *Modern Age*, XVII (Winter 1973), folder 11 or see the Imaginative Conservative.
25. Eric Voegelin, *From Enlightenment to Revolution*. Op. cit., p. 17.
26. Ibid., p. 38.
27. Ibid., p. 38–39.
28. Ibid., p. 159.
29. J. L. Talmon, *Political Messianism: The Romantic Phase* (New York: Praeger, 1960).
30. Eric Voegelin, *From Enlightenment to Revolution*, op. cit. p. 181.
31. Henri de Lubac, *The Drama of Atheist Humanism*. Translated by Edith M. Riley, Meridian Books, World Publishing Company, 1965.
32. Voegelin, *From Enlightenment to Revolution*, op. cit., p. 159.
33. Ibid., pp. 240–271.
34. Voegelin's final chapter is called: "Marx: The Genesis of Gnostic Socialism." (Ibid., pp. 272–302).
35. Ibid., pp. 227–233.
36. Ibid., p. 196.
37. Nicolas Berdyaev, *The Origins of Russian Communism*, translated from the Russian by R.M. French, London: Geoffrey Bles, Ltd., 1937, 1948, reprinted 1953.

· 1 0 ·
CLOSING COMMENTS

The title of Norman Jacobson's article "The Autonomy of Political Theory" in Rolland Young, ed., *Approaches to the Study of Politics*, is significant on two counts.[1] Firstly, the subject he is studying is something called "political theory" and not political philosophy as Strauss and the classics would have it. Political philosophy has been transformed into political theory, a subdivision of political science which is itself a subdivision of modern social science. Secondly, it is on the "unity" of political theory by which, I believe, Jacobson means the autonomy of political theory. Political theory is an autonomous discipline much as economic theory, sociological theory, psychological theory, and anthropological theory are unified and autonomous disciplines each within its own subfield. In what, then, does this unity or autonomy consist? Jacobson's answer is presented in the form of two critiques. The first is a critique of Strauss and the tradition of the natural as a philosophy. The second is a critique of Lasswell and the philosophy of behaviorism prominent in Yale in the work of Dahl and his students, Wildavsky, Polsby, and Wolfinger at Berkeley. At the heart of the dispute is the question of values. Here is where Jacobson divides sharply from Strauss and Voegelin.

To Strauss "values," that is to say natural right, was immanent in reality, that is to say nature. And the discovery of nature understood philosophically was the event in the development of the political philosophy. Not so for Jacobson who likens this to the perpetuation of a crime with Strauss as the "perpetrator," - the word is Jacobson's own. What then is the status of values in a world of fact? Jacobson's answer is clear, simple, and decisive: Values are created by the men, societies, and the cultures of which they are a product. Are there better or worse values? I think he would say "certainly," just as there are better and worse works of literature, music, and paintings. But they are all man-made and cultural creations. And herein lies the autonomy or "unity" of "political theory." The clash with the classical views of Strauss and the medieval or Catholic view of Voegelin could not be sharper. As against nature (and ultimately God) man has emerged as a creator of the ultimate yardstick in measure of all things in the debate since the *Protagoras*. As an ally of Strauss and Voegelin, Willmoore Kendall replied by defining this (namely the social contract) as the ultimate issue between conservatives and liberals.

The second contribution by the Berkeley school was made by Sheldon Wolin in his study of *Politics and Vision*.[2] In the opening pages of this widely read work, Wolin tells us that "the concepts of a political theory can be likened to a net." What the fishers will catch will depend on the net and where he chooses to cast it. Plato chose one brand and cast it in the polis. Marx chose a very different brand and cast it in the modern world of capitalism. Small wonder they came up with very different kinds of fish at the end of the day. Presumably there are better and worse nets and better or worse places to fish. But there is no ideal net or perfectly right place to fish. There are better fishermen and worse. Among the best were Machiavelli and Hobbes. Plato does not rank all that high, and Marx who merits only a mention caught no fish at all. His view of the proletariat as the Adonis of the historical process was exactly wrong. History, Wolin tells us, played a cruel trick on Marx. Instead of the proletariat emerging as Adonis, it emerged as Quasimodo. Now that would certainly be a cruel trick if it were ever played. But there is no evidence that it was, and every evidence that it was not. As is well known, in the *Economic and Philosophical Manuscripts of 1844* Marx describes the condition of the proletariat as cruelly disfigured under the conditions of alienated labor in modern capitalist manufacture and looked to the experience of revolution as transforming that condition.

Wolin followed this up with a study of "Hobbs and Epic Tradition of Political Theory."[3] Now if there was ever an epic thinker in the latter half of the nineteenth century it was surely Karl Marx. The three volumes of *Capital* constitute an epic achievement as epically wrong. His fundamental vision produced an ethical and political inversion on an epic scale and has been universally abandoned. "The true descendant of the theory of the natural law," Tawney once remarked, was "the labor theory of value. The last of the school men was Karl Marx" (see page 83, endnote 9). But the day of the school man is over and a commanding work of political philosophy has yet to appear.

A curious feature in Wolin as a political theorist is his latter-day conversion to inversion as a fundamental concept in political theory analysis. He does this with the concept of totalitarianism which he applies to the United States presenting it as a case of "inverted totalitarianism." Now in the field of education which is our entering wedge into the culture wars, we have public schools, charter schools, private schools, parochial schools, and evangelical schools. We now even have home schools and homeschooling for those who would like none of the above. We have, in brief, pluralism running wild ... and to no avail. And plural-ISM is the very opposite of totalitarianism. The inversion here would appear to be in the mind of the critic and not in the political domain.

Our third critic is Hans Kelsen. But he can only be called a Berkeley critic by courtesy since he merely spent his last few years at Berkeley. He was educated in Europe, a member of the circle surrounding Max Weber, and a professor who had the young Eric Voegelin as his assistant in his lectures on law and political science. Kelsen's critique, brief as it is, is the most interesting we have from the side of positivism and the case for liberal democracy. Of the criticisms leveled against *The New Science of Politics*, Voegelin's Walgreen lectures,[4] the critique by Hans Kelsen is certainly the most clear-headed, concise, and consistent.[5]

Kelsen focuses on the problem of democracy and more particularly on the problem of representation in a modern democracy. There have been two types of democracy in the Western tradition, the direct democracy of the ancient city and the representative democracy of the modern state. Kelsen's focus is exclusively on the latter and it is within this context that he presents his critique under the title "A New Doctrine of Representation."[6] The new type turns on a distinction made by Voegelin between the "elemental" form of representation and the "existential" form. The elemental form is characteristic of the liberal democracies and consists of making marks on a piece of paper against the name of the candidate favored for President, Prime Minister, etc., etc. This is the procedure of elections via the secret ballot extended to an electorate consisting of the people as a whole. The existential type, by contrast, focuses on substance rather than the procedure in the representation of a people articulating itself in readiness for action as a power unit on the stage of history. There can be debate as to whether the Soviet government represents the people, says Voegelin. But there can be no debate as to whether the Soviet government represents Soviet society.[7]

Kelsen notes right away the deprecating quality of the description Voegelin makes of the elemental type of representation in terms of mere marks on a sheet of paper, a superficial procedure when contracted with the real substance of effective representation. This corresponds exactly to the distinction made by Marxist theory between a purely formal representation characteristic of bourgeois democracy and the real representation of the workers, the toilers, and the poor, characteristics of socialist democracy. The ink on the Treaty of Versailles had barely dried, Kelsen tells us, when a variety of the totalitarian movements in Italy and Germany and much of Europe arose in favor of autocracy of one kind or another.[8] Fascism and national socialism challenged democracy directly in favor of dictatorship, whether the dictator be called the Führer or the Duce. In the socialist case autocracy, rule by the Communist Party was defined as democracy for the "immense majority" from the Communist Manifesto to the writings of Lenin and Stalin and the new Soviet Constitution. But the basic struggle remains the struggle between democracy and autocracy. The fundamental definition of democracy is "government by the people," where *demos* means the people and *kratein* means to govern. To substitute the concept of "government for the people" is to make no answer at all, for all governments can say that they are acting for the people.

According to the new science of politics, Kelsen points out, these marks on a sheet of paper also known as the process of elections refer merely to society that exists if not in the external world. But where else, he asks, can society exist if not in the external world? More: To say that an autocratic government such as the Soviet Union is acting "for" the people because it is attempting to realize "the common good" in heart in the needs of the people may be good propaganda, but it is bad political theory since there is no objectively ascertainable "common good." What is good to the Whig may not be good for the Tory. As I write, Robert Reich has just come out with a book called *The Common Good*. But Kelsen would say, if I read him right, that what looked good to one half of the electorate from President Obama to candidate Clinton looked bad to the other half (minus three million) from Mitch McConnell to candidate and now to President Donald Trump. The point is slurred over, especially in socialist rhetoric, by referring to something called "the will of the people." But this is merely a figure of speech: the collectivity has no will. Will is a characteristic of the individual as I think even Robert Reich would agree.

More controversial is the extended footnote reference to the three-volume work by J. R. Talmon on *The Rise of Totalitarian Democracy*[9] which traces the spread of these ideas from their inception in the Enlightenment and French Revolution to the political messianism of Karl Marx. At the time a very knowledgeable writer like E.H. Carr could refer to "Soviet democracy" as another and different type of democracy from the Western constitutionalist type. And Carr is credited with having read Talmon's manuscript. But I think it would be a mistake to see Talmon, who reads quite conservatively to me, as venturing that far. If we are to look anywhere it is to the work of Willmoore Kendall who explicitly favored absolute as against limited majority rule vested in a congress to exclude heresy in the political sense and exercise thought control. Making reference to John Courtney Murray and his study *We Hold These Truths*, Kendall argued that it is the right of society, this people, to exclude its opposite, namely the communists in the heresy hunt marked by the Hatch Act, the Smith Act and McCarran Rider, in what came to be known as McCarthyism. For Kelsen, however, the basic distinction is between restricted and unrestricted popular sovereignty in a democracy. And as a liberal he favors restricted government in the interest of freedom of conscience, of thought and of speech. And it is, I would say, even more mistaken to think of Eric Voegelin, an arch conservative, as extending favors to the Soviet Union. Where, then, is the problem in this paradoxical reading of the text?

A clue to the resolution of the paradox lies in the fact that existential representation is representation even when there are no parties. Apart from the city states of the ancient world small enough to enjoy direct democracy it was only in the Middle Ages that we have the representation of the realm without political parties. Existential representation is designed to explain this form of representation as a reality and to do so without making any value judgment on the content of political articulation in the real world. It is a value-neutral concept applying to all forms of articulation to be in the Lombards, or Attila the Hun, or Genghis Khan, or Lenin and the Soviet Union. In his three-volume study Talmon traces the rise of a second form of democracy, turning on the unrestricted right of the community, which he calls "totalitarian democracy," and he traces this from Rousseau and the French Revolution to the political messianism of the contemporary Marxist movement. Now Rousseau's foremost disciple in the world of contemporary right-left politics was precisely the young Willmoore Kendall, the boy prodigy who returned from Spain to become a flaming conservative and supporter of the Franco regime. Kendall accepts Franco's framing of the problem as the war between Spain and anti-Spain or the threat of the world communism penetrating deeply into Republican ranks. In Spain, Kendall tells us, American-style democracy was not on the agenda with Franco's unforgiving attitude toward his enemies. Back in the United States Kendall swiftly made a reputation for himself as a "majority rule democrat." But the majority he favored was not the limited majority of reigning liberal political theory but the absolute majority of unrestricted popular sovereignty as expressive of the community in its development, destiny and perfection. Nowhere is this better seen than in his dispute with Herbert McCloskey who had written on "The Fallacy of Absolute Majority Rule."[10] Kendall's reply in the next issue of the journal was titled "Prolegomena to Any Future Work on Majority Rule" and is as shattering a reply as anyone can find in a learned journal.[11] The McCloskey–Kendall dispute is the debate between the Locke of constitutional democracy and the Rousseau of totalitarian democracy in the liberal–conservative class from the House on Un-American Activities Committee to the elections, Presidential and Congressional. Kendall starts with Rousseau as the philosopher of the neighborhood community and defends its right, right mind you, to ward off "the liberal revolution," and perhaps even regain some lost ground!

The most notable part of Kendall's reply is the final section on the relationship between ethics and politics and the method appropriate to this distinction. Between ethics and politics and the method appropriate to this distinction, there is a sharp line which McCloskey crosses and recrosses to the confusion of the reader. Ethics is the domain in which a man (or community) makes his basic moral decisions. Ethics is logically prior to the politics and controlling of the political which is itself value-neutral. Political theory is a value-neutral and purely professional enterprise. It is foolish, writes Kendall, to argue about politics until you have clarified your position on the prior level of morals and metaphysics. This Weberian stand, presently popular in American political sociology, sets Kendall at odds with Leo Strauss whom he nominated as the first of his two great teachers (the second being Eric Voegelin). Strauss rejected the fact-value distinction in his critique of Weber and the claim of political theory to the status of an autonomous discipline. A law, Strauss argues plausibly, can be wrong: We often speak of unjust laws. Kendall takes Rousseau to be right and he says, "If a people wishes to do itself harm who is there say to it nay?" And the answer Kendall gave is "No one." This is the core of the Kendall position developed in the seven articles and reviews which make up the book. Its most elaborate presentation is in "The People Versus Socrates Revisited," first published in *Modern Age* and now available in *Contra Mundum*.[12] But we also see it in the article on Conservatism, on "The Two Majorities in American Politics," and on "McCarthyism." Each and every one of these is crafted in Socratic form, in the dialectical pairing of an argument and counterargument that first came to light in the *Dissoi Logoi* and the birth of philosophy in the Western world. But the presentation is no longer primitive as in a document dating back as far as the seventh century BC. On the contrary the quality of the craftsmanship is very near perfection in its literary and dramatic style. But the position developed over the course of a dozen years is bursting with problems of its own. Consider the internment of the Japanese by the liberal Roosevelt administration. Was the Government right to take this step to ward off a foreseeable danger? The Kendall position would answer "yes" in the light of the danger to the security of the community. Was it then wrong in the Korematsu decision of some years later? The position would have to say "no, it was right again." But this is impossible: Morally and constitutionally it could not be right both times, and we all now believe it was right the second time and wrong the first. In "The Majority Principle and the Scientific Elite," his first article on the topic,[13] Kendall makes the case for the purest relativism in moral as opposed to scientific judgment, arguing that the people are the equals of the elite in the morals and art. Such relativism robs the notion of value of its validity in any sense, and Kendall would soon abandon it in favor of "absolutism." But the problem remains and is intrinsic to the Kendall–Rousseau formulation. Rousseau's formulation substitutes effectiveness, which is a political fact, for right, which is a moral fact. And the fact that there is no one to say it, does not make it right as a political judgment. And least of all it does so if a lone dissenter like Socrates is condemned to death on patently false charges of atheism and corrupting the youth. But the paradox of supremely gifted Socratic inquiry remains to be appreciated in this singular contribution to the left–right clash in political education and the war in culture.

Here we begin not with the abstractions of classical political philosophy but with concrete realities of current American politics in the postwar years defined in terms of the left–right clash, the liberal revolution, and the growing conservative resistance. And the big news Kendall has to report on the war is the fact that the conservatives are winning the war. While the substance of the analysis derives from Rousseau, the form is purely Socratic, with Kendall as his own Plato writing up the clashes as democratic encounters. He begins by telling us what this book is not. It is not the work of a historian doubling in brass like Russell Kirk, or of a talented young man like M. Stanton Evans having his first go at things, etc., etc. It is, on the contrary, the work of a professional political theorist and there to be judged by stricter standards. Unlike Strauss he is not writing from a point of view outside modern political theory but very much as an insider challenging the prevailing orthodoxy from within the ranks. This extends to his conservative colleagues at *National Review* whom he dismisses as "the literary intellectuals" who mistake the failure to win in the journals for a failure to win in congress and in reality. And he goes about his task like this:

Kendall likes to begin with a problem to which his study is offered as a solution. For the conservative, intellectual movement the problem is framed by the question: What is American conservatism as it shapes up in the immediate postwar decades? The question is "up", make no mistake about it, and some very highly placed mouths are asking it. He cites a series of answers from president Eisenhower who sees no value in the liberal-conservative distinction, to von Mises and his adepts, who equate it with the free market, to the religious minded, who equate it with belief in a God-centered universe, to Ayn Rand and a rampant materialism, atheism, and success in the capitalist marketplace, to Clinton Rossiter, who sees the liberal as the most optimistic of the pessimists and the conservative as the most pessimistic of the optimists, etc. Kendall moves swiftly to show the weakness in each of these proposed definitions. How does belief in a God-centered universe account for Sidney Hook now among the staunchest of anticommunists? And so on down the line. On one thing, however, the witnesses generally presuppose a line of division between the liberal position and the conservative. "*The Nation*" is a Liberal magazine, the "*National Review*" is a conservative magazine. Senator Humphrey is recognizably a liberal, Senator Byrd a conservative. So there is a line connecting the individual positions, and it is a line of battle, of political warfare in which it is essential to draw it correctly and bring in intelligence reports on a war in progress. Kendall's solution is to draw the line with precision by turn tabling the question before the house.

The question correctly put is "what do the liberals want? And what is their program for getting it?" When framed in these terms we see right away that the various liberal positions are parts of an interconnected whole which forms "the liberal revolution" in both of two senses of the word, namely the Industrial Revolution and the French Revolution. Give the liberals their way and the United states would no longer be the republic the framers intended as shown by the Federalist Papers. What the liberals want is an egalitarian, multicultural, statist society run in the form of a plebiscitary democracy. What we face, therefore, is liberal revolution and conservative resistance, liberal negation of what America stands for and conservative affirmation of its virtue and success. One example is immigration traditionally based on a quota system. The quota system has been abolished. But immigration policy still follows something like the quota lines with Anglo-Saxons favored over Albanians. Another is tax policy with liberals favoring progressively higher taxes in a soak-the-rich program. But when the bill becomes law you will find that the loopholes are still there. Americans, writes Kendall, want the right to get "smacking rich." Or take the TVA modeled as the precursor to a series of such authorities. The liberals got their TVA in the give and take of politics in the rough and ready. But the notion of a series of such authorities replacing private capital was stopped dead in its tracks. Nor is there anything so dead, Kendall writes, as the idea of socialism in America.[14]

This turning of the tables marks the decisive point in the development of the Socratic style which became the hallmark of Kendall as a critic. To recapitulate for a moment: It begins with a clean cut between ethics and politics. The ethical is the domain in which the community develops its standard of validity. The political is the domain in which it is applied via the process of decision making of which the majority principle (as distinct from unanimity) is one example. The former, choice of an ethical standard, is as value laden as the latter, choice as a method of decision making, is value neutral. If C.E.M. Joad tells us this to abandon the problem to the "irrational," then Kendall's first answer is that it is always wise to know where the "rational" leaves off and the "irrational" begins. The later Kendall was to refine this position. While the choice of a method of decision-making is value neutral, the domain of the moral is the domain which is conservative of character to make us what we are. Liberals and conservatives are both Americans. But the eastern seaboard liberal is a different kind of American from the American from the heartland or from the South like Idabel, Oklahoma from which Kendall came, to Yale and the Eastern seaboard.

Here, then, is the answer to Bambrough and the liberal contention that knowledge, if it is to be counted as knowledge, must be reducible to *a techné* capable of instruction as passed on by the shoemaker, builder, etc. Nonsense, Kendall would say, for the two types of knowledge are radically different. Men and women are both human beings. But they are beings of a different sort with different perspectives leading to different choices in the moral world of the family and society. Each makes a choice, and the choice is necessarily subjective and made within a horizon. But the two horizons are not the same, and this leads to the war of the sexes.

The imperative which flows from this is the demand that you must take sides if you are not the village idiot. The sides are drawn up for you by the realities of American politics in the mid-twentieth century. The tension between the two sides makes the dynamics of American politics in the state and local as on the presidential level. The claims made are often very different, sometimes even diametrically opposed. The result is Executive-Legislative tension in a conflict in which you must assess the comparative validity of the claims of each side. This assessment forms the theme of "The Two Majorities in American Politics,"[15] the second of Kendall's two finest works as a political theorist to which we now invite your attention.

Form and substance, substance and form: Kendall's next contribution is his study of "The Two Majorities in American Politics"[16] with which we are plunged into the center of the left–right clash in the fifties and sixties. The conventional critic is likely to fix attention on the content, which is conservative in the extreme. But it is more interesting, I suggest, to fix attention on the form which is original and in the tradition of Socratic investigation. He opens with a problem little noticed in the literature, the problem of legislative-executive tension. Executive-legislative tension is a symptom on the surface of our politics. But why does it continue year after year, and what, way down deep, does it signify? This is the Socratic question, the "What is X?" question for which Socrates was famous. The next step is to lay out a series of issues on which the two sides take consistently different positions, and the lines are drawn.

The issues generating the tension are clearly these:

1. Internal security: a lax executive authority and the need of close Congressional oversight in the drafting of legislation.
2. The pork barrel practice of congressmen versus the welfare of the whole.
3. Protectionism and tariffs versus the doctrine of free trade.
4. Foreign aid versus a greater reliance on the military might of the US.
5. The national debt and it's size: the Keynesian view and its precursor.
6. Immigration policy: a functioning quota system or open immigration.
7. A bullish view of air power versus boots on the ground.

8. A general nationalistic outlook versus the family of man and the prospects for a world community.
9. A willingness to ally oneself with right wing dictatorships versus a polity designed to keep Franco and the Dominican Republic at bay.
10. The drive toward a plebiscitary political system revolting around the presidential election versus the Congressional government of the Framers.
11. A reform of the party system and abolition of the filibuster and seniority principle. And the continuing conflict over civil rights.

Kendall frames the conflict fairly, with care and precision. But the interesting point is the cast that he always frames it from the liberal side as the best liberal spokesman would see it. The liberal features above form the counterposition. And Socratic investigation all comes in two parts. The first is a value-neutral analysis flowing from the question framing the problem on the level of the *doxa* or common sense. The second is value oriented and frames the solution offered but now on the level of the *logos* or moral understanding projected on the level of deep theory or what we call moral philosophy.

These four constituent elements (the problem, the question, the critical analysis, and the counter position) constitute the framework of all genuine Socratic investigation. The problem, first appearing on the surface of things is one which all sides will agree is a problem forming a common universe of discourse. The question is framed to investigate the deep roots of the problem beyond the symptomatology of understanding on the level of *doxa*. The textual analysis is designed to confront the best statement of the counterposition available in the literature. The position defended is generally left in broad outline form as something for the critics to think about more deeply in a step or two toward the *logos*. By contrast with the traditional approach in the style of the lecture, Socratic education is characteristically problem-posing education. No problem, no Socratic investigation either by the master or by the pupil. And Kendall's execution of this classic method accounts for his status as a political theorist of rank, some would say the first rank, in the annals of American political theory.

Now the point to note about the first three elements is the fact that they are all value neutral. The problem is recognized by all as a problem. The question is phrased to get to the heart of the problem. But when we come to the critical or textual analysis we see right away that it is at one and the same time value neutral in execution and value oriented in approach. For only this latter makes it genuine political theory and not sociology or narrative political history. Kendall's restatements of the McCloskey or liberal position are an early and fine exposition from the conservative perspective. The critical analysis of Dahl's celebrated Walgreen lectures, takes this one step further.[17] In the choice of Dahl, Kendall is once more selecting the best on the opposing side or counterposition. The problem is the continued existence of executive-legislative tension and the search for its deeper meaning and significance.

The answer formulated in *The Two Majorities* is most interesting from the perspective of method. In terms of method Kendall always proceeds from the concrete to the abstract, the particular to the general. In this respect as in others he differs widely from Strauss whom he regarded as his first and greatest teacher since his student days. The problem of executive-legislative tension arises typically with the executive wanting to do something and facing Congressional resistance. In this tug of war Kendall sees conservative victories where others all see conservative defeats. To clarify their optical illusion Kendall proposes two simple questions: Whether to have something and if so, how much? What, then, were the concrete issues laid out in the form of a series, and how does his pair of questions prove Congressional victory where others have seen only defeat? He then turns to Dahl's Walgreen lectures as a paradigmatic statement from the best on the opposite side. And, finally, he closes with Rousseau and his band of Swiss peasants engaged in dialogue under an oak tree as a metaphor helpful in assessing the quality of discussion in the two sides, liberal and conservative, in the course of the electoral process. This is noteworthy as Kendall's case made in terms of Socratic technique to be perfected in the chapter on McCarthyism.

The issues dividing the American people run as follows:

1. Should we have an open or "relatively" closed society?
2. Should we drive toward an egalitarian society with an ethic of redistribution or a capitalist society with high income differentials?
3. Should we press on toward the welfare state with expanded regulation by the government or retain the capitalist society of the Framers?
4. Should our form of government be shaped progressively by the ideology of progressivism issuing from the academy or remain staunchly conservative?
5. The executive is (in principle) for world government and the outlawing of war. The Congress is firmly nationalist and not averse to the use of force.

6. The executive looks to the brotherhood of man and its policies are oriented toward the weak and lowly, etc. Not so the Congress.
7. The liberals favor absolute freedom of thought and speech. Conservatives and Congress favor certain clear restrictions on both. Liberals favor science, the scientific outlook, and the expertise flowing from it. In Congress, meetings in both houses begin with a prayer.
8. Civil Rights: The executive is prepared to extend full civil rights across the states under the authority of the Fourteenth Amendment. Congress believes the Tenth Amendment still stands and protects the states in the differential application of civil rights to "differently situated people." In these and all such matters the President has the nation's professors, pundits, moralizers, and the press behind him. So if he appears to embody knowledge, unselfishness, and high principle, it follows that Congress embodies selfishness and bigotry, low principle or no principle at all. In that case there is nothing to be said, and the debate is closed. But the urgent task, Kendall argues, is to reopen the discussion in mutual respect and good faith and the belief that there is something to be learned by attending to the space for both sides, Congressional and well as Presidential.

On the level of method the next step is of critical significance. First off, Kendall redefines the issue now in more fundamental terms. He then restates the liberal-conservative conflict now in terms of the *basic* dividing of two sides. The issue restated is this: How is it that we as a people regularly send to the White House a president pledged to do certain things and, at one and the same, send to the Hill a group of men pledged to short circuit the program in part or as a whole? Here we have the unexplained mystery underlying executive-legislative tension in Washington politics. And until we resolve it we no more understand ourselves as a people than a *schizophrenic* understands himself as a man. He then reframes the nine or so issues as encountered in the political marketplace in terms of a couple of basic issues on which the two sides are radically divided. The first of the two is the question of "the open society": Do we want an open society or a closed or partly closed society? And, second, as to the form of government: Do we want a plebiscitary democracy ruled by a President armed with a majority mandate or a Republican form of government vesting sovereignty in the people via their duly elected representatives in Congress? Kendall's answer takes two forms which blend into one. And here it is:

The Republican form of government with sovereign power vested in Congress is the form defended in the Federalist Papers, the Constitution, and the Bill of Rights. It is the authentic American political tradition making for a deliberative assembly with no room for mandates arising out of temporary popular majorities. The solution to our mystery lies in the fact that there are in fact two majorities, two numerically distinct majorities: one representing Congress and the other representing the President. And the problem for American political theory is to assess the relative merits of the two majorities and not act as if one of them did not exist, as Dahl does throughout his book. The Presidency with its ever more sweeping powers is a later development "engrafted" on the system. Give it its full head of steam and it cannot but end by destroying the system as designed by the Framers. More: the essence of liberal politics is the sustained drive toward the open society in which all opinions, no matter how evil some may be, are tolerated. But this is an impossibility and Mill's attempt to prove it is bad political theory. Kendall's study of McCarthyism reopens the case for the closed society in the persecution of the communists. And his critique of Mill which forms the center of the book is the case for the consensual as opposed to the fully open society. When men come together to form a society, writes Kendall, they always do so in terms of a consensus to be developed and expanded over time. And they will not lightly set it aside to accommodate the opposite or heretical view. And the articulation of this process forms the substance of the analysis of McCarthyism which is the most remarkable of the many studies published on the phenomenon.

But the discussion to which Kendall invites us can as readily be framed from the opposite direction. The ambiguity is in the term "engrafted." Substitute the term "developed" and the argument reads very differently. All later developments can be seen as "engrafted" as the system searches for new ways and means to deal with a changing and vastly different world. How do the merits of the two majorities shape up in reviewing domestic and foreign policy from the New Deal to Kennedy and the Cuban missile crisis? The New Deal was only partially successful in addressing the problem of unemployment and underproduction. But in the broad it displayed imagination and initiative in the creation of government agencies to review the problems of the nations as a whole from social security on up. The New Deal breathed a new spirit and the President was reelected three times. The problems of the infrastructure (highways, roads, bridges, etc.) can only be conceived as a whole to be addressed in the Presidential program and not District by District. The District by District approach is eminently suitable for the rendering of constituent services to business. But the big problems of the infrastructure, particularly education, cannot be handled on that basis. On the grand questions of foreign policy such as policy toward China, Europe, and the Soviet Union, the conservative view was wrong and the liberal view proved to be successful. The conservative view was articulated by Congress members Mundt of South Dakota and others on the Foreign Relations Committee. And Kendall can speak of Chiang "pawing the ground in Formosa." But Chiang was by then in desperate straits and protected by the US Navy. Shortly thereafter he stopped pawing the ground and started pushing up the daisies. But China has evolved and the days of the Communist autocracy would appear to be numbered, and a world war fought in China was averted. And Marshall's dictum "the wrong enemy in the wrong place at the wrong time" was profoundly right.

Were the US to become fully engaged in a war in China there would be nothing to stop the Red Army from sweeping to Paris. Instead, the President and his liberal advisors formulated the Marshall Plan, formed NATO, and announced the Truman Doctrine protecting Greece and stabilizing the European economy, and the rest is history. And this history continued to Kennedy and the Cuban missile crisis and finally to the implosion of the Soviet Union and the end of the Cold War. But the most striking case which Kendall, the gifted exponent of Socratic teaching, fails to notice is the case of education in which the President viewing the problems of the nation as a whole proposed a National Science Foundation whose team of educators were to develop the methods and techniques of Socratic or discovery teaching for schools across the nation with a special focus on minority education. From the conservative side, by contrast, we had nothing except for the empty rhetoric of A *Nation at Risk* some years later.

The most fascinating aspect of Kendall's study of McCarthyism is its presentation in purely Socratic terms. Kendall is unique among conservatives as a theorist who comes to the table from the Socratic side, developed in his Oxford days under Collingwood. He begins with a well-known fact agreed to by all to establish a common universe of discourse. In the clash on McCarthyism both sides got boiling mad and stayed angry till the dispute was resolved. Such tension is rare in American politics. American politics in normally a low-key politics. Only thrice before have we experienced such high tension. The first was the issue of loyalism. The second was on the alien and sedition acts. And the third was on the issue of slavery. Since then, namely for a hundred years, we have enjoyed a form of low-key politics. And the question arises: What was everyone so mad about?

Kendall next proposes three commonly held opinions, held at the level of the *doxoi*, and proceeds to show their merely partial truth or falsity. What then are the tests which a fuller and more complete explanation needs to meet if it is to serve as a solution to the riddle implicit in our question? Kendall formulates the tests for a correct solution in a brief section and, finally, proceeds to offer his solution. The three answers taken together form the counterposition encountered in the marketplace of political controversy. And Kendall is careful to present them precisely as their protagonists see them. This is the "objective" or value-neutral dimension of the critique to follow. Answer One is the simplest of the three and readily disposed of. According to Answer One the problem was Joe McCarthy himself. He was rude and crude, overbearing, and intimidated witnesses. He invited government employees to break rank and spill confidential material to him directly. He brandished a fake list of alleged suspects in the State Department, produced no legislation, and was a demagogue. He was a hater and a poison in the system which had to get rid of him and did so after the Army-McCarthy hearings.

Kendall does not concede the point but enters a demurrer. The facts even if correct do not prove the case they were intended to. McCarthyism, the phenomenon under analysis, preceded McCarthy by some half dozen years before the Wheeling, West Virginia Speech. In terms of actual history we should understand that the movement produced McCarthy, and not McCarthy the movement for all that it took his name. Remember the Hatch Act, the Smith Act, and the McCarren Rider. Conservative America was entering the business of proscribing communism as an un-American activity long before the Senator stepped on the stage in 1952. Answer One is, therefore, bad history and worse political theory.

Answer Two fixes attention on the spread of world communism and the challenge of Soviet power. With Soviet control of Eastern Europe and the sweep of Mao's armies across the land, Congress and the American people had every reason to feel threatened. The Korean War continued to develop, now with the infusion of a hundred thousand crack Chinese soldiers. Soon there would be talk of socialist encirclement. In a word, the issue was world communism now spreading like a prairie fire. And once more Kendall is careful to state the case from the opposite side. Answer Two is clearly a deeper and better answer than Answer One and we are tempted to accept it as final and return to the day's work. But here Kendall enters a word of caution. Answer Two frames the issue as one of foreign policy. And Americans do not as a rule get all that mad about an issue in foreign policy. Remember our question:

What were people so mad about? Why did the liberals consider the McCarthyites to be so hateful and such bad people? And the issue could not be one merely in foreign policy. In brief, the issue is not one of an error in policy and the stupidity that underlies it. It must be one that goes beyond intellectual error to the roots of our being as moral subjects and the charter of liberty that informs our lives and traditions as a people. The issue, in other words, must be one that we can grasp with hooks in a policy dispute. Consider the fervor on both sides in the Hiss-Chambers case and the galaxy of eminent Hiss supporters in the two trials. Answer Two is superficial and fundamentally misleading because it directs our attention to the mind, the intellect, and not to the moral subjectivity that makes us who we are in the liberal-conservative war in culture. To reach the issue we must go beyond cerebration and words. Yet it must be capable of being stated in words. Kendall believes he knows what it is and can state it in words. But only after presenting Answer Three.

Answer Three frames the issue in Constitutional terms as one involving the separation of powers in Federal union. Congress and the McCarthyites were clearly and all too often invading the domain and prerogatives of the executive. And this without proper Court trials with respect for the rights, especially the First Amendment right of the witnesses so that their rights could be ensured. Once again, the issue can be symmetrically stated beginning with the liberal side. And once again the issue as stated is too legalistic, too formal and technical to arouse the anger it evidently did on both sides. The only correct answer which meets the tests of validity laid out is that the fundamental issue raised by organized communism is the issue of heresy rising up in our midst to undermine the American consensus, tradition, and way of life. To this the liberals with their views of relativism and moral skepticism, and the open society to which it leads, have no answer. Hence the war between them which is ultimately the war between the open society and a society closed to Communist thought and belief, and to the curtailment of freedom of thought, and not simply the curtailment of speech as protected by the First Amendment. McCarthyism was a heresy hunt and make no mistake about that. It slammed the door shut with no nonsense about John Stuart Mill and the fantasy of the open society.

The Kendall view of the nature of communism was not without precedent in high places. Back in 1970 Winston Churchill voiced the desire "to strangle the Bolshevik monster in its cradle," and the British sent an invading army to overthrow the new regime. But the problematic character of the position as a whole emerges most clearly in the context of contrasting arguments. In the Introduction to his translation of Alfredo Rossi's *A Communist Party in Action*,[18] he dramatizes the armed threat posed by the Red Army and is sharply critical of economism and Marshall Plan thinking. Indeed, Kendall argues, the possibility of its success, however modest, might itself prompt the command for the Red Army to march to Paris. The refutation of this entire outlook came from a most unlikely source, the Soviet leader himself. In his "Secret Speech" of 1956 Nikita Khrushchev spelled out "The Crimes of the Stalin Era" and a hitherto expanding world communism began a process of systematic disintegration. Kendall's vision was a precise inversion of the shape of things to come from Khrushchev to Gorbachev and the final collapse of the system. All that remained to haunt Europe was a specter. And the same was true of the United States where the Communist Party dissolved itself and put the heresy hunter out of business. In fact, when we read the minutes of the House hearings on Alger Hiss, the Ware Group, the Perlo Group, and the Silvermaster Group there is no suggestion of a heresy hunt. Even the most conservative Congressman such as Herbert spoke of loyalty and subversion, placing communists in high places in government, and ultimately of espionage. Henry Collins, Lee Pressman, and others had been open about their beliefs all through the thirties and forties. And Alger Hiss would never have been convinced were it not for "the immutable documents" there to convict him of perjury and espionage. But Kendall, now a convert to Roman Catholicism, presses on to the charge of heresy to explain why people got all that mad.

This extreme quality in Kendall the logician mars his analysis of the Socrates trial.[19] The charges of atheism and of corrupting the youth were clearly charges of heresy *avant la lettre* and before the Church. But the witness for the prosecution argues the case on grounds of consensus destruction and not heresy. Socrates was seventy, and typically argued with people one at a time. This was a necessary feature of his teaching since his discussion was philosophical, often concerned with abstract technical considerations. He had no mass following and was anything but a demagogue. And the charges were patently false. Philosophy, as Socrates practiced it, can enable the youth. It can never corrupt it. Yet Kendall sees a danger to the status quo in the undermining of the consensus and proceeds to brand Socrates "a revolutionary agitator," thereby deserving the penalty of death. Anything less, we suppose, would lead to the threat of a relatively open society and the prospects of inevitable disintegration of the political community. In premodern classical political philosophy politics presides over ethics, and the laws preside over Socrates.

The singular quality of Kendall as a theorist of consensus emerges when the Socrates case is read in the light of McCarthyism. For we now see how the charge of heresy is blended with that of the "revolutionary agitator" bent on the destruction of the consensus. The intimate blend of the two charges is revealed most fully in his debate with Mulford Sibley. The debate was billed as "War and the Use of Force: Moral or Immoral, Christian or Unchristian," and packed the large Dinkelspiel auditorium at Stanford. Kendall was at his sizzling best in the polemic and opened with a couplet defining the two moral terms:

> "Pale Ebenezer thought it wrong to fight
> But Roaring Bill who killed him thought it right."

Sibley was a tall, somewhat pale figure of a man. And there is no doubt who Roaring Bill might be. In a dazzling display of erudition Kendall presented the Christian tradition developed in the Middle Ages and the theory of the just war in St. Thomas and others. This was the tradition in its concrete reality and Sibley had betrayed it. And with this Kendall turned to an attack on Sibley himself. "Heretic, barbarian, parasite," this was the profane trinity defining Sibley, the paradigm of the pacifist, socialist and humanitarian side. Heretic, barbarian, parasite, and we all know what we should do with parasites.

But the most singular quality in Kendall as a theorist was the inverted quality of the fundamental vision and the policy recommendations flowing from it. His retrodiction of the past was always perfect. But the future always turned out to be the precise opposite from anything we had been led to expect. This was the weak side of his argument. But it also concealed a dangerous side in foreign policy. As mentioned above, the ink had barely dried on his Introduction to Alfredo Rossi's *A Communist Party in Action* when the process of destalinization began to pave the road toward the elimination of the Soviet threat. Much the same inversion would manifest itself with the election of Ronald Reagan a dozen years later, and continue with the election of George W. Bush, and now Donald Trump. Readers of "The Two Majorities" will recall the fact that the Kendall theory predicted a liberal President, be he a Democrat or a Republican. According to the theory a liberal presidency was built into the electoral system and structure of campaign for the office. Instead we have had three conservative Presidents and several liberal Congresses. So the charge of quixotism built into a liberal Presidency and requiring a healthy dose of Sancho Panza from a conservative Congress would have to be scrapped along with a policy of rollback for Eastern Europe with the probability of nuclear war with the Soviet Union.

As revealed in the Introduction, Kendall's method was to postulate an adversary, a counter Kendall, as smart, ruthless, and reckless as himself and make his countermoves with this adversary in mind. But the Soviet hierarchy from Khrushchev to Brezhnev and Gorbachev contained no such player in the highest offices in the Party, and we were spared a nuclear conflict of worldwide dimensions. His method involved the same fine analysis, some would call it hair splitting, of language. To Albert Schweitzer's use of the term "intolerable" in referring to the consequences of nuclear war, Kendall counters with "intolerable" or merely highly "undesirable." And the answer is not merely intolerable but also proven to be unnecessary. So, too, is his case for a sharply increased tightening in a (relatively) close political system even as American society continued to open the channels of communication in every direction from D.H. Lawrence to Playboy and the variety of radical opinions in books and magazines and heard on the air. Is there a danger in the extreme dispersion of opinions and feelings? Perhaps there is. And it is to this that we now turn in Kendall's critique of Mill and the open society.

"The Fallacy of the Open Society"[20] is the finest piece of work in the Kendall repertoire. Indeed, it could readily be ranked among the six finest articles to be published in an American journal of scholarship. In terms of method it develops as a paradigm of Socratic investigation. It is a masterpiece of "problem-posing education." The problem, the counterposition, the paradigmatic adversary, the critical question, and the counterarguments flowing from it, and the challenging solution now at the level of the *logos*, are all there in perfect and symmetrical order. It remains only for the listener or reader to choose. In their fundamentals the issues are the same with Protagorean relativism, subjectivism, and moral skepticism as the main issues on a stage in which man is the measure of all things that are. In their play Kendall washed away "the acids of skepticism" to affirm the ontological reality of moral morns with Plato as a witness and God as the measure of all things that are that they are, and of all things that are not that they are not. With this and only with this can nihilism and the void be banished as that most unwelcome guest now knocking at the door.

Kendall frames the issue in bipolar terms with the American conservative confronting the liberal. In other words, the culture clash is within the borders of modernity, concretely on the stage built by that most modern of modern nations formed as the United States of America with the Federalist Papers as its new testament and charter of liberty. But, in fact, there was a third guest at the table in the form of Leo Strauss branding the Federalist Papers as carrying "the evil teaching" of Machiavelli across the Atlantic. And Strauss' students kept their distance from Kendall and the *National Review*. Much the same is true of Voegelin and his followers none of whom ever contributed to the *National Review*. If Strauss represents the classical city and pagan philosophy, then Voegelin may be said to represent Catholic culture and the articulation of the Word in Thomas and medieval philosophy. The Church has long been critical of capitalism and modern culture. Much of its work has been oriented toward the poor and suffering. It has been a conscience warning the multimillionaires that it is easier for a camel to pass through the eye of a needle than for a rich man to enter the kingdom of heaven. Natural law teaching condemned usury or the charging of high interest rates without which the lines of credit for capitalist expansion would have been completely unavailable. In the eyes of the Church the issue of credit (and the credit card) is at bottom a moral issue in sharp tension with the Christian way of life.

Kendall blends the two traditions, ancient and modern, with his thesis of "We the (Virtuous) People." But the two traditions, premodern and modern, stand in sharp conflict with one another and Strauss is right (or at least consistent) in drawing attention to the revolutionary significance of the social contract in Hobbes, Locke, and Rousseau. So, too, is Voegelin profoundly correct in drawing the line at the Enlightenment and the heritage of modern culture which he brands as spiritually all but dead.

But, one might say, these are disputes at the peak of culture and the pinnacle of high scholarship. What has any of this to do with the culture clash as experience by the literate public and the populace at large? This is a good sharp question and merits a good sharp reply which I should like to make as follows. Few have read Voegelin (and his reference to Cardinal De Lubac and Church doctrine) but everyone has read *The Godfather* with its many references to prayer and Catholic culture. And the message is remarkably the same in broad outline. Puzo presents a critique, nay, an indictment of a people and a society steeped in vice, in exploitation and sexual corruption which we still read about today with movie moguls and porn queens. Nothing has changed and nothing will. But I reserve an excursus for my concluding statement and return to Kendall and the critique of the open society.

Mankind should be reminded, Mill tells us, "that there was once a man named Socrates." Quite so, replies Kendall, and it should also be reminded that there was once a man named Plato who set out the story of his master's trial in two famous dialogues. Kendall supplements his Mill critique with a study of them in "The People Versus Socrates Revisited" and followed this up with an analysis of "Cicero and the Politics of Public Orthodoxy," reprinted in *Contra Mundum*.[21] So the lines are drawn between Mill, the paradigmatic liberal, and Kendall, the paradigmatic conservative. But the issue of the Socrates trial is more than that. The clue to its subtlety lies in the fact that in a sense the legal correctness of the procedure could stand beyond challenge. Politically, writes R.H.S. Crossman at the close of *Plato Today*, the guilt of Socrates was proved to the hilt. And Crossman was a liberal and labor MP! How is it that a liberal Professor of Plato Studies could join a conservative on this decisive point? The answer lies in the choice of the second of Kendall's two corroborative studies, namely the study of "Cicero and the Politics of the Public Orthodoxy." Notice that this, too, is a classical or premodern study and the pieces fall into place. The underlying issue which gives the Socrates' case its subtlety is the radical difference between the modern and the premodern world on ethics and politics and their relationship to one another. From Rome to Greece the premodern mind saw ethics as radically subordinate to politics and the public orthodoxy. The modern mind can hardly conceive of this and sees ethics as an independent and autonomous sphere to which political decisions must be referred to gauge their justice or injustice. A twentieth-century parallel might be the case of Sacco and Vanzetti who were probably innocent, but sentenced to death in the fear and hysteria of the time after due process of law. In the Mill critique as in "McCarthyism" Kendall's genius is to unite the premodern and the modern and to apply the ethics of the former to the politics of the latter via the ambiguous case of his master Jean-Jacques Rousseau. Socrates himself had no doubt of his innocence and referred to his accusers as "you who are my murderers." But he also had no doubt of the hierarchical relationship between himself and the laws of the city, and their right to pass final judgment. The laws had the right to pass final judgment and he had the duty to obey even if the content of the judgment was wrong. The charge goes to the root of things political because the charge of atheism is in effect the charge of heresy *avant la lettre*. And this the majority could not abide for such is the politics of the public orthodoxy. But meanwhile, on to Kendall's critique.

The Rousseau connection emerges at the outset of the critique and shaped the point of its concluding and most salient point of attack. Every society is founded on a consensus, a body of shared belief which defines it and makes it what it is, and which it will not lightly set aside in response to this or that critic who questions it. Mill misunderstands the very nature of society which is anything but an Oxford debating club. The idea of an open society, a society without a consensus, a public truth to hold it together, is a contradiction in terms. Its inner emptiness marks the nihilism to which skepticism and relativism, to the extent to which it is put into practice in the schools and channels of communication, must ineluctably lead.

Mills likewise mistakes the nature of man who is not likely to stand idly by while he sees his most sacred truths desecrated as with, shall we say, the crucifix plunged in a bowl of urine. Truth is, of course, a value, and the freedom to pursue it is likewise a value and perhaps a very high one. But it is one and only one of many values which society is pledged to pursue. But when elevated to the rank of the highest and final value, the absolute value, it loses its quality as a value and becomes society's ultimate principle of order to which all else must be subordinated. And this leads to bedlam or an incoherence at the heart of things.

The Swiss connection now emerges more fully in the figure of Rousseau to dominate the remainder of the discussion. A fine passage is quoted from *The Social Contract* and supplemented with reference to *The Government of Poland*, *The Discourse on the Arts and Sciences*, and the well-known *Letter to Mirabeau*. The contrast drawn by Rousseau and Kendall alike is between the healthy functioning of a political system with a tight well-knit body of public truth and one sick with a *dissesus*, a conflict of values, at the heart of things. The whole stock of Rousseau's wisdom about things political, says Jouvenel in another quote, lies in his contrast of the one with that in which the dispersal of feelings and opinions has proceeded a pace. It was for this reason that Rousseau had reservations about the development of the arts and the sciences and, though a Protestant himself, about the introduction and spread of Protestantism in France. But the very structure of the open society makes precisely this dispersal of feelings inevitable in matters of political opinion at the fundamental level. Feelings and opinions are two sides of the same coin. And, as in Weimar Germany, their progressive discussion makes democratic government impossible. The open society confers freedom on all its members at the cost of its own freedom as a society. This is Kendall's case for the contradiction at the heart of liberal theory and practice.

Kendall's case is presented as a tightly reasoned logical argument immune to criticism from the outside. This was very much the form in which he made the case for "a more vigorous policy toward the Soviet Union" of rollback, liberation, and victory before the Kremlin felt impelled to order the march of the Red Army to Paris. His analysis was based on the immediate past with the fall of Eastern Europe, China, and Vietnam. But the immediate future and final collapse of the Soviet Union proved to be the exact opposite. This inversion, readily seen in a comparison with historical reality as it unfolded in the future, points to some singular features and flaws in the overall analysis.

Strauss and Voegelin agree that the United States has evolved into a mass society. Strauss uses the phrase "mass democracy" more than once. And Voegelin speaks of a man who can say that he spent his life making a particular piece of Grand Rapids furniture. Kendall is alone in portraying the populace in the mid-twentieth century as the community of virtuous people and not the lonely crowd of liberal theory. The fundamental virtue of the American regime from the days of the Federalists to his boyhood days in Idabel, Oklahoma, is critical to his theory. The destruction of the indigenous culture of the Indian Tribes and the practice of slavery are never confronted. Nor are the appalling facts of segregation in the Southern schools and the conditions of life of the Negro people - for a century before since the Civil War. In fact, Kendall spent his last days on a series of lectures called the Vanderbilt lectures developing a critique of Lincoln (and his legacy) as constituting a derailment from the American tradition as it developed from the Mayflower Compact on down.[22]

His method was to favor the most vigorous internal critique of a model set up as an ideal type. But if things changed, as they always seemed to, he would change the basic assumptions or point to some built-in disclaimers which he liked to call "verbal parachutes." So in "The Majority Principle and the Scientific Elite"[23] he favored a complete relativism in policy-making by the majority. In his later, more mature writings, he saw this as part of the liberal line and championed absolutism in morals and Christianity in religion. In the "Prolegomena to Any Future Work on Majority Rule"[24] he tells us that democracy would be "a fraud and a racket" if it did not let the other side (the socialists or communists) have their way with the statute books on winning a free and fair election. In "McCarthyism"[25] and other writings he would make this impossible with a series of sanctions amounting to the persecution of the counter consensus. In one article he confidently predicts "the coming of Constitutional Crisis" but when the coming constitutional crisis did not come he points to his "verbal parachutes."

In "McCarthyism"[26] he tells us why the liberal answers are wrong and why the real issue is heresy and not the clear and present danger test of liberal rulings. And if this is not seen, why next time around folks might get a whole lot madder. But with the demise of the Soviet Union (and the dissolution of the Communist Party) there has been no next time and people have not gotten a whole lot madder. In "What Is Conservatism?" and again in "The Two Majorities" he tells us that there is nothing so dead as socialism in America. But the rousing response to Bernie Sanders in the primaries including the fifty million raised in small donations tells a different and indeed opposite story.

Summing Up

On the level of method the key move Kendall makes is to transform a teaching in "pure" political theory into one in "empirical" political theory where it can be tested against the facts. Do this (A, B, and C), Mill tells us, and you will get that (X, Y, and Z). Now is this in fact true, Kendall asks, as a matter of rational political expectation?

His answer as we have seen, is a round NO. The press toward an open society must "ineluctably" lead to progressive disintegration and eventual collapse. But it has not done so in the century or more after Mill wrote those words. In the second part of the argument a critic will want to test Kendall's teaching by the same empirical test. Did the spread of world communism continue unabated? No, it did not. The international movement soon broke up, first with Tito in Yugoslavia and then with Mao in China, and with de-Stalinization in Eastern Europe, the disintegration became unstoppable. Did the Soviet Union make any move toward Paris with the Red Army? No again. In fact, the Eastern European satellite states regained their independence and in time East Germany joined the West in a united German republic.

The same pattern of inversion is revealed on the domestic scene. The United States began as a relatively more closed republic with slavery and the restrictions of the vote. But as it developed and expanded it developed in the direction of a relatively more open society. The right to vote was extended to Black people and to women, etc. "Separate but equal" gave way to school integration albeit with dismally low standards of funding, staffing, and performance. In his review of David Spitz's *Democracy and the Challenge to Power*[27] Kendall answers the question "Which God?" i.e., which tradition, with the answer, the God whose name is Yahweh and so forth down the line and in "Whom we trust" as inscribed on the nation's coinage. But with a progressively more multicultural society Spitz's question still stands. And the increasing secularization of society makes Kendall's reply increasingly irrelevant. More irrelevant yet is his demand for a heresy hunt as the fundamental solution to the crisis in consensus. Next time, he warned, people will get a whole lot madder. But there has been no next time and people are not madder or even much concerned about what is by now only a specter from the past. We see the same inversion on all major and most predictions. The structure of Presidential elections which ensured a liberal president proceeded to give us three conservative presidents and some quite liberal Congresses. The liberal-conservative split has remained at something like fifty-fifty, with liberal candidate Clinton ahead in the popular vote and Trump ahead in the vote in the Electoral College. And the two together constitute the consensus with weights on very different sides of the political equation from Trump to Bernie Sanders. And this places the problem of consensus in a very different light.

As Kendall well knew (and knew better than most) consensus, like the temperature, comes in various degrees. In a high consensus society like Britain it can be increasingly open and not merely tolerant but even hospitable to radically different ideas. In a relatively low consensus society like the United States it is likely to fear dissent like the boogie of anarchism in the Sacco-Vanzetti case and communism in the Sweezy case. Britain was wise enough to provide a Hyde Park for open dissent to the point of idiosyncrasy and open the doors of the University to such fine scholars as Charles Taylor and C.B. Macpherson etc., etc. and our culture has only been the richer for it. In the US, we had the case Sweezy versus New Hampshire, with no University, not even Berkeley, opening its doors to a first-rate economic historian and economist. Kendall would brand this as outlaw and shut the doors ever tighter in the name of the consensus. But the healthier the consensus the more it can tolerate and even welcome the scholar with radically different opinions. Consensus we must have, else society is impossible. But the answer to a heresy hunt is the building of a deeper and higher consensus in which the evils and injustices of the past are frankly admitted and not forever rationalized from "The People Versus Socrates Revisited" on down to their recrudescence in the form of McCarthyism. And this is the task of education beginning with the family and community and going on to the schools, colleges, and Universities, and the entire publishing and communications network. The Kendall paradigm is one example of an inversion that made this impossible via its influence on conservative thought prominently including Buckley and Bozell, Kendall and Burnham. In like fashion, I contend, Socratic teaching, developed as a craft of teaching in which the student is "the discoverer of new truths," is the most effective alternative to the traditional mode in the rebuilding of culture in the schools and community. Kendall's contribution to this form of investigation is his most distinctive gift to scholarship precisely as his flair for it made him the finest classroom teacher I have ever seen in four different universities. When the value-oriented part is placed in parentheses the value-neutral critique of the counterposition remains as a permanent contribution to method in analysis from Gramsci and Freire on the left, Kendall on the right, with Bruner and associates showing how it can be done in mathematics and science. And this is the innermost connection between my first lines in my first chapter and these last with which I close the text.

It was somewhat by accident that I met James P. Burnham who follows the Big Three in the development of the conservative critique. The phone rang late one morning and a stranger mentioned that Burnham would be visiting Berkeley the next day and would I care to act as his host for the visit. I readily agreed and we met at Cruchon's off Telegraph Avenue for lunch and a stroll through the campus. Burnham was a tall, well-groomed gentleman, with a courteous and extremely polite manner. His conversation was fluent and easy but tinged with an air of the supercilious verging on the haughty. I questioned him about some of his interesting colleagues at *National Review* like Whittaker Chambers, Russell Kirk, Frank Meyer, and Willmoore Kendall, but he did not seem inclined to talk much about them so I let the matter drop. He was more interested in talking about Berkeley and the wave of liberalism that had produced the Free Speech Movement. He saw the hand of the Faculty in this turn to the left and wondered how they divided in the liberal-conservative split. I said that the faculty in the professional fields was rather conservative but tended more toward the center and the left in the liberal arts. In that case, he said, why not abolish the liberal arts. I was sure he was not serious and made no reply. He was himself a Professor of Philosophy at New York University, a friend of Malraux, and at home with French literature.

Burnham entered the political scene as a follower of Trotsky and advocate of world revolution as against "socialism in one country." At that time the disciples of Trotsky were split into two groups, the Canonites and the Shachtmanites. The Canonites took their name from James P. Canon, author of a well-known book on *The Struggle for a Proletarian Party in America*, whose work was studied by Lenin, and Max Shachtman, a popular and plausible speaker, and closer to Trotsky himself. During this period, Burnham wrote prolifically for the main journal and papers supporting Trotsky along the Shachtman lines in the twists and turns of Soviet policy and changes on the world scene in the Europe of the late twenties and early thirties. Then something happened (or did not) and Burnham broke with the movement entirely saying that Marxism had come to mean nothing to him for several years now. And with this he began his journey step by step to the far right. In time he would break with *Partisan Review*, the highly intellectual cultural magazine sympathetic to Trotsky and the critique of the Soviet Union over the issue of ex-communist witnesses and the role of the Government toward them. Burnham was moving one step at a time toward the far-right position, and a break with the Editorial. In time he also went on to join the CIA and met the young William F. Buckley, then vacationing in Mexico. Burnham obtained a minor position for Buckley, but it did not last long as Buckley gradually became bored with the triviality and tedium of the work in this junior capacity. It was, however, the beginning of collegial relationship marked by cordiality and mutual respect over the years at *National Review*.

Burnham exercised a strong influence over *National Review* always pressing it to be ever more professional in form and substance. Of all the senior editors, he is perhaps the most warmly remembered for his editorial contribution often in the midst of a fractious Board. He also wrote prolifically and his articles are among the best to appear in a magazine which could boast of such writers as Richard Weaver, Ernst van den Haag, and John O'Sullivan. He also wrote some very well-known books such as *The Managerial Revolution: Defenders of Freedom*[28] and a study of Congress titled *Congress and the American Tradition*,[29] and contributed a small study on the role and powers of Congress to *The Committee and Its Critics*.[30] Indeed, with the notable exception of Willmoore Kendall no one has made a greater contribution to the development of the conservative countercritique than this former follower of Leon Trotsky.

Burnham's intellectual origins cast light on his singular position in relation to the foundational writers of the conservative movement on the level of deep theory. Unlike Kendall he began with a deep conviction on the desirability, perhaps the inevitability, of "world communism." Unlike Voegelin, he began as a Marxist with an embrace of modernity and no nostalgia for the Middle Ages and "the world we have lost." Unlike Strauss, he never looked back to philosophy in its classic sense as the true philosophy. Nor did he see Machiavelli as the perpetrator of the crime of the century. Quite the contrary, one of his late works was titled *The Machiavellians: Defenders of Freedom*,[31] and devoted to a sympathetic study of Sorel, Mosca, Michels, and Pareto. It opens with a fine Introduction[32] contrasting the utopian Outlook in Dante with a more realistic analysis of the time including the war between the Guelphs and the Ghibellines, a topic on which he could write with the authority of a specialist. But the study of the individual Machiavellians is purely narrative, not critical. If you want a lucid, chapter-length narrative on Sorel, Mosca,

Michaels, etc. here is where you will find it But the critical edge is blunted, if it is there at all. It does not enter the Machiavelli controversy created by Strauss, and to which Voegelin, Mansfield, Pocock, Isaiah Berlin, and Sheldon Wolin were all to contribute sooner or later. And so it is with *The Managerial Revolution*, which Deutscher tells us in passing, has its genesis in a book published earlier by a French follower of Trotsky, and is today all but forgotten.[33] One thing it failed to predict is the revolution in the computer and information technology soon to follow and in which the major capitalists, allied with the big banks, dominate the managerial elite. But the most startling feature in the Burnham transformation from the moralist of the revolution to the realist of reaction is the switch from utopianism to realism of a hard-headed type and the moral fervor or the lingering remains of pure utopianism at the heart of rollback at the price of a nuclear war with the Soviet Union. All prudence and moderation would seem to have gone with the wind.

Notes

1. Rolland Young, ed., *Approaches to the Study of Politics*, Evanston, IL: North Western University Press, 1958.
2. Sheldon S. Wolin, *Politics and Vision*, Boston, Mass: Little, Brown and Company, 1960.
3. Sheldon S. Wolin, "Hobbs and Epic Tradition of Political Theory," Chapter six in Nicholas Xenos, ed., *Fugitive Democracy and Other Essays*, Princeton, NJ: Princeton University Press, 2005 and 2016, pp. 117–148.
4. Eric Voegelin, *The New Science of Politics*. University of Chicago Press, Chicago, IL, 1987, originally 1952.
5. Hans Kelsen, "Foundations of Democracy," *Ethics: An International Journal of Social Political and Legal Philosophy*, Vol. 66, No. 1, Part 2 (Oct. 1955), Chicago: University of Chicago Press, pp. 1–101.
6. Ibid.
7. Ibid., Voegelin, quoted by Kelsen, p. 10.
8. Ibid., "A New Type of Representation," p. 1.
9. J. L. Talmon, *The Rise of Totalitarian Democracy*, Boston, MA: Beacon Press, 1952.
10. Herbert McCloskey, "The Fallacy of Absolute Majority Rule," *Journal of Politics*, 11 (1949), 637ff.
11. Willmoore Kendall, "Prolegomena to Any Future Work on Majority Rule," *The Journal of Politics*, 12, no. 4 (Nov., 1950): 694–713.
12. Willmoore Kendall, "The People Versus Socrates Revisited," Nellie Kendall, ed., *Contra Mundum*, 1971 and reprinted by the University Press of America, Lanham, MD: 1994.
13. Willmoore Kendall, "The Majority Principle and the Scientific Elite," *The Southern Review*, (Winter 1939), 463–473.

14. Willmoore Kendall, "The Two Majorities in American Politics," chapter 2 in *The Conservative Affirmation* and "What is Conservatism?," chapter 1 in *The Conservative Affirmation*, pp. 13–14.
15. Kendall, "Two Majorities," pp. 21–49.
16. Ibid.
17. Roberts A. Dahl, *A Preface to Democratic Theory*, University of Chicago Press, Chicago, IL, 2006.
18. Angelo Rossi, *A Communist Party in Action*, translated by *Willmoore Kendall*; New Haven, Conn., Yale University Press, 1949.
19. Willmoore Kendall, "The People Versus Socrates Revisited," *Modern Age*, (Winter 1958–59).
20. Willmoore Kendall, "The Fallacy of the Open Society" in the *American Political Science Review*, Vol. 54, Issue 4, (December 1960), pp. 972–979.
21. Willmoore Kendall and Frederick D. Wilhelmsen. "*Cicero* and the Politics of the *Public Orthodoxy*." *Pamplona*, Universidad de Navarra, 1965; Nellie D. Kendall, ed. *Willmoore Kendall Contra Mundum* (Lanham, MD: University Press, 1971).
22. Willmoore Kendall and George Carey, *The Basic Symbols of The American Political Tradition*, Washington, D.C.: The Catholic University of America Press, 1995.
23. Kendall, "Majority Principle," *op. cit.*
24. Kendall, "Prolegomena," *op. cit.*
25. "McCarthyism: *Pons Asinororum* of Contemporary Conservatism" is Chapter 3 of Willmoore Kendall's book, *The Conservative Affirmation*, Chicago: Henry Regnery Company, 1963.
26. Ibid.
27. David Spitz, *Democracy and the Challenge of Power*, New York: Columbia University Press. 1958. Willmoore Kendall's comments are in the second review of his book, *The Conservative Affirmation*, Chicago: Henry Regnery Company, 1963.
28. James P. Burnham, *The Machiavellians: Defenders of Freedom*. New York: John Day Co., 1943.
29. James P. Burnham, *Congress and the American Tradition*, Chicago, H. Regnery Co., 1959.
30. William F. Buckley Jr., *The Committee and Its Critics: A Calm Review of the House Un-American Activity Committee:* New York: Putnam, 1962.
31. James P. Burnham, *The Machiavellians*, *op. cit.*
32. Ibid.
33. Isaac Deutscher, *The Prophet Armed: Trotsky 1879-1921, vol. I; The Prophet Disarmed: Trotsky 1921–1929, vol. II; The Prophet Outcast 1929–1940, vol. III*, New York: Oxford University Press, 1954, 1959, and 1963 respectively.

FINAL REMARKS

By way of conclusion I would like to circle in on the unifying structure of my argument by first considering the main criticisms advanced in the course of writing the initial two or three chapters. The criticisms made were always interesting and often enlightening and centered around my use of three figures, Sol Stern, Paulo Freire, and Mario Puzo. While Sol Stern is admittedly a minor writer, his article is a concise distillation of the view from the far right, and our literature is the richer for having it. If you want to know precisely how the far right sees the problem of Freire here is where you will find it, warts and all. Stern's article is priceless in revealing the mind and emotional structure at the center of conservative thinking on the problem of the culture wars and the clash in education. He titles it "The Pedagogy of the Oppressor" though Paulo had been the one in jail and oppressed no one. He spent his life on a literacy campaign for the workers and peasants, the "oppressed" of his title. And, except for the first two pages of Chapter Two, his book has nothing to do with education in the sense of school and culture. It is a book on consciousness-raising and not on education. In taking it for a work on education, Sol Stern has made a category mistake. This mistake pervades the conservative critique and gives Sol Stern's article its paradigmatic status.

Freire's real contribution to education, the tiny four-page article on "The Act of Study," is overlooked entirely by Stern and the critics. Its creation came about by accident in Freire's career, and the accident was never repeated. He had been asked to prepare a bibliography to serve as a bank of knowledge for the beginning student. No no, said Paulo, don't begin like that. Begin like this with the mind of the students. And this shift from the object side of the equation to the subject side constitutes the Freire revolution and gives it its significance. In "The Act of Study" there are no clichés, Marxist or otherwise. It is a fresh and original piece of work in pure cognitional theory developed in the Marxist tradition by the early Lukács and the later Bloch. This is the tradition out of which Freire wrote and there is nothing discredited about it. In Marx it goes back to his earlier writings down to the Theses on Feuerbach, especially the First Thesis. Freire conceives of the student himself as the creator and recreator of ideas in response to critical questioning by the teacher (and, perhaps, his fellow students). The teacher's role is confined to critical questioning embroidered from time to time with brief and suggestive counter arguments. Freire called this "problem posing education," and that is as good a name as any. Its likeness to the form inquiry developed by Willmoore Kendall can hardly be mistaken and reveals its value-neutral character.

I have preferred to dub it "Socratic" to bring out its more classical and ancient heritage as recorded by Xenophon in the practice of the historical Socrates and dramatized by Plato in a number of early dialogues, prominently including *The Theaetetus*, where Socrates likens Himself to a midwife, herself barren, who brings out the creation in the other. The key point in the dialogue as opposed to the lecture is the creation of ideas by the student. "Education," said Freire, "is suffering from narration sickness," and there is nothing in the Marxist line about that. In point of historical fact it is precisely in the line of thought developed by Gramsci in his brief article "On Education." This demonstrates the Hegelian or subject side of dialectic or dialogue in Freire, and Gramsci before him.

In talking to friends, liberal and not communist, sympathetic to Freire and Gramsci, I noticed how often they referred to the message as one of love or one of trust, and sometimes both. I was also struck by the fact that, unknown to them, Che and Paulo had used precisely the same words in fragments of conversation reprinted in the papers. In drafting an article on Moses Hess "Today and Destiny: The Judgment of Moses Hess" published in Plowshares magazine, I called this "the warm current" in socialism as distinguished from "the cold current" of economic and scientific analysis. The warm current was moral and the cold current was scientific and empirical. The former spoke to you as subject, the latter as object. Much of the success of the early socialist movement flows from the fact that they related to the people as subjects and addressed their needs in health and education, etc., binding them into a community of disciples and followers. If you read books like *Red Star Over China* or *Thunder Out of China* you cannot miss the message and its effectiveness. Much the same can be said on the other side of the world in *Greece: American Dilemma and Opportunity*.[1] There it is in its positive side, and its inversion to autocracy and despotism is one of the most striking inversions in the socialist movement. But the former was there as the study of EAM[2] in the book on Greece makes abundantly clear. How do we characterize it and explain its hold on the people in the premodern world of China, Kerala (India), and parts of Greece? My answer is to develop a theory called "The politics of friendship" to explain the rousing success of Fidel in Cuba, the EAM in Greece, Mao and Chou in China, and the hundreds of thousands or million(s) in Kerala. But the way to understand it, I suggest, is not to begin with the abstracts of theory but with a concrete depiction in practice as conveyed in a work of fiction addressed to the popular mind in all its simplicity. And Puzo's novel struck me as the perfect vehicle for this venture in pedagogy. Understand it and you will have yet understand the domestic politics of the cold war from the early Whittaker Chambers to the late Alger Hiss, from the solidity of the Hillary Clinton appeal to the rousing response to Bernie Sanders.

Puzo's novel was widely read as a work of entertainment centering around the theme of power. And sure there is much to be said for this View. All the elements of a gripping story are there. It recounts the story of a mafia family's rise to power, the striking Entrance of Virgil Sollozzo, the drug deal and the war of the Five Families, Michael's preemptive first strike, and the rise of a new Don. It's perfect symmetry making for a gripping tale, especially when larded with large doses of sex and violence provided by Sonny Corleone and Lucy Mancini, Luca Brasi and Al Neri. It's all there and impossible to miss, and a critic of Pauline Kael's caliber could dismiss it as "trash." This is the public view and so deeply contained that to question it might well seem perverse and especially at this late date. But the public understanding is only a partial understanding based on the surface of the book. As in all such writing, Leibniz comes readily to mind, the surface of the book presents an exoteric story, a narrative to satisfy the vulgar taste while concealing the true teaching in it. The elements of the esoteric teaching are, however, incomprehensible to the vulgar and it remains only to lay them out one beside the other for the real teaching of the novel to emerge to full light of day.

Puzo's novel presents a teaching about justice. Justice, and nothing less is the grand theme of the discussion between Don Corleone and Amerigo Buonasera; his opposite number represents America and modern society. And it is this theme which Coppola chose for the dramatic close up with which to open the movie. It was a stroke of genius. But of what is justice composed? This is the theme of the novel as indeed of the story of philosophy. Puzo's novel is one chapter in this story as told from the pre-modern point of view of the late Middle Ages. The esoteric translation shows all the elements in the critique of liberal democracy by contrasting two worlds: it is the world of liberal democracy with the world of the Corleones. The world of the Corleones is a closed society made up of a number of key elements. In contrast to the great world outside, it is a small local community of face to face interaction among people who know one another directly fenced in by the code of *omerta* or silence to the external world. Second, they are a homogenous society, all sharing a common language, culture, and religion. Third, this society is marked by a creedal unity. In terms of fundamental belief they think alike. When news of the killing of Fanucci spreads through the community, the young Vito Andolini is regarded as "a man of respect." Fourth, it remains pre-modern in its ethos, its economic, social, and familial structure.

Fifth, the bond uniting the family together is allegiance, or loyalty to the Don. "Why do you fear to give your first allegiance to me," the consensus which binds the community together in its hierarchical articulation from the Consigliori and the Capos, to the soldiers and the humblest men. Sixth, but this consensus, the consensus of a pre-modern community, comes at a price: The consensus, that is to say the political, presides over the individual, that is to say the ethical in a manner well understood by F. H. Bradley in his essay on "My Station and Its Duties" in *Ethical Studies*. From this point of view the abstract individual, the individual abstracted from his community, is a freak and a monster created by the liberal imagination. "She is a hitter and a thief," says Don Corrado Prizzi to Jack Nicholson of his wife, "*We* are your family." And Nicholson understood and accepted.

The contrast drawn by Puzo is between the pre-market society of the Sicilian underworld and the market society within which it functions. This contrast marks the transition from status to contract in the vocabulary of Sir Henry Sumner Maine, our most prominent scholar on the topic.[3] Market society and the moral climate it creates is marked by economic exploitation and political, social, and sexual corruption. It is visual through and through and from top to bottom. Of the two boys who beat up Bonasera's daughter nothing more need be said. The real counter evidence begins with the Judge who let them off. A second is Jack Woltz, the movie mogul and his virtual rape of a young girl of twelve. A third is Les Halley, the band leader with a personal contract for the singing of Johnnie Fontane, only to lease him out and pocket the cash. A fourth is the store owner who sold some furniture for two hundred dollars knowing he was declaring bankruptcy and would never have to deliver. A fifth is the case of the two young men who took the Don's furnace apart with the threat to leave it like that unless they were paid for re-assembling it. A sixth is Capt McCloskey who was in the pay of Sollozzo, and Capt. Phillips (who was) in the pay of the Corleones. In fact, the whole precinct collected its regular rake, off the bookies as a regular part of life in the city. And finally there was Billy Gough who collected from both sides and lost his life in a venture of extortion on the mafia. In fact, with the exception of Kay (and the Adams family) who are not organic to the story there is not a single representative of the counter world who is not exploitative and corrupt in one way or another. A liberal vote might ask if Puzo is not in sympathy with the hierarchical and the authoritarian world he portrays so well. For Puzo the question does not really arise as a live option, or the pre-modern world between, say, the age of Augustine and the rise of commercial capitalism in the city states; there was no such thing as representative liberal democracy. It simply did not exist.

The issue at stake in this excursus is the nature of the political obligation, and therefore, of justice in the well-ordered city. Are two major counterclaims (Strauss and Voegelin), ranging from the ancient city to the high Middle Ages, or are there in fact three carrying the story to the close of the age of feudalism, and the rise of liberal capitalism? Writing from the Straussian point of view, Professor Paul Rahe leaves us with two, by assimilating "friendship" in The Godfather, to the idea of "friendship" in the classics.[4] He performs this feat by recounting an anecdote at the close of his study. Anyone who comes to Washington and is looking for a friend, President Truman is quoted as saying, would do better to save his money and buy a dog.

By way of ending Professor Rahe concludes on a note of dramatic force. To Truman's observation on the condition of friendlessness in Washington he appends the observation that this is something Don Corleone would have understood completely and of course he would. He understood the modern world outside him thoroughly and rejected it completely. But the two concepts are not the same. In fact they are radically different. The former, whether in

Truman or Aristotle, is based on amiability, the bond uniting two or more individuals in a community of equals. Friendship here is based on equality. But "friendship," on the lips of Hagen to Jack Woltz or Don Corleone to Buonasera, is political friendship or alliance in a hierarchical relationship. In this relationship, your middle name was loyalty, not amiability. As Puzo makes clear, you did not need to be the Don's friend, and few, if any, were. All you needed to do was to bring some small gift from time to time to show your friendship with a gesture of loyalty to the Don. So when in the late thirties the Don surveyed his world he found it functioning much better than the world outside on the way to Munich. Then Sollozzo the Turk came with his offer of partnership in the drug trade and turned the world upside down.

But Professor Rahe operates with a two-factor theory called Ancients and Moderns. And what does not fit the one, in this case the moderns, must be fitted into the other, in this case the Ancients. The result is a partial, superficial and one sided reading of the text which misses the point of political obligation and justice completely. What is justice in the eyes of the Don and the world of the Corleones? As an actor in a small but functioning world with its norms and distribution of power, he can only see it as retribution with condign punishment. Your daughter is Still alive, he reminds Buonasera, and scales down the justice to condign proportions. Perhaps the greatest thing to the ancients are some words of Glaucon in the Republic. But the distance between the ancient city and the late feudal world is immense and to be measured in centuries if not millennia. And they have both passed and remain only as a memory in the mind of man.

Puzo is a realist and the narrative closes with Michael's plans for moving to Las Vegas where the Corleone family can fade somewhat into the world of the casino and business as usual. In the history of ideas *The Godfather* is correctly seen as the third of three consecutive statements in the conservative critique of modernity and liberal democracy. Nor should we be surprised by its presentation in the form of a novel with a flashy (Pauline Kael would say "trashy") exterior. Politics is often presented in the form of a novel. One has only to think or *Animal Farm* and *1984*, or *Lord of the Flies*, the early novels of Eric Ambler, Straw Dogs, and the films of Sam Peckinpah, of Turgenev and Dostoevsky, or Silone, Malraux, and many others all the way back to Swift and *The Adventures of Gulliver* in Lilliput. High scholarship has become critical scholarship in the analysis of ideas. But Puzo and the writers mentioned above are offering not "high scholarship" but a high order of vision and creative thinking in the form of a critique of what is and a vision of what could be and indeed has for a moment in time.

Notes

1. L. S. Stavrianos., *Greece: American Dilemma and Opportunity*. Chicago: Henry Regnery Company. 1952.
2. *Ethnikón Apeleftherotikón Métopon–Ethnikós Laïkós Apeleftherotikós Strátos:* in English, the National Liberation Front.
3. Henry Sumner Maine, *From Status to Contract* in. *Ancient Law, Its Connection with the Early History of Society, and Its Relation to Modern Ideas* (1st ed.). London: John Murray, 1861 (in the Internet Archive of the Harvard Book Collection). See also Peter Laslett, *The World We Have Lost*, London: Routledge, reprinted in 2000, (first published by Methuen & Company, Ltd., 1965).
4. Paul Rahe, "Don Vito Corleone, Friendship, and the American Regime," in Reinventing the American People: Unity and Diversity Today, ed. Robert Royal (Washington, D. C.: Ethics and Public Policy Center, 1995), pp. 115–35.

    Also see Paul Rahe: "Don Corleone, Multiculturalist," A Study Guide by Steven Alan Samson, Liberty University Digital Commons, 2005.

CONCLUSION

The Argument in Model Form

1) Q. Does consciousness exist?
   a) Consciousness does not exist (as an entity). (William James) It can be likened to a bodily process like digestion or photosynthesis. (John Searles)
   b) Consciousness does exist (as an entity) though not as material object. (John Dewey, Bernard Lonergan SJ)

2) Q. Does the self exist?
   a) No! When I look onward I cannot perceive a self or anything like it. (David Hume)
   b) The self does exist, though not as material or sensible object. The self is a subject which can then be objectified and studied though not precisely like a material object. (Albury Castell, Bernard Lonergan)

3) Q. Is the subject–object distinction fundamental to moral philosophy?
   a) The subject–object distinction is not fundamental to philosophy. In scientific philosophy we think in terms of sense contents which form the fundamental units. (Russell, Ayer)
   b) The subject–object distinction is fundamental to moral and political philosophy by placing the experience of the subject at the foundation

of moral and political philosophy. Consciousness is experience, and not perception, which can only be of an object. (Lonergan, Polanyi, Marx, Lukacs, Gramsci, Freire)

4) Q. Is there any such phenomenon as "insight" or "intuition"?
   a) No (by inference). It plays no role in the writings of the critical philosophers from Hume to Russell on down.
   b) Yes is the Weighty Tome by Lonergan by that name, as well as by Polanyi and, more particularly, Beveridge.

5) Q. Is there an operation called *Verstehen* as a form of understanding?
   a) No. There is only rational comprehension as in sociology and the sciences.
   b) Yes. While we see this most clearly in novelists and dramatists from Shakespeare to Dostoyevsky, it is also a significant feature of all good political and moral philosophy and gives it it's depth. (Dewey, Lonergan, Polanyi, Beveridge)

6) Q. What is history? How should it be understood and taught?
   a) History is the correct, precise, and accurate recording of events and ideas as they occurred, presenting the past as it really was. (Ranke and positivist historiography)
   b) No! Even in the hands of such very competent historians such as Diane Ravitch and Entwistle it has a two-dimensional quality known as "scissors and paste," or programmatic history. In paradigmatic history, however, we bring in the activity of the historian as a critical and creative subject with his particular horizon. (Collingwood, Carr, Becker, Beard)

7) Q. Are moral judgments fundamentally noncognitive, or can we know "the truth that sets one free"?
   a) Moral judgments are not cognitive because there is no way by which they can be verified on an inter-subjective basis. (Hume, Russell, Ayer, Oppenheim)
   b) Moral judgments are cognitive, and the moral falsehoods of the Stalin era were exposed by the rebels in Hungary and Eastern Europe after decades of officials lied as enforced by the Stalin regime. (Polanyi, Lonergan and the Catholic critics, Strauss, Kendall, and the Straussians)

8) Q. Is this the rationale for the liberal-conservative split in the culture war?
   a) The rationale is incontestable and opens the way to relativism, pluralism, and toleration, in a word to liberal and representative democracy. (Russell, Berlin, Ayer, Popper, Kelsen)
   b) The rationale is false and based on empiricism, positivism, and "the acids of skepticism." It paves the way to a lowering of standards and the debasement of a mass society in which the individual is nothing, and culture is a thing of the past. (Strauss, Voegelin, Kendall)

9) Q. Do we want to move still further toward pluralism and the open society?
   a) The open society is a contradiction in terms and a pluralism going beyond the American consensus is a recipe for intellectual and political disintegration. One way to arrest this decline is a sound education is our schools, colleges, and universities in the tradition of America, the Christian faith, and classical philosophy. (Kendall, Voegelin, Strauss, Weaver, Mayer, and perhaps Van den Haag)
   b) A Liberal, pluralist, and tolerant democracy is our best and only hope. While we have not met with success in our schools, our Universities continue to be the most respected in the world. (Berlin, Russell, Crossman, Polanyi, Beveridge)

10) Q. How should we Moderns best relate to Plato and Classical Philosophy?
    a) The philosophy of Plato has laid the groundwork for all later philosophy, especially in the discovery of nature and the rock of moral philosophy and God, not man, as the measure of all things. (Strauss, Voegelin, Kendall, as also Jaeger, Friedlander, Versenyi)
    b) In advocating autocracy in a small closed society, Plato has laid the groundwork for a fascist and totalitarian enterprise. (Russell, Crossman, Kelsen, and possibly Popper)

11) Q. How is the student best conceived? And what is the best form of teaching the student so conceived?
    a) The mind of the student is best conceived as a storehouse of knowledge of true and tested facts and algorithms. Teaching is the transmission of knowledge in the form of the lecture with the aid of the textbook as checked by regular tests. We need more homework, a

longer school day, and a longer school year. (E.D. Hirsch *et al.*, The Gardner Commission Report, etc.)

b) The student is best understood as "the discoverer of new truths," new that is for him, or the creator and recreator of new ideas in the course of dialogue from the simpler to the more complex and true solution. (Gramsci and Freire, Polanyi and Beveridge, Bruner and Associates R.L. and Paul Halmos)

Teaching in the traditional form readily spills over into indoctrination, a form of teaching frankly advocated by the far left and far right, by George S. Counts and William F. Buckley.

The form of the contrasting argument bursting through the placid surface of traditional discourse is a recurrent feature in the history of ideas. Its entrance on the scene was marked by the *Dissoi Logoi* of the Seventh Century BC and the practice of the historical Socrates. It favors the dialogue, the form chosen by Plato, over the lecture, article, or treatise, the forms chosen by his successors when a tradition has been established. Now it remains only to smooth out the edges, polish up the arguments, and collect the received body of knowledge in the form of a *Summa*, a *Dictionaire*, or *Encyclopedie Philosophique*. There it is, and it remains only for the schools and teachers to transmit the knowledge and information. Education becomes a process of transmission.

But the form of contrasting argument keeps breaking through the challenge of received wisdom in the form of a question and the counterargument flowing from it. So we have the *Sic Et Non* of Abelard, *The Dialogues of Hylas and Philonous*, Kierkegaard's *Either/Or* with the slash of decision, Marx's questioning and critique of everyone and everything. Since the time of Plato's dialogues and Aristotle's treatises, the two forms stand side by side, and the history of letters is the history of the exchange between them from "the quarrel between the ancients and the moderns" to the present-day quarrel between the moderns themselves. I have set this out in a series of chapters beginning with the dramatic case of Antonio Gramsci Whose thoughts on education have been transformed to fit into the ideologies of the left and the right as understood at the time. And I have, finally, presented them once more, now in more focused form, so that the division between them is clear and the need for choice imperative.

At this point it becomes reasonable to close by recommending the shift from "Plato" to "Socrates," where "Plato" represents the lecture and textbook, the article and the treatise, and "Socrates" is a metaphor for the inquiring mind, and critical question, the dialogue or conversation with the student as fellow subject engaged in a joint search for a new truth. This may not be feasible at the level of the University where the specialist transmits his knowledge to the results of his researches in the appropriate form of a lecture to his audience, the body of students, conceived as an object. But it is entirely feasible on the primary-secondary level, where the students should first learn to think for themselves and develop a critical grasp of the theories and perspectives underlying the rival bodies of knowledge in the liberal arts and various solutions and proofs in mathematics and the sciences. What is required is a change in perspective, and shift from "Plato" to "Socrates" or the universe of objects to the universe of subjects, and the rest will follow from the engagement of the teachers to the engagement of the foundations to give us the education and culture worthy of the American people.

CPSIA information can be obtained
at www.ICGtesting.com
Printed in the USA
LVHW080315010322
712301LV00003B/28

9 781433 151651